OXFORD STUDIES IN LANGUAGE CONTACT

Series Editors: Suzanne Romaine, Merton College, Oxford,
and Peter Mühlhäusler, University of Adelaide

Language Contact in Japan

OXFORD STUDIES IN LANGUAGE CONTACT

Most of the world's speech communities are multilingual, making contact between languages an important force in the everyday lives of most people. Studies of language contact should therefore form an integral part of work in theoretical, social, and historical linguistics. As yet, however, there are insufficient studies to permit typological generalizations.

Oxford Studies in Language Contact aims to fill this gap by making available a collection of research monographs presenting case studies of language contact around the world. The series addresses language contact and its consequences in a broad interdisciplinary context, which includes not only linguistics, but also social, historical, cultural, and psychological perspectives. Topics falling within the scope of the series include: bilingualism, multilingualism, language mixing, code-switching, diglossia, pidgins and creoles, problems of cross-cultural communication, and language shift and death.

Language Contact in Japan

A Socio-linguistic History

LEO J. LOVEDAY

CLARENDON PRESS · OXFORD
1996

Oxford University Press, Walton Street, Oxford OX2 6DP

Oxford New York
Athens Auckland Bangkok Bombay
Calcutta Cape Town Dar es Salaam Delhi
Florence Hong Kong Istanbul Karachi
Kuala Lumpur Madras Madrid Melbourne
Mexico City Nairobi Paris Singapore
Taipei Tokyo Toronto

and associated companies in
Berlin Ibadan

Oxford is a trade mark of Oxford University Press

Published in the United States
by Oxford University Press Inc., New York

© Leo J. Loveday 1996

British Library Cataloguing in Publication Data
Data available

Library of Congress Cataloging in Publication Data
Data available

ISBN 0 19 823559 3

1   3   5   7   9   10   8   6   4   2

Typeset by Graphicraft Typesetters Ltd., Hong Kong
Printed in Great Britain on acid-free paper by
Bookcraft (Bath) Ltd, Midsomer Norton

For
Satomi and George
Thank you for waiting

Preface

The major difficulty with a book like this is presenting the material in a way that is accessible to readers unfamiliar with the Japanese language and cultural background. I have tried my best to set out the information and research data in a style that someone with little or no specialist knowledge of Japanese should be able to follow easily. Wherever possible, however, additional references, especially in English, are cited for those in need of further clarification. The use of certain linguistic terminology could not be avoided, but I have tried to cut out as much superfluous jargon as possible.

However, I hope that in my efforts to popularize my research, I have not robbed it of its appeal for specialists. Where the work is deemed inadequate, I recommend consulting the original Ph.D. thesis out of which the book grew: 'The Sociolinguistic Evolution and Synchronic Dynamics of Language Contact in Japan' (Essex University, UK, 1990).

L.J.L.

Acknowledgements

As I tried to come to terms with the apparently straightforward topic of this study, its overwhelming complexity and immensity became increasingly obvious. Nevertheless, the book, even with its numerous deficiencies, would never have seen the light of day were it not for moral and academic support from various sources.

Many Japanese informants, relatives, colleagues, and friends have aided me in this project, but only a few can be named here. Professor Masāki Tatsuki of Doshisha University sacrificed considerable time to help with the interpretation of specialist texts and the carrying-out of computer analysis. I also wish to thank all my ex-students of the English department at Doshisha University for their indirect and direct inspiration, and for their help with the survey. I am grateful to the Department of English at Doshisha University for supplying me with the materials and conditions permitting me to undertake this research.

I also wish to thank Professors Trudgill and Mühlhäusler for their guidance with the early version of this work as a Ph.D. thesis. My thanks are also due to Professor Suzanne Romaine for her valuable criticisms at the editorial stage, as does Frances Morphy of Oxford University Press for her efficiency and encouragement throughout the publishing process.

Contents

List of Tables and Figures

Figures

Introduction

The Japanese are often stereotyped as a nation possessing a unique culture, having hardly any linguistic connections with other language-groups, a characterization which some Japanese admittedly also promote for ideological purposes. However, on closer examination of their linguistic and cultural history, a very different picture emerges, of a people avidly looking beyond themselves for inspiration and external contact—political environment permitting. It is the story of this surprisingly enduring, 2,000-year-long influence of other cultures and languages on Japan which constitutes the focus of this book.

The picture that will emerge provides important clues to the causes and patterns of language change in general and will be valuable for comparative purposes, especially to those searching for data to help them formulate cross-cultural universals in language-contact behaviour. Furthermore, it is now necessary to pay attention to language-contact processes in the long-neglected setting of a monolingual speech-community. Significant insights into the contemporary modifications undergone by the English language in a non-native, Asian context fundamentally different from one, such as India, with a colonial, British heritage, can also be gleaned here. In addition, it is hoped that some readers will be stimulated by the application of interdisciplinary theory and methodology in this case-study.

Approach

The reasons for, and results and dynamics of, Japanese contact with other languages are presented here mainly within a socio-linguistic framework, but the approach also includes an eclectic mix from diverse disciplines such as cultural anthropology, social psychology, and semiotics, as well as subfields within the domain of linguistics such as comparative and historical linguistics, stylistics, structural work in morphology/semantics, and functionalism.

A variety of research methods and data-collection have been employed, ranging from the use of bibliographic material (mainly for the historical study in Chapters 2 and 3) to participant observation, the recording and collating of data from the mass media, and a field-work-based, attitudinal survey (for later chapters).

Organization

The book is divided into seven chapters, which may be read as separate, self-contained units and so not necessarily in the order in which they are arranged. The first offers a unifying vision for understanding language-contact phenomena. Chapter 2 surveys and analyses the history of Japanese linguistic relations with Asian languages, concentrating on the social forces involved, while Chapter 3 deals with European language-contact from the sixteenth century until the Second World War, examining its channels, agents, motivation, and areas of occurrence, following the same analytic approach. Chapter 4 looks at the processes and typical contexts of contact with foreign words, focusing particularly on the socio-economic environment which is encouraging such absorption. Chapter 5 considers the patterns involved in assimilating foreign words on different levels such as sound and writing. This is followed by an analysis of 'deviant' changes in English word-formation by the Japanese. Chapter 6 explores current attitudes in the community towards foreign borrowing and mixing with Japanese; this is done by means of a survey which sets out to identify clearly those who support language-contact dissemination and those who favour resistance. The final chapter proposes an original, strategy-based, functional model of the contact behaviour of the Japanese today in relation to their social and individual needs. Although the later chapters may theoretically be the most difficult, even those with only a limited training in linguistics should be able to understand the arguments.

Introducing the Japanese Language

This section discusses only those aspects deemed to be vital or relevant to the body of this work; no attempt is made at a comprehensive description of the Japanese language, for which several high-quality reference-works already exist in English: Shibatani (1990), Hinds (1986), Martin (1975), Miller (1967), and others.

The origins of Japanese have been the subject of much controversy and speculation, since linguistic evidence remains too scanty for determining definite links. However, fundamental phonological and grammatical parallels with the Altaic family (including Manchu-Tungus, Mongolian, and Turkic) and with Korean have been identified, while only lexical links with the Austronesian (or Malayo-Polynesian) family have been uncovered; further data also suggest possible relations with Tibeto-Burmese. This mixed linguistic heritage, together with recent archaeological and anthropological discoveries of multi-ethnic and multi-cultural, prehistorical immigration to the islands from East Asia and the Pacific, support the view that Japanese may itself have developed out of a contact language. For instance, Lewin (1981: 1,729–30) claims that the base was probably a variety or varieties of Austronesian in contact with a variety or varieties of Altaic, with Japanese supposedly emerging as a fully developed language by the Yayoi era (300 BC–AD 200). Miller (1980: 163–7), on the other hand, refutes notions of a creolized beginning and attributes the Austronesian element to borrowing into an Altaic base.

It should be pointed out that Japanese is not at all related to Chinese, although it has drawn heavily on the latter's vocabulary and writing-system. It is not coincidental, however, that the earliest records of Japanese consist of several words found in a Chinese history-book, the *Wei chih*, of the late third century; for since earliest times Japan has maintained close affiliations with China and Chinese-influenced groups. Apart from a few words on swords and mirrors of the fifth and sixth centuries, the earliest Japanese writings date from the beginning of the eighth century. (See the following section for a brief historical guide to Japanese orthography.)

The language of the Japanese nation of 123 million is ranked as the tenth most-spoken tongue in the world, although it is hardly known outside the archipelago—except in Japanese immigrant communities in the Americas and among the ageing population of former South-East Asian colonies such as Korea and Taiwan. Its linguistic homogeneity is frequently overstated, without due recognition of other ethnic and linguistic minorities such as the Ainu and Okinawans, who are indigenous, and its 648,000-strong[1] permanent foreign resident communities such as the Korean and Chinese as well as newer groups such as Indo-Chinese refugees, the Indian community and the pool of Asian labourers from Iran and the Philippines in addition to the growing number of South Americans of Japanese ancestry.

[1] Figures from the Japanese Ministry of Foreign Affairs (1988).

Literacy is officially declared to be 99 per cent, which underlines the desired monolithism of the community. An officially promoted, oral and written standard variety based on Tokyo speech is generally acquired at school and superposed on the many, not all mutually intelligible, dialects which continue to survive despite standardizing pressures from mass media, social levelling, urbanization, and centralization. Language attitudes have been characterized as deeply ethnocentric, and beliefs in the uniqueness, superiority, spiritual power, unlearnability, and untranslatability of Japanese are apparently strongly held by certain members of society: see Miller (1977, 1982).

Japanese is a subject-object-verb language which is recognized as agglutinative, although contact with Chinese has introduced a massive stock of uninflected words and modified its synthetic character. Plural distinctions are not generally made, although words such as 'several' and 'many', as well as numerals and reduplication, may be employed to mark plurals. Nouns in Japanese do not inflect either for gender or for case. There are no relative pronouns, (the entire subordinate clause is placed in front of the nouns it modifies), nor any articles, and verbs do not indicate number or person, although present, past, and conditional time is marked. The subjects of sentences are sparingly expressed, but subtle distinctions in reference are made by means of either a subject marker or a topic marker.

Considerable complexity is also evident in honorific verb-inflections encoding the social context, reflecting the degree of intimacy and status, and among other factors, marking, the speaker's age and gender. Adjectives are traditionally analysed as having the same conjugational forms as verbs, functioning both attributively and as predicates. In Japanese all modifiers, whether single words or word groups, invariably precede the nouns to be modified. This is the opposite of the general pattern of English word-order.

In Japanese there are basically two word-classes: the *invariables*, such as substantives, determinatives, demonstratives, numerals, adverbs, and interrogatives, which ideally must be followed by postpositions but which often stand alone, particularly in colloquial speech; and *variable* words, such as verbs and adjectives, which cannot be used without functional suffixes.

Japanese is a syllable-timed language, with mora length phonemically distinctive and a tone pattern inherent to words that is also occasionally distinctive. In fact, Japanese has three kinds of morae: those constituted with a vowel, those constituted with a consonant, and those made up of a consonant plus a vowel.

In the contemporary, Tokyo-based standard variety, the velar phonemes are /k, g, n/, the fricatives /s, z, c, ʃ, t, ʧ, ʒ, ʤ, Φ/ and a bilabial voiceless /h/, the dentals /t, d/, bilabials /p, b, m, w/, vowels /a, i, e, o/, with an unrounded /u/ which, together with /i/, are usually devoiced after voiceless consonants, semi-vocalic /j/, an alveolar palatal /n/, and an uvular syllabic nasal /N/, a vibrationless tongue-tip alveolar flap /ɾ/, and a glottal stop which occurs before /p, t, k, s, ʃ, ʧ/, turning them into geminate consonants.

Native taxonomies for ecological items such as the weather, plants, rice cultivation, and fishing, as well as for social positions and relations, are particularly extensive. Linguistic markers of social identity relating to gender are also available through terms of self-reference, sentence-final particles, and the use of honorifics. There also exist a large number of onomatopoetic words and a set of numeral classifiers categorizing nouns according to qualities such as shape, size, and texture.

A Guide to Japanese Writing

This section offers a concise and limited introduction to fundamental aspects of Japanese orthographic practice, past and present, which are mentioned in this book or are necessary for a fuller understanding of various points. For detailed, comprehensive accounts in English consult Seeley (1991), Habein (1984), and Miller (1967). A minimal grasp of the basic development and workings of the present-day Japanese writing-system is essential to understanding the description and analysis of the contact processes with Chinese and English set out in the following chapters.

Chinese characters (known in Japanese as *kanji*) are supposed to have originated along the Yellow River *c*.1300–1100 BC, that is to say during the Yin dynasty, in the form of pictographs: 人 'man'; 木 'tree'. However, after various phases of development, the stylistic forms and signification processes became more sophisticated and complex:

- Existing pictorial representations were combined to create new meanings more economically: 休 'repose'.
- An element (often unrelated to the meaning) was added to some characters to indicate their (homophonic) pronunciation. Thus the character 每 (Chinese: *mei*) is added to 木 to produce 梅 *mei*, 'plum'.
- Certain characters were used to represent words of the same or similar meaning but with different pronunciations, and vice versa, which led to

multiple readings such as 楽 (Chinese: *yue*) 'music' or (*le*) 'pleasure', and, conversely, 萬 (Chinese: *wan*) 'scorpion' or 'ten thousand'.

- Varied methods of compounding characters were employed to increase lexical productivity. For example, hypernymous concepts were expressed by semantically related characters, and abstract concepts by antonymous characters; other methods such as rebuses were also used.

The Japanese possessed no indigenous writing-system and borrowed the character script from the Chinese. Although the earliest writing in Chinese characters so far discovered in Japan date from the fifth century, their introduction to the islands goes back one century earlier. The Japanese adopted different historical varieties for pronouncing characters (see Chapter 1), and this has led, in some cases, to multiple readings for the same character. Historical sound-change within China and Japan, together with Japanese interference, has led to a divergent pronunciation from contemporary Chinese readings of the characters.

The total number of characters is 50,000, but present-day Japanese generally employ only about 2,000 for everyday purposes, and the number for daily use has been limited to 1,945 by language planning, with a further 166 approved for names. However, members of the older generation and specialists in scientific and highly cultured fields know probably 1,000 over and above the required 2,000.

Texts written in characters with a surface appearance of Chinese are called *kambun*. *Kan/m* refers to the period of the Han dynasty (206 BC–AD 220) and *bun* means 'written composition'. The term excludes vernacular Chinese, and, as employed by the Japanese, includes Chinese texts both by Chinese natives and by non-natives such as Japanese or Korean, even though in the latter case there may be considerable divergence from Chinese linguistic norms. *Kambun* is especially associated in Japan with the now archaic writings of the bureaucracy, the aristocracy, Buddhist clergy, and academia. Some of Japan's most important ancient records, such as the *Kojiki* (712) and *Nihongi* (720), are composed in it. However, after late Heian times (*c*.900 AD) the need for, and competence in, *kambun* seems to have declined as mixed Sino-Japanese written varieties emerged and flourished. Nevertheless, *kambun* had a strong influence on many Japanese written varieties and was variously revived under Zen influences in Buddhist, philological, and poetic texts, and later by eighteenth-century sinologists for philosophical and scientific work. In fact, a strongly sinicized writing-style was maintained until the middle of this century, being employed typically as the official written style and in men's letters.

In their early encounters with Chinese texts, the Japanese developed a system of replacing the Chinese pronunciations of words symbolized by characters with their Japanese equivalents. This seems to have grown out of a simplified way of reading characters among the less educated. To help Japanese readers transpose a Chinese text into Japanese, a system of clues developed using diacritics around the edges of the characters. Some of these notations provided help to fill in Japanese suffixes, inflections, and postpositions.

Already by the eighth century a system for phonetically transcribing Japanese words using Chinese characters without reference to their semantics had been developed. These phonetically used characters are known as *manyōgana*. They were employed initially for rendering Japanese proper names and place-names but were subsequently developed for the transcription of the entire Japanese language—as demonstrated by their use in the ancient eighth-century collection of Japanese poetry the *Manyōshū*, from which their name derives. However, there existed a plethora of alternative forms, bearing no relation to efficiency or rationality but more to scribal preference and aesthetic values.

The origin of the present-day syllabaries shown in Table I.1 lies in the simplification and abbreviation of parts of *manyōgana*, together with a serious shrinking of the latter's polyvalency. Chinese characters had been conceived for an analytic language and were unsuited to the synthetic nature of Japanese. The syllabaries allowed for a closer representation of the phonological and grammatical character of Japanese. They emerged, from the tenth century, as a normal medium for writing Japanese texts such as poetry, diaries, and tales, and thus constitute an important step in Japanese emancipation from Chinese characters. The cursive style of *hiragana* (literally 'common *kana*') became the popular syllabic script, particularly associated with women. From the twelfth century, characters were introduced into popular texts encoded in the cursive syllabary intended for the general public, a practice that is now the norm of the present-day Japanese writing-system. On the other hand, the infusion of characters into script written in the angular syllabary known as *katakana* (literally 'one-side borrowings', because they derive from one side of a character) date from the ninth century, although this system was originally developed only as a means of notating Buddhist scriptures. Later, as

TABLE I.1. The Japanese Syllabaries[a]

H	あ	い	う	え	お									
K	ア	イ	ウ	エ	オ									
R	a	i	u	e	o									
H	か	き	く	け	こ	が	ぎ	ぐ	げ	ご	きゃ	きゅ	きょ	ぎゃ	ぎゅ	ぎょ
K	カ	キ	ク	ケ	コ	ガ	ギ	グ	ゲ	ゴ	キャ	キュ	キョ	ギャ	ギュ	ギョ
R	ka	ki	ku	ke	ko	ga	gi	gu	ge	go	kya	kyu	kyo	gya	gyu	gyo
H	さ	し	す	せ	そ	ざ	じ	ず	ぜ	ぞ	しゃ	しゅ	しょ	じゃ	じゅ	じょ
K	サ	シ	ス	セ	ソ	ザ	ジ	ズ	ゼ	ゾ	シャ	シュ	ショ	ジャ	ジュ	ジョ
R	sa	shi	su	se	so	za	ji	zu	ze	zo	sha	shu	sho	ja	ju	jo
H	た	ち	つ	て	と	だ	ぢ	づ	で	ど	ちゃ	ちゅ	ちょ	ぢゃ	ぢゅ	ぢょ
K	タ	チ	ツ	テ	ト	ダ	ヂ	ヅ	デ	ド	チャ	チュ	チョ	ヂャ	ヂュ	ヂョ
R	ta	te	tsu	te	to	da	ji	zu	de	do	cha	chu	cho	ja	ju	jo
H	な	に	ぬ	ね	の						にゃ	にゅ	にょ			
K	ナ	ニ	ヌ	ネ	ノ						ニャ	ニュ	ニョ			
R	na	ni	nu	ne	no						nya	nyu	nyo			
H	は	ひ	ふ	へ	ほ	ば	び	ぶ	べ	ぼ	ひゃ	ひゅ	ひょ	びゃ	びゅ	びょ
K	ハ	ヒ	フ	ヘ	ホ	バ	ビ	ブ	ベ	ボ	ヒャ	ヒュ	ヒョ	ビャ	ビュ	ビョ
R	ha	hi	fu	he	ho	ba	bi	bu	be	bo	hya	hyu	hyo	bya	byu	byo
H						ぱ	ぴ	ぷ	ぺ	ぽ	ぴゃ	ぴゅ	ぴょ			
K						パ	ピ	プ	ペ	ポ	ピャ	ピュ	ピョ			
R						pa	pi	pu	pe	po	pya	pyu	pyo			
H	ま	み	む	め	も						みゃ	みゅ	みょ			
K	マ	ミ	ム	メ	モ						ミャ	ミユ	ミョ			
R	ma	mi	mu	me	mo						mya	myu	myo			
H	ら	り	る	れ	ろ						りゃ	りゅ	りょ			
K	ラ	リ	ル	レ	ロ						リャ	リュ	リョ			
R	ra	ri	ru	re	ro						rya	ryu	ryo			
H	や		ゆ		よ											
K	ヤ		ユ		ヨ											
R	ya		yu		yo											
H	わ			を		ん										
K	ワ			ヲ		ン										
R	wa			o		n										

[a] H = hiragana, K = katakana, R = romanized.

the syllabic forms grew as large as the characters with which they were combined, they became the preferred syllabary for high-style texts such as official records and academic chronicles, prevailing in legal documents and scholarly work until the end of the Second World War.

Table I.1 presents the contemporary versions of these two Japanese syllabaries, with their romanized equivalents. The phonological unit represented by the syllabaries is the mora, which may be regarded as lying between a phoneme and a syllable; the analysis of Japanese sounds into this chart owes much to traditional Sanskrit linguistics.[2]

The angular syllabary, *katakana*, is generally only used, within present-day, standard texts composed of characters and the cursive syllabary (*hiragana*), for transcribing native onomatopoetic items, loan-words, and foreign names, and for extra emphasis—for example, to replace English italics. *Katakana* by itself is, however, employed for telegrams and, more recently, has been used for computer print-outs such as bank statements and salary slips.

The syllabary charts also represent a list of most of the possible phonological sequences permissible in Japanese; of course, the chart does not indicate gemination or vowel lengthening. The rules for combining the syllabic signs with Chinese characters to show native morphology are complex, and there is considerable variation in spite of official attempts at standardization.[3]

---

[2] It should be noted that voicing is represented by slanting ditto-like marks after the consonant that is voiced. Gemination (not shown in the table) is indicated by placing the small graph for *tsu* before the consonant which is doubled e.g. いった *itta* 'went'. There are two ways of showing vowel lengthening, depending on the syllabary. In *hiragana*, double letters are used in many cases, e.g. ああ いい うう, but because of phonological evolution, *ō* is written お う, and *ē* variously represented, depending on a word's history, either as ええ or えい. Vowel lengthening in *katakana* is simply indicated by a long dash e.g. ページ *peiji* 'page'. From the chart it may appear as if there is redundancy in some cases, but there are reasons for the apparent duplication. One is the object-marking particle, which means that *o* is written with the symbol を (*w*)*o*, in contrast to お. Similarly, the voiced graphs for *chi* and *tsu* (pronounced *ji* and *zu* respectively) are not interchangeable with the similar-sounding voiced derivations from *shi* and *su* (also pronounced *ji* and *zu*) but are only employed when they are either preceded in the same word by *chi* or *tsu*, e.g. tsuzuku つづく 'continue', or where voicing has occurred due to the formation of a compound, e.g. *hana* 'nose' + *chi* 'blood' > *hanaji* はなぢ 'nosebleed'. A recent innovation in the *katakana* syllabary has been the symbolization of the English /v/ consonant with the *u* sign and voicing marks: ヴ. However, this is not yet totally orthodox.

[3] The basic principle is to use the character for the root or stem of a word that remains after all affixes have been removed. In the following examples the character or stem element is represented with a capital letter and the part in *hiragana* with lower-case letters: 行く *I-ku/ YU-ku* 'to go'; 行かない *I-kanai* 'not go'; 行った *I-tta* 'went' (informal level); 行きました

The roman alphabet was first used to transcribe Japanese in the second half of the sixteenth century by Christian missionaries from Portugal and Spain. First arriving in 1549, these groups engaged in preaching, and this led to the need for publishing in Japanese; but persecution and exclusion from Japan put a complete end to their activities in 1635. The most productive were the Portuguese Jesuits, who first wrote Japanese according to Latin orthographic principles but later switched to those of Portuguese. On the one hand, Christian works were translated into Japanese; on the other, Japanese texts were made accessible to Iberian students of the language, sometimes in the contemporary colloquial variety. Although the Portuguese missionary's system of transcribing Japanese had no lasting effect, their profound knowledge of Japanese is reflected in the attribution of the innovation of the little circular diacritic (°) to indicate the *p* sound in the syllabaries to their linguistic efforts.

During the Edo period various systems of transcription based on roman letters were devised by Dutch, German, and French individuals, but it was not until the American missionary J. C. Hepburn (1815–1911) published the first English–Japanese dictionary in Shanghai in 1867 that a general model was established.[4]

In fact, after the Second World War the American Occupation Education Committee proposed that the Japanese ultimately entirely give up writing in characters and syllabaries and adopt romanization, but nothing concrete, apart from some intensive teaching of roman script in primary schools in the immediate post-war period, ever emerged from this proposal.

Today, the applications of the roman script are fairly limited; it is employed for transcribing Japanese items in many Japanese dictionaries of foreign languages; Japanese learn to transcribe their names in it for interaction with non-Japanese, and the names of many Japanese products in advertising are presented in it; it is also required for certain computer and/or word-processor keyboards used by the Japanese.

I-kimashita 'went' (formal level); 行う OKONA-*u* '*to carry out*'; 行わなければ OKONA-*wanakereba* 'if not carried out'; 行われる OKONA-*wareru* 'to be carried out'.

[4] Later, Japanese scholars produced their own romanized versions aiming at providing not so much a guide to pronunciation as a close correspondence to the syllabaries. In 1937 the government officially adopted one of these Japanese systems as the standard transcription (*Kunreishiki-rōmaji*), which was employed until the end of the war, after which the Hepburn system, used by the Americans, once again came into use. A 1953 ruling of the Language Planning Commision (*Kokugo Shingikai*) expresses a compromise position between the two systems, although generally advocating the *Kunrei* pattern. The main differences between the

Transcription

In this book, transcription of Japanese into the roman script will follow the Hepburn system, because it causes less difficulty for those who do not know how to pronounce Japanese.[5]

Hepburn and *Kunrei* transcriptions occur in the representation of alveolar and post-alveolar affricates and post-alveolar fricatives, e.g. (in the order H/K): tsu/tu, sha/sya, shu/syu; sho/syo; cha/tya; chi/ti; chu/tyu; cho/tyo; ja/zya, dya; ju/zyu, dyu; jo/zyo, dyo.

[5] Two minor modifications are introduced here. According to the strict observation of the Hepburn system, certain long vowels should be represented by overlining with a macron e.g. *ā*, *ū*, *ō*, while others such as *ii* and *ei* should not. Here, in contrast, this distinction is not maintained and a long *ī* and *ē* with a macron will be used throughout for the sake of regularity. Furthermore, in orthodox Hepburn romanization, phonemic /n/ before *p*, *b*, and *m* is indicated as *m*, as a true representation of pronunciation, e.g. *sammai*, while in more recent versions this appears as *sanmai*. However, the original convention which represents the phonetic or allophonic rather than the phonological is maintained here. Another device employed is the apostrophe which distinguished syllable-final *n* (ん) from syllable-initial *n* (な に ぬ ね の), e.g. *jin'in* 'personnel' and *jinin* 'resignation'.

1

Introducing Language Contact

This chapter will offer a brief introduction to the field of language contact and propose a universal typology for relating types of language contact to social settings which will be applied to the Japanese scenario throughout this book. Those readers already familiar with the theoretical background or wishing to proceed straight to the descriptive episodes concerning Japanese contact may dispense with it. However, it may be worth consulting the typology presented in Table 1.1 as the presentation proceeds.

Language contact is observable in almost every country of the contemporary world and is evident in the recorded history of nearly all languages. The term 'language contact' as employed here, covers an extremely broad range of phenomena, all of which relate to the direct and indirect influences of languages on each other. These reciprocal influences of one language or more on another may occur on any or every linguistic level and may also extend beyond these, to discourse and interaction. The words 'language contact' or 'language transfer' are employed here because they do not imply any normative judgements concerning the purity or legitimacy of the consequences of contact, nor suggest any degree of integration into a language during or after contact. Furthermore, the term 'language contact' indicates no particular source or type of influence and ascribes no volition on the part of speakers, which other terms such as 'mixing' or 'borrowing' might.

The subject of language contact has long been considered peripheral to linguistics, which has devoted its attention to the idealization of already standardized varieties within a prescriptivist and scriptist paradigm. Neogrammarians as well as generativists have failed to perceive the impact of other languages except in terms of proto-systems, thus neglecting historical and cultural influences. A further reason for the linguist's disregard of language contact is the existence of a negative folk-ideology concerning it. However, these academic attitudes have recently had to be revised in order to provide a more adequate account of the nature and development of language—for example, in seeking to explain language change, in identifying genetic relationships between languages, in

TABLE 1.1. A Socio-linguistic Typology of Language-Contact Settings and their Corresponding Contact-Phenomena[a]

Contact Phenomenon	Language-contact setting (minimal ⇐⇐⇐⇐⇐⇐⇐⇐⇐Degree of community bilingualism⇒⇒⇒⇒⇒⇒⇒⇒maximal)					
	Distant / dominant non-bilingual	Distant but institutional	Bounded and subordinate	Equal bilingual	Diglossic bilingual	Language-shifting
Areal features	*					
Interference		*	*	*	*	*
Interlanguage		*	*	*	*Temporary	*
Borrowing	*Small-scale		*Variable	*Variable	*Major	*Massive
Code-switching		*		*	*	*
Code-mixing				*	*	
Convergence			*	*	*	*[b]
Pidginization[c]	*	*	*			
Decreolization						*

[a] * indicates that the contact phenomenon only has the potential to occur in a particular setting and should be understood not as an obligatory feature but as a characteristic tendency frequently associated with a special set of socio-linguistic conditions.

[b] Convergence may occur during the final phase of language shift.

[c] Pidginization may occur in any setting in the early phases of learning a foreign language and may even, in certain cases, become a permanent condition. Pidginization in the form of 'foreigner talk' may occur in the dominant non-bilingual setting.

describing the varieties of second-language learners and the special con-
tact-varieties in bi- or multilingual communities, whether immigrant or
indigenous, and, above all, in coming to terms with pidgins and creoles.
Thus, the subject of language contact has already been investigated from
diverse and often unconnected perspectives; but in spite of the plethora
of descriptive studies focusing on particular cases, the many different processes and types of contact have never been unified into a single, general
theory, and this has resulted in a rather serious lacuna in the realm of
generalization and universal application. In fact, each research-field has
tended to generate its own terminology, which, sometimes even within
common areas of investigation, has not been systematized.

Although during the founding of modern linguistics language contact
received attention as *Sprachmischung* (Hermann, 1866) and 'language
mixture' (Whitney, 1881), it was not until the publication of *Languages
in Contact* by Uriel Weinreich in 1953 that it established itself as a dis-
ciplinary concern. Not only did this seminal work provide an exhaustive
survey of literature on the topic up to the time of its publication, but
its combination of rigorous structural analysis with a consideration of
sociological factors set up a theoretical framework that still dominates
the field. Surprisingly, there have been few groundbreaking developments
since Weinreich, although a multitude of case-studies have appeared.
However, the 1990s are witnessing a rekindling of theoretical interest in
the subject.[1]

It is important to realize that many concepts and subfields within the
discipline of linguistics are integral to the field of language contact. Among
these are phenomena such as areal linguistics, interference, borrowing,
language shift, diglossia, code-switching/-mixing, language convergence,
pidginization, and creolization. Although all these terms cannot be defined here, some will appear in the course of the following discussion.

It is now time for linguists to consider the common points between
these varied phenomena and establish a universal theory of language
contact applicable across communities by making a systematic study of
the causal factors but avoiding mechanistic explanations. It would, for
example, be theoretically valuable to identify the similarities in the linguistic phenomena termed 'interference' and 'convergence', since both
may involve the phonological, syntactic, and/or semantic *restructuring* of
a native language because of the influence of a foreign language. Likewise,

---

[1] See Thomason and Kaufman (1988); Jahr (1992); McMahon (1994).

the process of restructuring—this time of a foreign language on the basis of one learnt first—in differently termed phenomena such as 'interlanguage', 'borrowing', 'second-language varieties', and 'pidginization' also deserves recognition.

The degree of assimilation appears to be a significant factor in the terminological distinctions, where unassimilated items are generally treated under 'interference' and 'code-switching', while more normatively integrated types of transfer receive attention under 'borrowing'. Another distinguishing criterion is the participants' consciousness of language contact, according to which code-switching is apparently a more conscious process than 'interference' but less conscious than 'borrowing' because it rarely involves phonological adaptions. Not only the shared theoretical aspects of contact terminology but also their co-occurrence and interrelating dynamics require more attention, and it is the aim of the following synthesizing framework to provide this.

A Typology of Contact Settings

In the study of language contact, what has made any sort of comparison or generalization most difficult is the lack of a common system of reference. Before any general theory can be elaborated, the problem of comparability must be solved.

(Mackey, 1983: 71)

That no general typology for language contact in relation to its sociocultural setting exists is probably a result of the difficulty in formulating empirical and historical universals for phenomena which linguists have assumed to be more or less random and unsystematizable. Of course, contact situations are dynamic in that they can alter their characteristics at any moment in response to social change. The initiation, maintenance, reduction, and termination of language contact depend on a host of apparently heterogeneous factors which, admittedly, are difficult to codify.

There now follows a practical and simple typology—designed to cover all situations of language contact—which can serve as a convenient method for comparing and contrasting such phenomena in relation to their social setting and thereby allows a measure of predictability, as well as providing a unifying approach. This typology of contact settings will serve as the yardstick in the ensuing discussion of Japanese language-contact.

The minimum level of the local community is taken here as the unit of reference where appropriate.[2] The communities involved in language contact are categorized[3] according to their degree of bilingualism: 'no', 'little', or 'widespread' societal bilingualism. These levels obviously represent different points on a continuum, but more precise specification is clearly not possible, as bilingualism can vary considerably among individual members of a community. Furthermore, the degree of societal bilingualism may increase, decrease, or revert over time, in the same way as the amount of contact can. However, no more than a general profile of a community during a particular phase of development is taken as the stage of reference here; the duration of the contact is not indicated.[4] Likewise, the causes of contact are not given, as these are fortuitous and depend on a very particular socio-historical configuration. The diverse factors responsible for language contact include: the social proximity of a group speaking another language; military occupation; a superposed religious medium; institutional support for a foreign language; political affiliation; immigration; and economic activity. These may also occur in combination.

Of course, the extent of community acceptance of, or resistance to, language contact, although not directly shown in the typology, is evident from the number of contact phenomena observable in a certain setting, as well as from the degree of bilingualism associated with it.

In Table 1.1 a socio-linguistic typology of six archetypal contact-settings is proposed, based on my own interpretation and synthesis of various research and arguments. The contact settings presented here constitute general 'profiles' of the language behaviour of a particular speech-community.[5] The typology should be understood as a systematization of

---

[2] Of course, the *speech-community* is not necessarily congruent with a national entity, since there may be various speech-communities within one country or territory which do not employ similar languages for similar purposes.

[3] In defining a speech-community for purposes of comparison, the following variables should be considered: size, stability, geographic location, indigenousness, length of residence.

[4] It should be obvious that no contact-setting is necessarily stable, and accordingly that the contact may cease at any particular moment, depending on particular socio-historical circumstances. Transitional phases are not indicated in the framework (as this would overcomplicate the patterns), but it should be clear that such phases will involve either the expansion or reduction of contact phenomena—the degree of interference, code-switching, and convergence in one setting may be restricted as the community becomes increasingly monolingual.

[5] The characterization of speech-communities as 'bilingual' or 'monolingual' is, of course, not unproblematic. The language behaviour of demographically minor groups who wield political, social, or economic power also must be taken into account, since they can affect the socio-linguistic relations of the entire community.

patterns to be expected in certain situations. The six settings represent an increasing level of bilingualism in the contact language (when moving from left to right). However, particularly in the equal, diglossic, and language-shifting settings, the distribution of bilingual competence may be equally high among certain community members. The term 'bilingual' in the table is understood as including multilingualism. The concept of bilingualism today is broad and includes non-fluent interlanguage states varying in native approximation, as well as only passive knowledge of the written language, so that the the conception of perfect, native-like proficiency in both languages is recognized as an ideal rarely attained by most bilinguals.

The various contact-phenomena shown in Table 1.1 vary in the way they combine, depending on the community and their intensity at a particular moment, so that, for example, borrowing may involve the transfer of 10 or 1,000 words. Nevertheless, there is a correlation between the number of loans transferred—that is, the intensity of contact—and the degree of community bilingualism, so that the settings on the right-hand side constitute the most fertile ground for contact. There now follows a brief characterization of each setting. This will allow the reader to gain a more concrete understanding of the socio-linguistic conditions involved.

The Distant or Dominant Non-bilingual Setting

This refers to the case where, among the members of a particular community, which may be either monolingual or socially bi- or multilingual, the knowledge and use of one (or more) contact language(s) is not widely distributed. Although there may well be some individuals familiar with the contact language(s), they are not representative of the community as a whole—for example, knowledge of Japanese among the British. The key characteristics of such a setting are that the community maintains no community-wide relations with speakers of the donor language and that it does not socially require the acquisition of that language. Contact in this setting is usually limited to lexical borrowing, which may start, increase, decrease, or terminate during certain periods; indirect contact may also be evident in loan translations or even stylistic influences.

Contact in this setting may be initiated through various channels. First, it may start with individual cases of diffusion into the community; but it is not introduced directly through bilingual interaction. The initial agents of contact may come from within the recipient community, or they may be outsiders familiar with the donor language and having a certain level of influence. Other possible agents are those who venture beyond the bounds of their community—travellers, explorers, and temporary emigrants—who bring back the language contact to their own group.

A second channel of contact is not directly personal but involves the transmission of the donor language in oral form, via radio, film, record, cassette, or video, and in written form via printed and handwritten material. Mediating agents, again usually within the recipient community, draw on these sources and initiate contact. In such cases, agents need not have been in direct contact with a foreign community; they need only have had access to the foreign language via indirect channels, and be in a sufficiently influential position to diffuse items from it into their community. Thus, they tend to be specialists of various kinds, such as journalists, translators, religious, academic, scientific, or technical researchers, even innovative artists and craftsmen. The subsequent integration of such contact will depend on the general socio-cultural significance of the items to the community at large.

A clear example of this setting is the contemporary contact with English in countries where the latter is not used as an official language nor employed to fulfil any internal function—see the inroads which English has made into modern German. This kind of contact community is located at a considerable physical distance from the donor source (England and the USA) and the phenomena observed tend to be limited to small-scale lexical borrowing with varying degrees of change on phonological and semantic levels.

Another type of distant non-bilingual setting is that in which the donor language of contact is employed by a subordinate group within the territory of a socio-economically and ethno-linguistically superior recipient community, the majority of whose speakers are ignorant of the donor variety. Typically, there exists considerable social distance between these contact groups, so that the only form of contact in the dominant non-bilingual community, if there is any, tends to be lexical borrowing on a limited scale, often for place-names, terms for local fauna and flora, and cultural items specific to the subordinate group. This situation is well exemplified by the behaviour evident in the contact between English and indigenous groups who were subjected to British colonization—Aborigines, Maoris, Native Americans, Eskimos. Further back in history, there is the case of the paucity of Celtic loans in southern dialects of Old English due to the social distance between the conquering

Germanic tribes and the enslaved Romanized Celts. Thus, in a dominant non-bilingual setting, contact other than small-scale lexical borrowing is rare. The principal characteristic of the distant non-bilingual setting is the unfamiliarity of the donor language in the recipient community.

The Distant but Institutional Setting

Similar to that which occurs in the previous setting, this kind of contact takes place when the acquisition of a foreign language is not part of community activities, unless in the domain of religion, but is promoted through an institution such as a school. This language-learning may be related to political dominance, as was the learning of Russian in East German schools; or it may be engaged in culturally for its own sake, as is the learning of Latin in Britain; or it may have a religious motivation, as does the study of classical Arabic by African Muslims. The purpose behind the teaching of the foreign language depends on the social history of the community.

It is essential to realize that learning a foreign language in school does not automatically lead to the creation of community bilingualism, for as Jakobvits (1971: 22) has bluntly pointed out: 'second language learning as a classroom subject is one thing, and being a bilingual person another and they often have little to do with each other'.

Unlike in natural settings of second-language learning, where many informal sources are available for reinforcement and practice, the institutionally taught 'foreign' language tends to be regarded as an end or product in itself rather than as a vehicle to achieve communicative goals. Among the most significant variables of this setting are:

- The range and depth of acquisition in relation to the skills imparted.
- The linguistic varieties (models) selected for acquisition.
- The methodology selected—for example, grammar-translation or rote memorization.
- The purpose of learning the foreign language—for example, to pass exams, have access to information, or read/maintain sacred texts.
- The social and psychological characteristics of the learners and their teachers: age, personality, previous learning-habits, amount of training and experience, attitudes and motivation.
- Aspects of the learning situation such as class size, curriculum and material, contact hours, teacher–student relations.

There are hardly any countries in the contemporary world which do not provide some of its citizens with the chance of institutionally acquiring a foreign language. Contact as a direct consequence of this on a societal scale, however, is very rarely observable. If it does occur on a community-wide basis, as with English in Germany, it is not due to instruction alone but involves other causal factors. In the case of English, of course, contributing forces such as the international use and status of English, world-power affiliation, and economic, technological, and scientific communication must be taken into account.

The contact phenomena typically associated with this setting are interference, interlanguage, pidginization, and code-switching in classroom-talk.

The Bounded and/or Subordinate Community

As can be seen from Table 1.1, the degree of bilingualism in this setting is higher than in the previous two, but it tends to be of a 'restricted' nature in that it is neither fluent, nor accurate, nor native-like. This 're-stricted' bilingualism arises from the restricted social contact maintained by the recipient or donor community, or both, towards each other. In the section dealing with the distant/dominant setting, a superior recipient community's contact behaviour was seen to be characterized by limited borrowing; but in a bounded or subordinate community, because of the increased presence of bilingualism, there tend to occur various phenomena such as interference, interlanguage, pidginization, and, more rarely, convergence.[6]

Often, cultural displacement and/or economic disadvantage or differing ethnicity leads to the social distance between the two communities. The term 'bounded' reflects the 'sealed-off' nature of the recipient community, which may be either self-imposed or externally constructed by the dominant community. This ethnic boundary may vary between 'soft' and 'hard', depending on distinctions such as skin-colour, facial features, dress style, cultural tradition, and values—as well as language. This

---

[6] The resemblance of this setting to Fishman's (1971) category of 'diglossia without bilingualism' should not go unnoticed: 'Here we find two or more speech communities united politically, religiously, and/or economically into a single functioning unit notwithstanding the sociocultural cleavages that separate them. At the level of this larger (but not always voluntary) unity, two or more languages or varieties must be recognized as obtaining. However, one (or both) of the speech communities involved is (are) marked by such relatively impermeable group boundaries that for "outsiders" . . . role access and linguistic access are severely restricted. At the same time linguistic repertoires in one or both groups are limited to role specialization.' As examples, Fishman cites the case of pre-First-World-War élites (Danish, Provençal, Russian, among others) who spoke French or some other fashionable High tongue for their intragroup purposes, while the masses spoke another language for their intragroup purposes.

setting lasts as long as the boundary remains stable; a sign of the collapse of the ethno-linguistic boundary is language shift.

Lewis (1978*b*) discusses different types of relatively stable bounded communities such as: (1) those existing in geographic isolation; (2) those which experience urban segregation; (3) ethnic-minority enclaves; and (4) those with their own tradition of restricted cultural contact.

Contemporary examples of each of these communities which are involved in language contact are:

1. Irish Gaelic speakers in the Gaeltacht; Gaelic speakers in the Scottish Highlands and Islands; Romansch speakers in Switzerland; Frisian speakers in Holland.
2. (First-generation) Pakastanis in Northern England; (first-generation) Turks in West Germany; Hispanics in the USA.
3. Albanians, Croats, and Greeks in southern Italy; Basques in southern France; Doukhobor Russians in Canada.
4. Conservative German-speaking Amish of Pennsylvania; Athapaskan and Pueblo Indians of the USA.

A further category is that of more mobile linguistic minorities such as nomads, gypsies, seasonal migrants, and involuntary immigrants such as slaves.

Typical of these communities is a markedly low level of bilingualism among permanent members, and, particularly, pidginization and fossilized interlanguages resulting from lack of access to the contact model and/or lack of assimilatory motivation. If the pidgin or interlanguage is limited only to the older generations, then the setting should be recategorized as either *equal-bilingual, language-shifting,* or *diglossic bilingual*. However, when learning a second language does not lead to greater mobility or entry into the dominant community, and when little communication with members of the dominant community takes place, restricted contact is likely to be longer-lasting for most members of the subordinate group. Educational opportunities in the mainstream language may or may not increase the level of bilingualism and inaugurate language shift. Exactly what keeps a community bounded for a certain period is community-specific; broad generalizations across time and space cannot easily be made here.

The Equal Bilingual Setting

This setting may entail one community employing two languages, or two communities in the same territory employing two languages, but the key feature is that neither of the languages is subordinate to the other and that either language may be employed for equal access in almost all social domains. This situation is infrequent, since communities tend to favour the employment of one language and there are often historical power-relations involved in the social evaluation of the two languages, even if their equality is legally guaranteed, as is the care for Flemish and French in Brussels, and English and French in Quebec.

For Pietersen (1978: 390) this situation occurs 'when two languages in a territory function for the same people and both can be used officially and at the dialect level . . . there is no high and low status . . . Both languages are used in almost all domains', although not 'haphazardly so that in practice there is probably a division of labor in which one language is used at home as the main language and not the other. But the point here is that both languages can be used in every domain.'

In communities where two languages are in principle equal to each other, their separate identities are not necessarily maintained. The norms of one may be renounced, and interference, borrowing, code-switching, code-mixing, and convergence are likely to appear.[7] An example of convergence is provided by Scollon and Scollon (1979) in their study of contact between French, English, Chipewyan, and Cree in a subarctic, multilingual Alaskan community where the four languages have syntactically and semantically coalesced in such a way that none of them exclusively symbolizes a separate ethnic identity, since their speakers in this setting share the same ethnicity. Such convergence has serious theoretical consequences for the traditional linguist's conception of language as a clearly distinguishable, self-contained system. In this setting, one mental system called a 'language' may be fused on various levels with another, originally separate, system. Such radical contact reveals the environmental dependency and elasticity of phenomena which linguists have up to now treated as stable and autonomous.

The Language-Shifting Community

The initiation, rate, and process of language shift vary considerably from case to case, but the procedure is observable in many contemporary

---

[7] e.g. Thomas (1982) mentions borrowing into Welsh from English on the written level as well as code-mixing which is a consequence of an earlier diglossic situation between the two languages. Fasold (1984: 56) cites extended borrowing of long phrases (code-mixing?) from English into Swahili in Tanzania. Interference on all linguistic levels is also to be expected with the increase in community bilingualism.

communities. In her now classic study of the shift from Hungarian to German, Gal (1979) mentions the occurrence of code-switching, borrowing, and interference. In addition to these contact phenomena, learner pidgins and interlanguage varieties have also been frequently documented, coinciding with the shift in culturally displaced and disadvantaged indigenous minorities, as well as, of course, immigrants.

The language-shifting community has frequently been regarded as the contact setting *par excellence*, and pioneering studies of language contact drew much of their data from such settings. Weinreich's seminal study, for example, draws heavily on the interference of immigrants to the USA; and Haugen's analysis is totally based on Norwegian immigrants' shift to American English.

From Table 1.1 it can be seen that convergence between the contact languages involved in language-shifting communities may also occur during the final stages of the shift.[8] Moroever, decreolization may also be regarded as a form of language shift—from the creole to the standard—which involves bilingualism and causes contact phenomena.[9] Of course, decreolization results from the diglossic relationship between the creole and the standard. Actually, language-shifting communities tend generally to appear in diglossic settings where the donor language belongs to a socially higher group.[10] A common reason for such a shift is a stronger

---

[8] Evidence for this comes from Dressler's account (1982) of language shift among e.g. Bretons and Austrian Croatians, where a restructuring of morphology, syntax, semantics, and pronouns on the basis of the majority language has been noted, together with 'lexical fading', i.e. massive borrowing from the language shifted to.

[9] In some Caribbean communities such as Jamaica and Guyana, there exists a post-creole continuum with a range of varieties from a close approximation to the standard to the deepest creole. Here it is speakers with an intermediate proficiency in the standard variety (termed the mesolect) and who are seeking upward social mobility who are attempting decreolization, and, in the process, evidence phonological and syntactic interference, relexification (borrowing from the standard), and code-switching 'up' or 'down' cf. Craig (1978).

[10] Fishman (1971), however, confusingly categorizes the situations of dislocated immigrants and their children as 'bilingualism without diglossia': 'without separate though complementary norms and values to establish and maintain functional separation of the speech varieties, that language or variety which is fortunate enough to be associated with the predominant shift of social forces tends to displace the other', with the result that second-generation immigrant children are 'particularly inclined to use their mother tongue and other tongue for intragroup communication in seemingly random fashion' (ibid. 87). Nevertheless, the dominant donor-language is the only viable one for High, official domains in immigrant communities, so that, although internally there may be no diglossia during language shift, there certainly exists external diglossia in relation to the mainstream monolingual society. Fasold (1984: 41) interprets situations of 'bilingualism without diglossia' as the result of 'leaky diglossia', where the formerly distinct functions of the High language intermingle or leak into the Low one.

identification with the dominant community and the renunciation of one's linguistic distinctiveness.[11]

The Diglossic Bilingual Setting[12]

A diglossic bilingual community is one where linguistic and role repertoires are compartmentalized, with each language serving High and Low functions respectively, but where the High language is accessible to members of the community—although usually only partial bilingualism in the High variety tends to characterize the majority. In diglossic bilingual settings the acquisition of the entire community-repertoire does not occur at home or in neighbourhood play-groups but through formal education, religion, government, or the work sphere. (This is the situation in present-day Paraguay.)

When it comes to the correlation of this setting with the listed contact-phenomena, considerable data are available from studies on high-status, non-native English varieties in many African and Asian states where local languages are assigned low status. Here, phenemona such as interlanguage, pidginization, interference on every linguistic level, borrowing from both sides, code-switching, and code-mixing[13] have all been observed.

[11] As an example of a case where language shift to the majority language is not occurring because social access into mainstream society is blocked is provided by Sandefur (1982: 10): 'Social mobility among Aborigines is *not* primarily in the direction of English-speaking white Australian society. Rather, it is in the direction of broader . . . Aboriginal social contacts . . . White Australians in general . . . do not accept black Australians on equal ground. This has reinforced today's resurgence of Aboriginal identity.' The result is that English is not the 'dominant language of Aboriginal communities. English is so little used in most everyday contexts and has so little instrumental value that it exerts little decreolization influence.'

[12] Fishman (1971) extended Ferguson's (1959) concept of diglossia to include bi-/multilingual situations where unrelated languages could also serve High and Low functions in the same community. The situation in Paraguay, according to Rubin (1968) and Fishman (1971), is diglossic bilingual, with more than half the population speaking both Spanish and Guarani but where the former language is employed in the domains of education, religion, government, and high culture, i.e. as the High variety, with Guarani for ordinary, informal, Low communication. However, it should be noted that if the élite in a society is monolingual in the High variety, as in tsarist Russia (where the aristocracy was exclusively French-speaking), or in the European colonization of Africa and Asia, the setting is classified as 'diglossia without bilingualism' because it involves two separate communities who do not employ each other's languages and corresponds to my 'bounded or subordinate setting'.

[13] See the research conducted by Tay (1982) on English–Chinese/Malay language-contact in Singapore; Jibril (1982) on the diglossic contact-setting of English in Nigeria; Zwengler (1982) on English in Kenya; Mehrotra (1982) and Kachru (1982, 1983a) on English-based language-contact in India; Gonzalez (1982) on code-switching/-mixing in the Philippines; and Gibbons (1983) on English–Cantonese code-mixing in Hong Kong. Additionally, when bounded groups lose their ethno-linguistic vitality and shift languages, they may become diglossic bilingual for

Finally, the case of areal features marked as potential under this setting needs to be briefly explained. Areal features may occur because of the physical proximity of different and distinct communities speaking different languages who share a long history of coexistence and some degree of social contact but do not employ each other's language on a societal basis (as indicated for the 'distant non-bilingual setting'). But they may also occur in a diglossic situation through the diffusion of a High variety across several neighbouring communities. Thus, the often-cited *Sprachbund* in the Balkan area, where Modern Greek, Albanian, Romanian, and Bulgarian share a rich fund of common vocabulary, morph-for-morph equivalents, and various syntactic devices, results from the unifying force of Byzantine civilization as represented by the Greek Orthodox Church, so that in many instances Greek can be recognized as the donor model for the shared language-contact.

Fishman (1971) attributes the contemporary proliferation of diglossic bilingual settings to modernization and growing social complexity. In a classic diglossic bilingual community each language has its own circumscribed functions, which are well-established, socially accepted, and maintained. As seen from Table 1.1, the contact features potentially occurring here are more far-ranging than any of the earlier settings; the two (or more) languages in contact each reveal greater 'permeability', but the high-status language tends to be less susceptible to change because of its overriding status and enshrined norms. The motivation for language contact in a diglossic bilingual setting appears to correspond closely to the classic Weinreichian factor of prestige or social advancement.

Armed with this introductory model of the nature of language contact in different communities around the world, the reader is now ready to interpret, analyse, and cross-relate the evolution of language contact in Japanese society.

a certain period: see the case of contemporary Scottish Gaelic as described by MacAulay (1982), where interference, borrowing, and code-switching are all observable. It is, however, important to recognize that diglossic bilingualism does not necessarily lead to language shift: e.g. in Europe, Latin persisted for centuries as a High medium in religious, academic, scientific, and some literary domains, but the vernacular languages survived.

2

Japanese Contact with Asian Languages

Japanese society has been involved in the processes of language contact since its earliest emergence. As was mentioned in the introduction to the Japanese language, the mixed linguistic heritage of Japanese points to the strong likelihood of it having gradually evolved through pidgin and creole stages of communication between Austronesian- and Altaic-speaking groups who migrated to the islands in prehistoric time (see Aikiba-Reynolds, 1983; Doi, 1984). Furthermore, the Chinese language has played a pre-eminent role in both linguistic and cultural development in Japan since the beginning of recorded history, but it is now being eclipsed by English-speaking cultures.

Table 2.1[1] offers a bird's-eye view of the evolution of Japanese linguistic contact with exogenous sources and of how this relates to historical periods and motivational forces. However, the cause for contact has been reduced to a very general, perhaps even over-simplified, notion. This chapter and the following two aim to provide substance and depth to this outline.

The Chinese Heritage

Research into Chinese-related language-contact is extensive and centuries old, since it has long been part of traditional Japanese education to be able to read and interpret classical Confucian texts. Furthermore, studies into Sino-Japanese relations are inextricably bound up with the history of the Japanese themselves, their linguistic evolution, the development of their writing-system, their classical culture and literature, their religious systems, their political and social order, and precisely for these reasons has occupied the attention of Japanese scholars since earliest times.[2]

---

[1] This table is my own adapted version of Umegaki's chart (1963: 32).

[2] As far back as the ninth cent., Chinese–Japanese dictionaries and glossaries, such as the *Shinsen jikyo* (completed 898–901) and the *Ruiju myōgishō* (1081), were being collated, and other Chinese-related research conducted by Buddhist priest-scholars. However, Chinese studies, with their focus on the correct reading and interpretation of classical texts—particularly

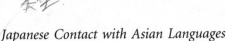

In this chapter a socio-historical orientation is adopted and the evolution of Japanese contact with other languages is described in terms of the typologizing framework proposed at the end of the Chapter 1. Apart from the categories of contact setting and type, related factors, such as the motivation, agents, channels, varieties, and effects of the language contact, will be considered here. The specific details of the transferred items themselves will not be extensively discussed unless this serves some special purpose: such precise explanation would require considerable familiarity with the languages in question (Chinese in particular) as well as Japanese. Readers interested in lists of Chinese-derived loans should consult Umegaki (1963) and Miller (1967).

The most pervasive and profound contact with any language in Japanese history has been that with Chinese, which was the medium carrying the cultural and technological innovation so crucial to the development of early Japan. Without the reception and assimilation of Chinese civilization, the Japanese would have remained in the Late Stone Age, as was the case for non-assimilating Ainu groups.

In fact, Chinese contact eventually contributed to the creation of a 'contact tradition' which provided a model for future types of interaction with external languages through the contemporary overlay of prestigious, foreign patterns of Chinese language and culture; this resulted from a diglossic, bicultural structure. Ultimately, of course, Japanese culture internalized the originally alien cultural elements in its own way. The cultural dichotomy is well represented in the historical division between indigenous, Japanese literary genres and those based on Chinese.[3]

It is important to understand that the phrase 'Chinese language-contact' not only refers to *direct* contact with Chinese people and culture (which was very limited) but includes contact with Chinese civilization via other groups, usually from Korea (see below on agents of transmission). Terms such as 'Chinese-related' and 'Chinese-style' refer to this

intense during the Chinese Confucianist revival of the Tokugawa period—declined from the mid-nineteenth cent.: Doi (1983). In their surveys of Japanese descriptive and historical linguistics, Hattori (1967) and Tsukishima (1967) provide commentated references to the most important Japanese researchers, past and present, in these areas. Yamada (1967) offers a detailed survey of historical and modern research into the Chinese-style writing-system of Japan, and Umetomo *et al.* (1961) give a comprehensive review of studies in Japanese philology and literature, many of which discuss contact with Chinese. In particualar, the research into Chinese borrowings conducted by Yamada (1940), and that of Kamei (1954) into prehistoric Chinese loans, is of considerable significance.

[3] Sansom (1928: 61) presents this diagrammatically: see App. 3.

TABLE 2.1. A Chronological Outline of Japanese Contact with other Languages

Period	Type of cultural motivation	Donor language
Heian (8th–12th cent.)	Buddhism, Confucianism	Chinese (Sanskrit)
Late 16th–early 17th cent.	Christianity	Portuguese, Spanish, Latin
Edo (17th–19th cent.)	Early Western science	Dutch
Meiji (1868–1912)	General Western culture	English, German, French
Pre-Second World War (1912–1940)	Mass Western culture (esp. American)	English, German, French
Present day	International culture	Mainly English; other languages

Korean modification and to subsequent Japanese transformation of Chinese culture—not uniquely, for example, in the integration of Chinese vocabulary, but also in the spheres of architecture, art, ideology, and social organization.

Unfortunately, a certain degree of simplification and generalization cannot be avoided in trying to synthesize the complex phases and results of 2,000 years of assimilating Chinese systems.

Phases of Chinese-Style Language-Contact

It is significant that the first historical reference to Japan is to be found in Chinese records dating from the first century AD,[4] though the major waves of influence and contact did not take place until the end of the sixth century. From this time, Japan, as a united country, officially launched a programme of massive sinicization, accompanied by the official adoption of Chinese Buddhism in AD 594. However, direct relations with China ended with the advent of an era of semi-seclusion, from 894–1401, during which only limited external communication was possible: Japanese were forbidden to travel overseas, and Chinese ships were excluded from Japanese ports. Nevertheless, in spite of the drastic reduction in Chinese-related contact, enough had been absorbed to permit the Japanese independently to elaborate and expand on Chinese social and linguistic patterns.

The Chinese heritage, enjoying a renaissance during the seventeenth and eighteenth centuries, managed to maintain a dominant position until the middle of the nineteenth, even though it was challenged twice by Western waves of learning and contact before then—this is the subject of the next chapter. However, it waned after Japan was forced to open up to American and European nations from 1854, a development which culminated in a passionate infatuation with all things Western. This in its turn declined before the arrival of the twentieth century. China's submission to British imperialism from the middle of the nineteenth century, its weakness in military encounters with Japan from 1895 until the end of the Second World War, the effects of the Cold War, and Japan's attainment of economic and technological superiority have all contributed to the decline and collapse of the Chinese model.

---

[4] The Chinese records reveal the payment of tribute from a northern Kyūshū state in AD 57: see Sugimoto and Swain (1978: 3). However, the first detailed report about Japan is found in a Chinese text called the *Wei chih*, composed towards the end of the third cent. AD, which describes a visit by envoys from the Han court to the Japanese kingdom of Wo. See Miller (1967: 12–27) for a full description.

Language-Contact Settings

As far as can be ascertained from the available evidence, prehistorical Japanese contact with Chinese corresponds to a 'distant non-bilingual' setting. Chinese material influences in fields such as techniques for rice and silk cultivation, metalwork, weaving, and building spread down from the Korean peninsula into northern Kyūshū and Japan from the second century BC and led to a shift from a nomadic, tribal society to a settled, agrarian one. By the fourth and fifth centuries AD Japan's external standing had grown to the extent where it maintained some kind of diplomatic representation in the southern tip of Korea; it also had direct, formal dealings with China. During these early centuries, for which no Japanese written records exist, limited borrowing of Chinese words for items that were transferred has been uncovered. Loans which have been suggested[5] include 'horse' *uma* (the animal seems to have been introduced from China), 'salt' *shio*, 'silkworm' *kaiko*, 'rice' *ine*, 'wheat' *mugi*, 'grind' *togu*, 'cleave' *saku*, 'flay' *hagu*, 'build' *tsuku*, 'house' *ie*, 'bamboo' *take*, 'boat' *fune*, 'pot' *kama*, 'sickle' *kama*, 'village' *sato*, 'state' *kuni*, and 'grave' *haka*. These indicate, above all, an agricultural, technical, organizational, and ritual importation of Chinese know-how.

By the Nara period (710–94) and the appearance of the earliest surviving texts in Japan, however, this language contact had dramatically changed into a diglossic bilingual setting (see Table 1.1), where the High second language was acquired through formal institutions, with native Chinese teachers and Korean immigrants knowledgeable in Chinese providing instruction. To what extent such groups held political power remains controversial, but according to the orthodox viewpoint, they constituted a prestigious minority that underwent assimilation. This contact setting prevailed well into early Heian times (end of the ninth century), with Chinese as a High variety used in the domains of administration and law, for many types of documentation, including official, academic, and private writing, for the state religion of Buddhism, and for works of High literature; many anthologies of Chinese poetry were compiled under T'ang influences—for example *Kaifūsō* (751).

The fact that knowledge of high-status, superimposed Chinese was not widely distributed among community members is typical of this setting,

---

[5] However, certain Japanese linguists have tried hard to refute almost the entire corpus: see Kamei (1954). On the other hand, Miller (1967: 237) notes that 'by and large Karlgren's list gives a good idea of the type and variety of these old Chinese loans in Japanese, and although items of detail may be questioned it remains secure as a body of evidence'.

where mastery of the High variety is frequently associated with the élite, who in this case were mainly made up of court nobility, the Buddhist clergy, and administrators.

It was because during this time the Japanese proceeded to adopt the Chinese writing-sytem wholesale, having none of their own, that they were forced to adopt the Chinese language with it. Thus, the initial employment of Chinese characters necessarily entailed bilingualism. Because of their copious copying of sutras and recitation of prayers in Chinese, Buddhist temples and monasteries appear to have played a key role during this period in the dissemination of skills in that language.

Of course, since our only sources of inference are written documents, it is difficult to assess the extent of oral communication in Chinese among the Japanese community but its occurrence seems likely in formal, ceremonial speech-events, particularly those linked to the imperial court. The fact that late Heian literature composed in Japanese reveals a steadily increasing number of well-integrated and established Chinese loans supports the view that Chinese forms were not restricted to a purely written level of communication. There is, moreover, evidence that the oral aspects of Chinese were seriously studied, under native Chinese teachers.[6] However, this oral proficiency in Chinese rapidly declined when methods for reading Chinese texts in an instantaneous Japanese translation established themselves. This was possible due to the fact that Chinese characters generally do not offer indications as to their pronunciation, thereby making possible their association with the sounds of a language other than Chinese.

Although borrowing in speech must have taken place on an increasing scale in this Nara/early Heian diglossic bilingual setting, it is not strongly evident in most of the few surviving, orally derived texts composed in Japanese during this period,[7] which maintain a strict division between the

---

[6] The *Nihon shoki* mentions that in 691 two 'professors of pronunciation' direct from T'ang China were employed at the court, and it is to be supposed there were many more.

[7] There are few texts composed in Japanese during this diglossic bilingual setting because Chinese was the High variety. Included among them are the following: an anthology of native poetry completed in 759 known as the *Man' yōshū*; imperial edicts (697–789) or *semmyō*; and ritual Shintō prayers or *norito* (eighth cent.). Both the *semmyō* and *norito* were routine formulas for oral recitation, their essentially spoken function explaining why they were notated in Japanese. The collection of native poetry also derived from oral transmission, and some of it was composed by people unfamiliar with Chinese. Furthermore, studies of the *Man' yōshū* reveal that the poems were composed with native Japanese vocabulary 'except for a very small number of Chinese and Sanskrit words mainly of Buddhist reference' (Habein, 1984: 15).

two languages, although they are influenced by Chinese literary styles. At first sight, the reverse might, in fact, seem to hold—namely, that Japanese was borrowed into Chinese—since items relating to the Japanese milieu appear, transcribed in characters, in texts written in Chinese during this period. But of course this is obviously not the case, for the Chinese texts were written for Japanese *intra*group purposes.

A further contact-feature notable in this setting is interference, which manifests itself, above all, in the phonological changes of Chinese[8] by the Japanese and in alteration of word-order patterns. The most significant results of this diglossic bilingual setting are undeniably the adoption of the Chinese writing-system, the development of which is diagrammatically outlined in Fig. 2.1, and the concomitant acquisition of classical Chinese vocabulary and syntax necessary to employ it.

From the tenth century, the situation regarding contact with Chinese, however, altered and evolved steadily into a diglossic setting without bilingualism, which was maintained with various degrees of intensity until the mid-twentieth century. In this new setting, contact with Chinese *per se* was made only in an institutional context, as it ceased to have a community function. Thus, it is necessary to distinguish between the socially employed bilingualism of the Nara/early Heian diglossic setting and the 'school Chinese' of the middle and later Heian period, which, as will be explained below, cannot be termed bilingualism.

The justification for this change from diglossic bilingual to institutional setting is subtle and complex and is closely connected with linguistic innovations and adaptions of the Chinese writing-system enabling its operation within a Japanese frame of reference. As mentioned above, there had arisen during the Nara period a method of instantly translating and thereby reading Chinese texts in Japanese (*kundoku*), which in turn encouraged the development of a method of writing in the Japanese language while maintaining a Chinese graphic and syntactic surface, so that

---

[8] The native-speaker pronunciation of eighth-cent. Chinese forms was altered during L2 acquisition, e.g. *pat* 'eight' and *tap* 'answer' were pronounced by contemporary Japanese as *pachi* and *tafu* but have since undergone further sound-changes (Hattori, 1974: 96). The Japanese lack of equivalents for Chinese 'l', vowel + consonant sequences, and certain vowel distinctions, together with a conflicting syllabic structure, led to the Chinese monosyllables *liao* and *liang* both being rendered as the polysyllabic *ri-ya-u*. Chinese dentals, diphthongs, and final-position nasals were also transformed (Hamada, 1955). Although possessing a pitch system that can be occasionally distinctive, the Japanese were unable to preserve the complex phonemic tone-patterns of Chinese, with the result that phonologically similar Chinese loans which were tonally clearly differentiated ended up as a proliferation of homophones.

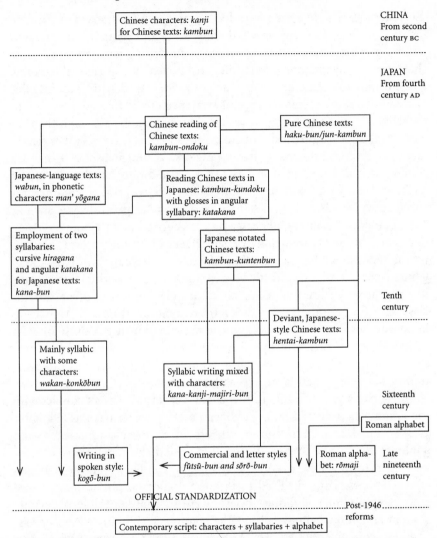

FIG. 2.1. The evolution of orthographic contact in Japan. This diagram presents a synthesis of the fundamental developments in the history of Japanese writing, but since these are very diversified, only the most important innovations and stages have been included. Although the names in the boxes represent generally recognized, major writing-styles, many texts conform only in varying degrees to such categorization. Notice that the diversity of styles ceases towards the end of the nineteenth century, when the forces of national unification, Western-style modernization, and mass education create a strongly centralized, bureaucratically organized society.

a Japanese text could be made to look as if it were composed in Chinese (*kambun*). Thus, the Japanese had come to reconceptualize reading and writing in Chinese characters as reading and writing Japanese in Chinese characters. Many intricate developments occurred during this orthographic redefinition, and the most important ones are captured in Fig. 2.1. Because of this fundamental change of awareness, from foreign to native, of the language that was being represented by characters, although the surface script appeared basically unchanged in high-status texts, it is necessary to recategorize the setting from + diglossa + bilingualism to + diglossa − bilingualism. However, it needs to be pointed out that the reading of a Chinese text with Chinese pronunciation (*ondoku*) was maintained for special purposes and eventually fossilized in ritual speech-events such as chanting aloud from Buddhist scriptures (derived from China).

It must be recognized that the later Heian institutionalized contact-setting was still a diglossic situation, since the presentation of Japanese in Chinese form was reserved for high-status domains, with Chinese loans filtering down to lower ranks such as ordinary priests and the warrior class. As a result of there being less requirement for Chinese bilingualism, knowledge of Chinese drastically declined—except in Buddhist monasteries, where it was rigorously cultivated. However, the decline in Chinese skills did not affect the productive, assimilatory expansion and integration of Chinese elements treated as Japanese.

Other factors contributed to this change of setting. Direct contact with the donor language of China had been curtailed as far back as 894, after which time Japan embarked on an era of semi-seclusion that would continue for five centuries; during this period the Japanese were prohibited from travelling overseas. Civil war in China and power-struggles at the Japanese court had led to the termination of political and social contact with China. Buddhist priests were the only ones given permission, in exceptional cases, to leave the country during this period of self-containment, which lasted until 1401. Even more important perhaps was the fact that after several centuries of intensive sinification, the Japanese had reached a level of cultural autonomy allowing separation from their Chinese model.

A significant linguistic indication of, and source of stimulation for, this recently won self-sufficiency was the emergence of the Japanese syllabaries (*kana*), which were widely used by the upper classes from the tenth century onwards; the syllabaries permitted the representation of Japanese without resorting to Chinese characters. Nevertheless, the superior value attached to knowledge of the characters, because of their symbolic association with political power and with the religious and scientific spheres, persisted, as is indicated by the discriminatory habit of teaching only the syllabaries to females, whereas men learned characters as well. In fact, until about the twelfth century, a division was maintained between a superficially Chinese-looking text (*kambun*)[9] written in characters, and a Japanese text transcribed in the syllabaries (*wabun*). Eventually, the two systems intermingled, culminating in the contemporary mixed script of characters and syllabic symbols—a century-long process depicted in Fig. 2.1.

As for the contact features of this institutional setting, certain processes such as continued borrowing and assimilatory changes are observable which would not normally be expected in such a situation but occur because of the unique dependency on, and daily recourse to, the Chinese writing-system. Since the Japanese decided to maintain a Chinese structural and graphic surface for their high-status texts, even though the purpose was to represent Japanese, a very special type of contact with Chinese was encouraged which had far-reaching consequences. Because the Chinese component remained ever active as a prestige model in high-style written Japanese, it became an inexhaustible source of linguistic inspiration. It was acquired and promoted in educational and institutional contexts such as private tutoring for the nobility, Buddhist temple schools (*terakoya*), and, before the introduction of mass education in the late nineteenth century, officially supported schools for the samurai class. In fact, reading and writing in Japanese was never explicitly taught during the Tokugawa period (1600–1867) but was picked up on the way to acquiring competence in reading and composing Chinese texts.

Once the fundamentals of the Chinese lexicon and Chinese stylistics had been assimilated, the Japanese were able to develop and rework them according to their own needs. Furthermore, though successive revivals of Chinese as a foreign language were instigated in institutional contexts such as Zen Buddhist monasteries (from the twelfth to the fourteenth

[9] The term *kambun* is confusingly vague and covers both native and non-native varieties. Thus, *kambun* can refer to:

1. a native Chinese text to be read in Chinese;
2. a non-native (Japanese-produced) text in Chinese to be read in Chinese;
3. a native Chinese text that can be read in an instantaneous Japanese translation-style;
4. a non-native (Japanese-produced) text superficially composed in Chinese but to be read in instantaneous Japanese translation-style and, therefore, essentially conceived of as constituting Japanese, although presented in Chinese form.

centuries[10]) and by Tokugawa scholars linked to the 'school of ancient Chinese learning' (*kogaku-ha*[11]—particularly during the eighteenth century), very few Japanese paid attention to Chinese as a living foreign language, mistakenly believing it to be identical to their own.

An obvious outcome of this was the apparently unusual situation of the Japanese language creating language contact from within itself. Actually, by the middle of Heian period (eleventh century), contact with Chinese was regarded less as a matter of interaction with a foreign language and more as a question of dealing with a special type of prestigious, Japanese 'style'.

Introducing Linguistic Data from Sino-Japanese Contact

In the following review of contact features occurring in this setting, which covers a period of more than a millennium (from the tenth to the mid-twentieth century) only items of general significance will be focused upon.

During Heian times, Chinese loans were being increasingly transferred from High domains such as political and administrative organization, Buddhist theology, Confucian ideology, military affairs, and areas of science such as astrology, mathematics, and medicine, into the Low oral sphere of Japanese and into texts written in Japanese. This phase of borrowing seems to fit in with the classic explanation of lexical gaps being created and filled through contact with a high-status donor-language. As the Chinese items were transferred, special constructions were developed to handle their radically different grammatical structure, as exemplified in reversed verb-object predication and the existence of passives and relatives. Furthermore, since the loans were represented in their corresponding Chinese characters, they were orthographically marked off as distinct from

[10] The early priest-founders who established Zen in Japan, Eisai (1141–1215) and Dōgen (1200–53), had both studied in China when Sung culture was flourishing. Some of the temples they helped to establish produced notable Chinese poetry, e.g. *Kūgeshū*. The influence of the Zen Chinese revival is also evident in the new pronunciations introduced to Japan fresh from China during this time—*sōon* (Sung pronunciation) or *tōon* (Chinese pronunciation)—as well as in certain new Chinese loans such as 'quilt' *futon*, 'paper lantern' *chōchin*, 'bean-jam bun' *manjū*. In fact, it was due to the suggestion of the Zen master Musō that the first official mission in five centuries was sent to China in 1325.

[11] For background information on *kogakuha* scholars cf. Yoshikawa (1975). A leading figure of the *kogakuha* was the Confucian philsopher Itō Jinsai (1627–1705). Many of these scholars adopted a philological approach to their study of the Chinese classics and elaborated new interpretations of them. Scholars such as Okajima Kanzan (1674–1728) and Ogyū Sorai (1666–1728) both argued for the retention of the 'pure' way of reading Chinese as Chinese.

Japanese, a device which also helped to preserve their initially separate phonology and structure.

By the end of Heian times, however, as mixed writing-styles simultaneously employing the syllabary and characters became common, so that ultimately even Japanese items were encoded in Chinese characters, the orthographic distinction between Chinese loans in Chinese characters and Japanese words in syllabic symbols became blurred and broke down.

The Chinese model is also discernible in converging word-formation processes. Thus, compounds for new customs and techniques imported from China during the Heian period follow Chinese morphological sequencing of verb plus noun, which is the reverse of the Japanese noun-plus-verb order for compounds: *makie* 'inlaid lacquer' < *maku* 'scatter, spread' plus *e* 'picture'.

The process of creative adaptation, particularly in the employment of Chinese characters, is striking in its diversity and duration. Adaptive change is visible in certain commonly employed character-compounds such as 今日 'now' plus 'day' to represent *kyō* 'today', and still continues in the infinite potential of new character-combinations to designate new concepts. Nativization can also be observed in the reshaping of the actual form of characters, sometimes also inaugurated by governmental language-planning.

Another part of assimilationary change not treated here (which can also be interpreted as 'interference' from Japanese) is the important reorientation from external to internal Japanese norms for pronouncing Chinese loans and composing written texts in a sinicized style (*kambun*).[12]

The most significant step in the Japanese nativization of Chinese characters, obviously, is the association of Japanese vocabulary with Chinese graphs evolving out of the translation-reading style (*kundoku*). In addition, over the centuries Chinese characters were selected to represent Japanese items, and their original, native meaning shifted or changed. For example, the character 文 in Modern Chinese means 'written graph' or 'decoration' but in contemporary Japanese means 'prose composition' or 'sentence'.

As well as these semantic changes, the Japanese introduced a number of innovations which would never have been permitted by Chinese norms:

[12] In fact, there existed a recognized L2 pronunciation of Chinese characters known as the 'peasant reading-style', *hyakusho-yomi*, which seems to have been an institutionalized variety of interlanguage which eventually established itself over native norms to constitute the general Japanese pronunciation of Chinese items. See Hayashi and Yamada (1955).

1. They gave more than a one-word reading of a character, e.g. 昔 *sono kami* 'once upon a time'.
2. They made Japanese compounds for one character: 志 *kokorozashi* 'resolution'.
3. They used two characters to be read as a single Japanese word: 大人 *otona* 'adult'.
4. They created compounds with three characters or more: 山下風 *arashi* 'storm'; 春夏秋冬 *shun-ka-shū-tō* 'spring-summer-autumn-winter'.

The most prolific area of orthographic nativization was the creation of new compounds out of Chinese characters. A particularly productive phase of this occurred at the end of the nineteenth century, when Japan needed to find a way of referring to freshly encountered Western intellectual, scientific, and technological items and concepts. During this period, the Japanese generally chose not to borrow but to calque: 汽車 *kisha* 'steam train'; 民主主義 *minshu-shugi* 'democracy'.

The creation of authentic-looking Chinese characters by the Japanese (*kokuji*) also deserves mention here. Interestingly enough, these graphic coinages are already evident as far back as the Nara period, appearing, for instance, on the ancient seals of the imperial storehouse. Certain Japanese-made characters are still employed and include the following: 働 *hataraki* 'work', 畠 *hatake* 'field'. What has happened in these cases is that innovatory combinations of various Chinese components (some of which were originally whole individual characters) have been made to form new single characters. As well as engaging in orthographic innovation, the Japanese sometimes supplied their home-made characters with artificial, but credible, Chinese pronunciations: for example, it was decided to pronounce the second, Japanese-made character in the compound 田畠 'fields for rice and vegetable cultivation' as *baku*.

In the Japanese assimilation and elaboration of the Chinese writing-system, not only its flexible graphic potential but also its inherently rich morphological and semantic productivity continued to be exploited centuries after initial contact.

Finally, it must be pointed out that even though the period from the Heian period until the mid-twentieth century has been fundamentally characterized as a diglossic setting, a very limited amount of borrowing from outside Chinese sources did take place which also makes this a non-bilingual distant setting. Thus, Japanese contact with Chinese was predominantly internal but also involved very small-scale external transfer.

However, in the latter case, the loans are limited to the filling of lexical gaps and the importation of new cultural items.[13]

Channels of Sino-Japanese Contact

As for agents responsible for the millennia-long contact with Chinese, many different types are involved. Apart from the certain influx of immigrants from the Asian continent lost to written history before the fourth century, there was a phase of settlement in Japan—primarily by Koreans, but also by Chinese émigrés fleeing war and persecution—from the fifth to the seventh century. The majority came voluntarily to meet the demand for their skills and knowledge in an as yet underdeveloped Japan; others were captives brought back after military action; and a few outstandingly learned ones were especially presented by Korean rulers to the Japanese sovereign. The early expatriates tended to be silkworm farmers, horse-breeders, artisans such as weavers, potters, and metalworkers, while later ones are associated with government administration, the dissemination of Buddhism, and—of linguistic significance—the field of Chinese learning and writing. Already from the fifth century, expatriate scribes had formed guilds (*fumibe*) to serve the Japanese nobility and state. In fact, many new arrivals from the Asian continent, and their descendants, held important posts in diplomacy, in military and economic affairs, and in Buddhist and Shintō institutions; many formed wealthy clans and married with the Japanese, or, in many cases, into the Japanese aristocracy.

It is necessary to point out that face-to-face contact with Chinese in China was limited, until this century, to a small number of privileged Japanese. During the ancient phases of contact, eighteen Japanese missions were sent, at odd intervals between AD 607 and AD 838, to the Chinese capital for one-year study-periods. They comprised officially selected Japanese priests, diplomats, technical specialists, physicians, pharmacists, academics, artists, and craftsmen. Although these Japanese who experienced first-hand Chinese contact played an important supportive and

---

[13] The main time for this contact was during the Kamakura period (1192–1333), when Zen Buddhist priests who had studied in China introduced new objects such as household items and food, the Chinese designations of which entered as loans, e.g. *manjū* 'bean-jam bun', *yōkan* 'sweet paste', *udon* 'noodle', *isu* 'chair', and *futon* 'bedding'. Recent Chinese loans, however, are clearly marked as foreign in their representation in the angular syllabary (*katakana*) and not in Chinese characters; they mainly relate to food, e.g. *rāmen*, *gyōza*, and *wantan*, and may have been transmitted via nineteenth- and twentieth-cent. contact with English.

extending role in Japan's sinification, the principal agents were undoubtedly the Sino-Korean expatriates.

With the change of setting in mid-Heian times, and a decline in Chinese writing, the main sinological cultivators and guardians were court nobles and Buddhist monks. Later, from the twelfth to the fourteenth century, a handful of Japanese priests went to China to study Zen and Confucianism and introduced various innovations in pronunciation and vocabulary. In fact, as major agents of Chinese contact in Japanese society, the role of the entire Buddhist clergy cannot be overestimated. It was they who maintained proficiency in the language for the longest period, and preserved the most conformist styles of Chinese writing.

Even though Japan sealed itself off from the outside world between 1633 and 1853, some very restricted social contact was possible with Chinese traders in Nagasaki. Furthermore, as society became more secularized, a great revival in Chinese studies took place, encouraged by state Confucianism. Face-to-face contact, of course, occurred during Japan's military action in China from the end of the nineteenth until the mid-twentieth century, but, because of a reversal in dominance between the two countries from the 1860s, no notable influence from Chinese occurred.

Chinese Contact-Models

As for Chinese varieties of contact with Japanese, the diversity of historical models is conspicuous. The main model of pronunciation for the phonetic use of characters in Japan between the fourth and late sixth century was called the *go'on* pronunciation in Japan and was based on the variety of the Six Dynasties period. This was superseded by the northern T'ang standard pronunciation or *kan'on* during the seventh and eighth centuries. Attempts to make the latter method of reading Chinese texts official initially resulted in confrontation with the conservative Buddhist clergy, who wished to maintain the *go'on* model; but the *kan'on* reading-style eventually won widespread acceptance. Later, in the thirteenth and fourteenth centuries, a middle Chinese variety, which was the standard of the Sung dynasty, was introduced through Chinese missionaries and Zen priests who had studied in China. This became known as the *tōsō'on* style, and various terms from Zen Buddhism finding their way into colloquial Japanese were modelled on this last variety. Because of the diversity of contact models, certain characters have multiple readings. For example:

下 *shita*　　Japanese reading (basic meaning: 'under')
下 *ka*　　(Kan'on)　　Chinese reading
下 *ge*　　(Go'on)　　Chinese reading
下 *a*　　(Tōsō'on)　　Chinese reading

With further reference to the phonological level, contact with Chinese led to certain innovatory additions to the Japanese sound-system which are related to convergence. These include: the establishment of previously impossible word-initial sequences with *g, z, d, b*, and *r*; the development of glides such as /*kjau*/ and /*gwen*/; the introduction of consonantal gemination and possibly of a final syllabic nasal as well.

Effects on Japanese Vocabulary

Regarding vocabulary, Sino-Japanese contact has led to as much as 48 per cent of modern Japanese being derived from Chinese. This proportion surprisingly exceeds that of native Japanese words, which stands at only 37 per cent (Japanese National Language Research Institute, 1964). However, it is essential to balance these statistics with frequency counts and a consideration of the contextual distribution of Japanese and Chinese elements if one is to gain a proper understanding of their respective roles in the community's language behaviour. As for contemporary usage, there appears to be a strong correlation between the level of formality and the presence of Chinese elements (cf. the Latinate component in English).

In certain lexical areas, Chinese elements have attained a high level of integration. For example, a few Japanese first-person pronouns derive from Chinese: *boku* ('I' for males) and the exclusively imperial *chin*. Even more significantly, the number-words over ten are all Chinese, reflecting the need to replace the ancient vague and cumbrous native system. Furthermore, the semantic range of numerous Japanese words has been extended through their representation by Chinese characters which symbolized additional meanings; for example, *kusa* natively means 'grass' but, through Chinese graphic association, also 'draft for a manuscript' or 'literary sketch'.

Means of Integration

With regard to the grammatical aspects of Sino-Japanese contact, 99 per cent of Chinese items have been transferred essentially as nouns into Japanese. It is important to understand that Chinese syntactic classes are non-inflecting, and that the assignment of fixed grammatical classes to classical Chinese forms is problematic, since such forms could perform any function permitted by their semantic potential, changing from verb, adjective, or noun according to their position in the sentence and context. Consequently, the Japanese ended up treating multifunctional Chinese items as nominal bound bases to which they attached class-converting elements:

Adjectival Class Conversion		*Verbal Class Conversion*	
健康な		勉強する	
ken kō	+ *na*	*ben kyō*	+ *su ru*
'health'	+ copulative suffix	'study'	+ 'to do'
CHINESE	+ JAPANESE	CHINESE	+ JAPANESE
CHARACTERS	SYLLABIC SIGN	CHARACTERS	SYLLABIC SIGNS

Orthographically, the hybridization is evident in the use of characters for nominally transferred Chinese, while Japanese syllabic symbols represent their functional conversion.

The Consequences of Chinese Contact

The structures of the two languages in contact were radically different: Japanese was polysyllabic, agglutinating, and inflecting, in contrast to monosyllabic, analytic Chinese, with reversed word-order. However, Japanese profoundly modified its structure by grafting onto an inflected stock a numerically preponderant uninflected element, the morphological simplification of which it has even come to idealize.

Only a few points concerning the contextual distribution of Chinese contact can be mentioned here. From the beginning, Chinese-style texts (*kambun*), with their varying range of approximation to pure Chinese, have been associated with the recording of Japanese factual information, as in historical and legal documentation; but prose and poetry totally influenced by Chinese traditions have also been produced by the Japanese. Of course, *kambun* has also been the medium of Buddhist scriptures and commentaries and most of secular scholarship. Furthermore, Chinese characters and Chinese-style composing were historically regarded as a male preserve.

Today, there seems to be a correlation between the degree of linguistic sinification and the perceived 'heaviness' and intellectuality of the style. Moreover, the degree of prestige and of oral unintelligibility tend to increase with sinification. The Emperor Showa's highly sinicized speech calling on the nation to surrender at the end of the Second World War failed to be understood by many, and was even mistaken by some for a declaration of victory. An extremely diglossic situation prevailed in Japanese society until post-war reforms imposed democraticization on the writing-system and ratified its desinification.

Resistance to Chinese Linguistic Influences

Japanese relations with China were, from the start, marked by mixed feelings of inferiority and assertiveness. Cultural resistance to total sinification is observable from earliest times in, for example, the maintainence of Shintoism in the face of Buddhism and in the production of literature in the Japanese tongue. Sinophilia was also virulently countered by the Japanese national-language scholars of the Edo period, the *kokugogakusha*, whose emergence was a reaction against Chinese studies during the Tokogawa period. They instigated investigation into ancient Japanese texts and they intellectualized Shintoism as opposed to Chinese Buddhism.

Linguistically, the persistence of the Japanese base should also be recognized. The case particles, for instance, were never destroyed by Chinese contact, and much of the Chinese lexis (*kango*) still remains restricted to the written sphere and is inappropriate in everyday oral contexts.

The subject of Japanese contact with Chinese language and culture obviously can and deserves to be explored beyond the limits necessarily imposed here. The Chinese heritage is truly vast and still strongly evident. Even though Chinese-style composition has become archaic and associated with a feudal past, Chinese-derived lexical items may still continue to be productive for contemporary purposes. One example is the new compound (itself made up of two character-compounds) 文字放送 *moji-hōsō*, literally 'written symbol' + 'broadcast', coined in the mid-1980s for the establishment of the Japanese Teletext service.

Other Asian Languages

In spite of the strong likelihood that Japanese itself evolved out of prehistoric contact amongst the Altaic and Austronesian languages of Asia, this section will be restricted to the Asian influences on Japanese after its stabilization and codification. In sharp contrast to the Chinese permeation of the Japanese world, these influences have been negligible, a reflection of the markedly distant position of the Japanese towards these peoples and their languages.

Ainu

The Ainu language, which is not related to Japanese[14] but is indigenous to Japan, has been variously linked to Indo-Germanic, Palao-Asiatic, Uralic, and Caucasian. Today, it is on the verge of extinction and, if heard at all, occurs only on the islands of Hokkaido, Sakhalin, and the Kuriles, although it existed on the mainland one millennium ago. The total number of persons identifying themselves as Ainu in 1979 in Hokkaido was 24,160, but of these only an estimated 200 are not the offspring of mixed marriages.[15] Since early times the Ainu have been regarded as a different and inferior ethnic group by the Japanese, whose cultural development advanced beyond the Ainu under early sinicization. Thus, for centuries, in spite of physical proximity, the Japanese maintained a distant non-bilingual setting *vis-à-vis* the Ainu, so that contact from the Japanese side has been restricted to very limited borrowing, which is mainly discernible in a few place-names in Hokkaido ending in *-betsu* (> pét 'river')—for example, *Ebetsu* and *Shibetsu*—together with a handful of loans related to the ecological sphere: 'salmon' (*sake*), 'sea otter' (*rakko*), 'reindeer' (*tonakai*), and 'seaweed' (*kombu*).

Korean[16]

There are various settings involved in contact with Korean. The first may be categorized as distant non-bilingual, with the Japanese sharing an alliance with continental states of south-west Korea known as Paekche and Koguryō as early as the fourth century. After the invasion of these states, in the seventh and eighth centuries, there entered into Japan a stream of highly skilled and cultivated *émigrés* (*kikaijin*), some of whom occupied powerful posts during the sinification of the Japanese state in the Nara period (710–94 AD). It can be supposed that this particular group of refugees soon initiated a language-shifting setting, as many intermarried with the Japanese aristocracy and smoothly integrated into Japanese

[14] The phonological and grammatical similarities between Ainu and Japanese are generally regarded as a result of minority Ainu-speakers converging towards the dominant language over the last centuries. Hence it is difficult to analyse the vocabulary common to both languages, but it seems likely that borrowing from Japanese has taken place, as Ainu is subordinate.

[15] See Motomichi and Bowles (1983).

[16] Korean and Japanese share many typological features, but it seems these are insufficient for absolute genetic linking. The similarities are often close enough to allow word-for-word translations.

society thanks to their high status. These pre-eighth-century Korean immigrants played a formative role in the cultural and political growth of early Japan and have left a legacy which is only now beginning to be acknowleged by the Japanese. The only contact of these early settings that has been uncovered is borrowing, which reveals itself in ancient place-names such as Nara (< Korean: *nara* 'land'), in architectural terms such as 'temple' (*tera*), and in a small number of names for imported objects: 'needle' (*hari*), 'bean paste' (*miso*), 'helmet' (*kabuto*). The channels of contact were purely oral, since the shared written variety was Chinese. The fact that the number of historical Koreanisms remained low despite the prestige of the immigrant community must be attributed to their rapid language-shift to Japanese, and to the overwhelming prestige of Chinese for both speech-communities.

The second phase of Korean contact occurred after Japan's colonization of Korea in 1910, when the setting is clearly identifiable as distant non-bilingual from the Japanese perspective; however, this setting was diglossic bilingual for the Koreans, who were required to speak and write in the High variety, that is to say Japanese, in all pubic domains. Thus, it can be understood that lingustic contact for the Japanese was limited and unnecessary. The small number of recent Korean loans belong mainly to slang (for example, 'bicycle' *charinko*) and were introduced by Japanese repatriates from Korea at the end of the Second World War and/or resulted from the existence of a Korean community in Japan who had undergone forced expatriation as slave labour.

Sanskrit

Contact with Sanskrit was initiated through academic Buddhist study, starting from the eighth century. One principal concern was with Sanskrit orthography, which is now recognized as having provided the model for the fifty-sound tabular organization of the Japanese syllabaries (a contemporary version of which is shown in Table I.1) and with the correct interpretation of the Indian sutras, which had been translated into Chinese. This setting can be characterized as of the distant but institutional type, but it was short-lived because the Heian period, with its culturally confident and autonomous attitude, ushered in emphatically locally rooted forms of Buddhism. The very few direct loans are, predictably, related to religion—'nun' (*ama*), Amitabha (*Amida*), 'the ruler of Hell' (*Enma*), 'temple roof-tile' (*kawara*)—but the majority entered indirectly, as calques, through the medium of Chinese doctrinal texts.

Twentieth-Century Asian Contacts

Through contact with English, Japanese has indirectly adopted loans from other Asian languages during this century. The following examples are listed in their English forms: *khaki, jungle, shampoo* (all from Hindi); *mango* and *curry* (both from Tamil); and *teak* (Malay). The setting is clearly identifiable as a distant non-bilingual one. It is worth noting that Asian languages are almost totally ignored in contemporary Japanese education, including university level. The appearance of the first Japanese dictionaries of Malay, Tagalog, Siamese, Burmese, and present-day Chinese during the Second World War constituted the first serious linguistic attention paid to South-East Asia. The military occupation of this region during the Second World War was too short to lead to any significant language-contact for the Japanese speech-community, but perhaps as Japanese companies are now increasingly establishing branches and factories there, new influences will appear in the next century.

3

The Social Evolution of Japanese Contact with European Languages

Today, at the end of the twentieth century, the English language features extensively in everyday Japanese life, even though Japanese society is monolingual. For those unfamiliar with the historical evidence, it might easily be assumed that contact with English and other European languages is a recent, post-war phenomenon. Thus, it may come as a surprise to some to discover that contact with English began 200 years ago, and contact with other European languages reaches as far back as 500 years. In fact, as Japan and the West are now moving into a relationship of closer mutual evaluation, it seems appropriate and valuable to consider why and how European language-contacts evolved, and to do so by exploring their formative dynamics.

Gairaigo: Alien Vocabulary

It is not coincidental that Japanese linguists have treated Euro-Japanese language-contact as a distinct topic from that of Chinese influence, and have subsumed it under the native category of *gai-raigo*, literally 'words coming from outside'. The full implications of the first component, *gai-* (外), in the compound deserve attention, since this element stresses the external, non-belonging nature of the succeeding component and does not correspond to the conception of partaking as implied by the English 'borrowing' or 'loan'. Consider, for example, its occurrence in the following compounds, where its function of indicating something lying outside the Japanese territory or 'organism' is evident:

gai-koku 'abroad, anywhere outside Japan'
gai-kokujin 'non-Japanese person'
gai-mushō 'foreign ministry'
gairai-shoku/dōbutsu 'exotic plant/animal'

According to data derived from a vocabulary survey of the popular press conducted by the Japanese National Language Research Institute in

TABLE 3.1. Proportion of Loans Derived from Contact with European Languages in Modern Japanese

Donor	% total Japanese lexicon
English	7.29
French	0.55
German	0.31
Italian	0.15
Portuguese and Spanish	0.14
Dutch	0.13
Russian	0.08
Other (Latin, Tamil, Polynesian, etc.)	0.52

1964, 10 per cent of the Japanese lexicon is made up of non-Chinese and non-Japanese words, not including hybrid elements, which make up 6 per cent. The majority of these non-Chinese and non-Japanese items are the result of borrowing from Western languages, English being the major contemporary donor, as Table 3.1 reveals.

Gairaigo is an important concept because it encodes the Japanese perception of an alien lexical stock which is usually represented in the angular syllabary *katakana*, thereby symbolizing and emphasizing the foreignness of the transferred item. As is well known, metalanguage, particularly the popular kind, can often be taken as an index of the ethno-methodological workings and socio-psychological attitudes of the community. In this connection it must be noted that Japanese academic terminology does contain more neutral terms such as *inyūgo* (移入語) 'imported, shipped-in words' and—the closest to the English equivalent—*shakuyōgo* (借用語) 'loaned words'. However, these are not part of everyday usage. Furthermore, it is worth noting that that before the Meiji Restoration in 1868, European-derived loans were referred to as *bango* (蛮語) 'barbarian words' and later *hakuraigo* (舶来語) 'foreign-made or imported words'. It may also be worth considering the subtle German distinction between *Lehnwort* 'loan' and *Fremdwort* 'foreignism' in relation to this question.

The division between the Japanese and Chinese-based lexicon as the 'national language' (*kokugo*),[1] and European-based vocabulary as *gairaigo*,

---

[1] Academically, a division is made between pure Japanese items (*wago*) and Chinese-derived items (*kango*).

originally arose out of the difference between character-using and alphabet-using codes. In fact, the angular syllabary (*katakana*) has been used for loan-words only since the end of the Second World War, and before this time efforts were made to write phonetic equivalents of alien loans in characters which were called *ateji* 'a substitute character unrelated to meaning': in pre-war days, for example *garasu* ('glass') was represented in characters as 硝子 but today is written in the angular syllables ガ ラ ス. The application of the angular syllabary to loans should be regarded not as primarily constituting a method of orthographic discrimination but as an aid to literacy. However, the inevitable consequence of its restrictive application to alien loans has resulted in its unique symbolization of vocabulary from Western languages by marking them in a script which is not applied to Japanese or Sino-Japanese words, except in special conditions such as to denote onomatopoeia or exclamation, and in modern computer-printed texts such as bank statements.

The division is further reflected in the fact that Chinese-derived vocabulary is codified in 'national-language dictionaries' (*kokugo-jiten*), which, of course, contain Japanese words. Although Chinese-derived items were once 'foreign' they are not usually conceived of as belonging to the set of alien vocabulary and do not appear in the special, mainly European-based loan-word dictionaries (*gairaigo-jiten*). Similarly, earlier transferred loans from Asian languages are not usually considered part of the alien lexicon, because they are represented in characters—for example, from Ainu: *kombu* 昆布 'seaweed'; from Korean: *miso* 味噌 'bean paste'; from Sanskrit: *ama* 尼 'nun'. However, a tiny portion of the alien lexicon, which I estimate at 0.2 per cent, is made up of rather recent contact with non-European languages, some of which has most likely been filtered through English. Examples are: Arabic *yashmak*; Tibetan *yak*; Mon-khmer *khsier*; Hawaiian *hula*. However, these loans tend to be part of international vocabulary, and generally refer to culturally specific phenomena of the country of their origin.

Additionally, it must be pointed out that the identification of a *gai-raigo* item and its differentiation from the direct transfer or quote from a foreign language (*gaikokugo*) is problematic because there exist no absolute defining criteria. Strictly linguistic judgements concerning the way an item is pronounced or its faithfulness to the donor meaning are not sufficient to determine its *gairaigo* status. The main determining factors for recognizing *gairaigo* would seem to be: the degree of the item's historic assimilation, and its general level of intelligibility in the community, both of which reveal themselves in the extent of its orthographic and phonetic conformity to Japanese norms, and in its increased occurrence.[2]

The earliest scholarly interest in European contacts can be found as far back as the beginning of the eighteenth century,[3] but it was not until the country was opened up to stronger Western influences in the late nineteenth century, and the effects of this were felt, that Japanese lexicographers began to concern themselves with the topic.[4] Today, the most comprehensive codification of the alien lexicon is that of Arakawa (1977), which contains 27,000 entries.

A Socio-linguistic Chronology of Early European Contacts

The following section offers a succinct social history of Euro-Japanese linguistic assimilation, with sections devoted to individual cases. Some of this pre-twentieth-century contact was on an extensive scale, but the transfers have, in many cases, become obsolete. The part played by these early European contacts as role-models in the socio-linguistic adaption of diverging phonology, morphology, and syntax should not be underestimated.

Contact with Christian Proselytism: Portuguese, Spanish, and Latin

As leading maritime colonizing powers of the sixteenth century, Portugal and Spain were the first and most influential European countries to establish links with Japan. Portuguese contact lasted for almost a century, from 1542 to 1639, while that with Spain endured only thirty-two years, from 1592 to 1624. The curtailment of this commercial and missionary activity was due to the isolationist policy of the Tokugawa government. The latter perceived a threat to its sovereignty from the growing conversion to Christianity of its citizens by the Hispanic groups, which it connected with potential foreign colonization. Spain had annexed the Phillippines in 1569, following missionary activity. In fact, by the beginning of the seventeenth century it has been estimated that as many as one million Japanese, including feudal lords, had converted to Christianity.

The Portuguese, together with other Europeans active at this time in

---

[2] Cf. Umegaki (1963: 7–11, 29–30).

[3] The famous scholar Arai Hakuseki (1657–1725) discussed and analysed Dutch loans, names, and orthography in his works *Seiyō-kibun, Sairan-igen* (1712), and *Tōga* (1717).

[4] In 1884 an article by Otsuki Fumiko entitled 'Gairaigo-genkō' ('Original Thoughts on Loan-Words') appeared; cf. Umegaki (1963). Otsuki was the first to include xenolexical items in his general Japanese dictionary (1889).

Japan, were important to the Japanese for their introduction of West-ern scientific information and technological discoveries in fields such as firearms, shipbuilding and navigation, mining, metallurgy, and printing, and in the academic areas of astrology, mathematics, and medicine.

The setting was generally that of a distant non-bilingual type, but in devout Catholic circles on Kyūshū, a much higher level of bilingualism in Portuguese was attained for a limited time, as indicated by the 4,000 loans which entered the local dialect. Certain Hispanicisms are preserved in regional varieties such as the dialect of the Nagasaki area (where Jesuits were most active) (see Umegaki, 1963, for examples). However, because of the thoroughness of the Tokugawa authorities in their efforts to stamp out Christianity, only fragmentary records remain.

The agents of the language contact were mainly merchant-traders, seamen, and Catholic priests and monks—who travelled widely around the country; some of the latter were sufficiently fluent to compile and print Japanese grammars and readers. Channels of contact were both oral and written, and some Latin texts were also published in Japan.

The use of Portuguese loans was fashionable, prestigious, and widespread enough to provoke some consternation, and even condemnation, among conservative prescriptivists. The power-holding sectors of Japanese society which felt threatened by the new teachings and cultural-political challenges set up social, and eventually physical, resistance to the Europeans.

Given that Latin was the High language of religious communication, quite a few Latinisms, such as *anima, spiritus, ecclesia*, and *pater*, entered Japanese. On top of this, special coinages using Chinese characters were devised at the time for certain terms such as *Biblia, Beato, Oratio*, and *Graça*. However, following ruthless persecution, nearly all transferred Christian vocabulary, including many other religious terms borrowed from Portuguese—*penitencia, mysterio, inferno, Domingo, baptismo, Charidade, Missa*—was tabooed.

It seems that the sixteenth- and seventeenth-century Japanese preferred borrowing to calquing and were desirous to maintain the original, foreign form. Of the thousands of transferred lexical items, only about 200 survive in modern use; many of these were reinforced later through contact with Dutch. Most of the loans refer to European cultural items of food and clothing introduced at the time; among those still in currency include 'bread' (*pan*), 'batter fries' (*tempura*), 'sponge cake' (*kasutera*), 'tobacco' (*tabako*), 'Christian' (*kirishitan*), 'soap' (*shabon*), and 'undershirt' (*jiban*). Since these words are often written in Chinese characters, many Japanese today are under the impression that they are originally Japanese words. The use of the *katakana* syllabary for non-Chinese and non-Japanese items had not yet emerged; characters were chosen to represent the foreign pronunciaiton without consideration of their meaning.

Japanese contact with Romance languages terminated in 1639, when the Portuguese were finally expelled for their political meddling and zealous proselytising and Japan sealed itself off from all dealings with Europeans, apart from the extremely controlled exchanges with the Dutch.

Dutch Mercantilism

When the Japanese closed their doors to the potential Hispanic colonizers, they decided to maintain very limited contact with the strictly commercially minded Dutch, who had established trade ties with Japan in 1609.

Because of severe seclusionist measures, the Dutch, unlike the Chinese, were not allowed to live in Nagasaki but were confined to an artificial offshore island, where a score of Dutch personnel were always in residence until the opening-up of Japan in the late 1850s. Face-to-face contact was limited to oral transactions in Dutch conducted through officially appointed Japanese interpreters. In fact, the study of Dutch was practised as a secret, hereditary art, carried out by only a few officially authorized interpreter-families for the first century of contact. From the late eighteenth century, growing numbers of selected aristocratic scholars were allowed to pursue their iconoclastic interests in Western science and medicine and engage in the study of the Dutch language.

As for the Dutch stationed in Nagasaki under constant Japanese surveillance, most were ordinary traders and navy personnel of generally low education. The exceptions were the doctors regularly assigned to the microcosmic community, some of whom were skilled enough to bring important advances in Japanese medical knowledge.

Until well into the eighteenth century, the oral channels of contact with the Dutch were monopolized by the state's interpreter-families, who lacked academic training and passed on their 'barbarian' language-skills orally, sometimes with simple notes. There was a ban on the import of European books until 1720, and the very limited number of translations and commentaries before that time, some surreptitiously circulated, reveal only minimal, indirect contact via the written channel before the mid-eighteenth century.

The Dutch, for their part, were not allowed to study the Japanese language, and the Japanese interpreters were also subject to official control.

Thus, the latter tended to avoid any contact with the 'barbarians' beyond the call of duty, and any behaviour which might be misinterpreted as collusion with Christians. As late as 1765 the printer's blocks for a harmless Japanese book about Holland were destroyed because they included the Dutch alphabet in illustrations; all copies of the work were confiscated. Clearly, the policy of this time was that no knowledge of the Dutch language whatsoever was to be disseminated among the general Japanese public.

Given the humiliations for the Dutch, and the potential dangers to the Japanese, it is surprising that contact was maintained for two and half centuries. Nevertheless, the motivation for both sides was strong: the Dutch sometimes made financial gains, but, most of all, they valued the prestige of being the sole European representatives in the country; the Japanese, meanwhile, were interested in importing products unobtainable from the Chinese, and in having access to information about the outer world.

It is indicative of the contemporary xenophobic response to things Western that linguistic reference-works on Dutch vocabulary and grammar did not appear until the very end of the eighteenth century. However, the field known as *ran-gaku* ('Dutch studies'), involving the teaching and application of a body of translated Dutch scientific texts, had already emerged among progressive academics of the mid-eighteenth century after the official relaxation of censorship on non-Christian, Western material in 1720.

Institutional contact with the Dutch language started very late. Not until 1811 was the first government bureau 'for the translation of barbarian books' established, to be followed by the foundation of a few private Dutch-language academies in later decades. These constituted the breeding-ground for many educational and political reformers of the late nineteenth century.

Resistance to Dutch–Japanese contact can be observed throughout the duration of that contact. It should be remembered that the authorities, together with traditional medical practitioners, Neo-Confucianist scholars, and academics belonging to the nationalistic school of 'Japanese learning', had a jealous and negative, if not openly hostile, attitude to Dutch studies—which at that time stood for the whole of Western civilization. Of course, the new knowledge threatened to undermine their position of power. Even as late as 1839, some of Japan's most eminent Dutch scholars were prosecuted and either imprisoned for life or forced to commit suicide because their criticism of government foreign policy had been unwelcome among influential conservative groups. Takano Chōei, who was branded the leader of this 'barbarian circle', had studied medicine under the Nagasaki surgeon Philip Franz von Siebold, who himself had earlier been expelled because of his overzealous cartographic interest in Japan.

The Dutch–Japanese setting is somewhat complex because bilingual competence in Dutch existed among a tiny, élite group of scholars and physicians and yet Dutch had no diglossic function in Japanese society. It was government policy to keep the situation as 'distant non-bilingual' as possible. Understanding of Dutch, however, expanded, particularly in the nineteenth century, among the younger, male upper class, although throughout the phases of contact with Dutch, it tended to be acquired primarily for translation purposes rather than as a vehicle of communication *per se*. In the final stage of contact, during the years, after 1853, when Japan was forced to end its isolation, Dutch enjoyed semi-official status as Japan's medium of external diplomacy. It was used verbally and in writing in commercial treaties and political relations with Western powers until the 1870s, when it was replaced by English.

It is obviously difficult to capture these various socio-linguistic stages under one classification, but as far as the general experience of the entire Japanese society is concerned, the characterization of contact with Dutch as a distant non-bilingual setting seems the most appropriate, although knowledge of Dutch was disseminated on a small-scale, institutional basis, among a handful of progressive scholars and selected, official interpreters.

As should be expected from the above comments on the complexity of the setting, the contact features observable here are richer and deeper than in most distant non-bilingual settings, although borrowing takes first place.

In some cases the origins of certain so-called Dutch loans are not Germanic at all, with Dutch merely serving as the 'carrier' for items derived from other languages: *ēteru* 'ether' from Greek, and *arukōru* 'alcohol' from Arabic. Additionally, it seems that some Dutch loans are really only reinforcements of earlier transfers from Portuguese: for example, *bisuketto* (< Dutch: *bescuit*) reinforced the earlier loan *bisukōto* (< Portuguese: *biscoito*), and a similar pattern holds for *koppu* ('beaker') derivative of both Portuguese *copo* and Dutch *kop*. A considerable number of Dutch borrowings were later supplanted by English loans or Japanese calques, or became obsolete. One such is *erekishiteito* (< Dutch: *electriciteit*) replaced by *denki* (< Sino-Japanese). The low level of surviving Dutch loans may be attributed to the fact that the language was hardly taught at all after the 1870s and was abandoned in favour of other, more prestigous European languages of the late nineteenth century. However, as many as 160 words of Dutch origin are still employed in modern standard Japanese,[5] and a score more survive in contemporary dialects, having undergone subsequent semantic changes: *dontaku* (< Dutch: *zondag* 'Sunday') in Tottori dialect signifies 'a sly dog', while in Hiroshima it means 'stupid'.

Because the early phase of oral communication was strictly limited to matters of commerce, with both sides scrupulously avoiding any intellectual or religious topics, seventeenth- and early eighteenth-century Dutch loans typically refer to physical objects. Borrowings relate to imported materials such as 'rubber' (*gomu*), 'glass' (*garasu*), 'gingham' (*giganjima*), 'diamond' (*giyaman*); items of food and drink such as 'ham' (*hamu*), 'beer' (*bīru*), 'coffee' (*kōhi*); and shipping terms such as 'captain' (*kapitan*), 'sailor' (*madorosu*), 'hook' (*hokku*), 'mast' (*masuto*), and 'compass' (*konpasu*).

After 1720, with the relaxation of restrictions on the importation of European books, there was a significant increase in loans of a scientific nature, particularly in the medical field. Terms for 'scalpel' (*mesu*), 'influenza' (*infurenza*), and 'black death' (*pesuto*) entered the language, as did loans for scientific instruments such as 'telescope' (*teresukoppu*) and 'thermometer' (*tarumomētoru*); herbs such as 'camomile' (*kamitsure*) and chemicals such as 'morphine' (*moruhine*) appeared in treatments. In the field of engineering, items such as 'pump' (*ponpu*), 'chain' (*ketchin*), and 'drill' (*bōru*) were taken over. According to some calculations,[6] as many as 3,000 Dutch loan-words were employed in technical and scientific terminology from the mid-eighteenth century.

Syllabic clipping to adapt Dutch transfers morpho-phonologically also took place, as shown, for example, in the creation of the term *ran-gaku* ('Dutch learning'), where *ran* is an abbreviation from *Oranda* 'Holland' and *gaku* 'learning' derives from Sino-Japanese; this also illustrates the creation of hybrid compounds from Dutch and Japanese elements, of which there were many.

Related to lexical transfer is the extensive Japanese reproduction of Dutch terminology in the form of loan translations and coinages in areas

---

[5] See Vos (1963) for a list of examples.   [6] See Saito (1968).

such as medicine, astronomy, botany, physics, and military technology: *byō-in* 'hospital' (< Dutch: *zieken-huis*): 'illness' + 'public building'; *kai-gun* 'navy' (< Dutch: *zee-macht*): 'sea' + 'army'.

Rare for distant non-bilingual and institutional contact-settings is the convergence with Dutch on the syntactic level, which seems to have resulted from the conventionalization of a translation variety from Dutch into Japanese. Among the innovations which surfaced at the time were:

1. The frequent use of the pseudo-copula *de-aru* in sentence-final position.
2. Use of *tokoro-no* to render the Dutch relative pronoun.
3. The usage of inanimate and abstract referents as sentence subjects.
4. The frequent use of personal pseudo-pronouns such as *kare* 'he' and *kanojo* 'she'.

It perhaps also deserves mentioning that Dutch grammatical analysis, itself based on a prescriptive, classical Greek framework, was applied to the Japanese language during the early nineteenth century by scholars in contact with European linguistics. For example, the concept of mood and tense in Dutch seems to have been first applied to Japanese grammar in 1833 by Tsurimine Shigenobu (1788–1859) in his *Gogaku shinsho* ('New Book on the Study of Language'); the new Western paradigm intensified as the century continued.

To conclude, it must be recognized that Dutch–Japanese cultural and scientific contacts laid the foundations for the extensive programme of modernization undertaken in the Meiji Restoration, beginning in 1868. Already during its period of national seclusion, Japan had slowly but steadily acquired knowledge of a Western language and civilization transmitted and studied through the Dutch written medium.

Minor Contact with European Languages since the Nineteenth Century

It was not until the nineteenth century that words from European languages other than Dutch and Portuguese/Spanish entered into Japanese, and ever since that time this general Euro-Japanese language-contact setting corresponds to that of the distant non-bilingual type, where borrowing predominates.

The study of French began with the temporary annexation of the Netherlands by France in 1808, when official interpreters in Nagasaki were ordered to learn it. Of course, this tiny sealed-off group specializing in foreign codes, to which all other Japanese had either extremely controlled or absolutely no access at all, must have found the task daunting without native speakers to guide them. Later, in the 1850s, Dutch officers were given the task of training Japanese troops and introduced French military terms into Japanese, French being the variety they used for this domain. French was subsequently retained as the special foreign language taught in all Japanese military academies until the early part of this century but declined in social popularity with the coming of the Meiji Restoration, as the French had not given diplomatic backing to the Meiji founders. Today, French borrowings are typically associated with fashion, food, and art forms; the following list offers a representative sampling (the items are given in their original French form): *à la mode, beret, chemise, haute couture; cognac, omelette, bifteck, consommé, chou (à la) crème; surréalisme, dessin, montage, chanson.*

Russian contact is supposed to have begun when an official translator was ordered to learn it in 1813 from a captured Russian ship-captain and managed to compile the first grammar of the language in that year.[7] However, cases of Japanese castaways being stranded in Russia had been recorded as far back as the seventeenth century. Furthermore, Russia carried out raids on the northern coast of Japan throughout the eighteenth century and unsuccessfully sought trade relations with Japan in the 1790s. For these reasons, Russian was initially considered an important language for self-defence purposes. Later, because of the Russian Revolution and the popularity of socialist and communist literature in intellectual circles, certain Russian political terms entered Japanese; two examples (here given in their romanized Russian form) are: *kampaniya* > *kanpa*; *intelligentsiya* > *interi*. Contact with the occupying Russian forces in the Japanese colony of Manchuria at the end of the Second World War also brought some Russian borrowings—for example, the Japanese *norma* 'amount of assigned labour' (in a work-camp). Mainstream Japanese had already integrated other, culturally specific Russian items: *samovar, troika, balalaika,* and *vodka.*

Contact with German started much later than with either French or Russian, when the respected German physician von Siebold took up a teaching-post at the government's translation bureau from 1861. Consequently, German became the preferred medium of instruction and diagnosis selected by the Western school of the Japanese medical profession. Its popularity increased with the establishment of the German empire from the 1870s and with the enthusiasm for Prussian government and society, as reflected in the modelling of the Meiji constitution (1889)

[7] See Doi (1983).

on the Prussian one. The penetration of German into Japanese up to the Second World War, especially in the fields of medicine, mountaineering, and academic study (politics and philosophy), was notable. Loans appeared which were derived, for example, from the following German forms: *Allergie, Tuberkulin, Röntgen* 'X-ray', *Karte* '(medical) chart'; *Seil* 'rope', *Hütte* 'hut', *Gelände* 'ski-slope'; *These, Thema, Ideologie, Demagog, Seminar.* German items were also transferred in student slang of the early twentieth century, as a result of the use of German in higher education; examples are items based on *Arbeit* 'work' and *Gewalt* 'violence'. In fact, German held a position of high status in relation to all other European languages except English, which it rivalled until 1946. After this its occurrence in the domains of medicine and higher education drastically declined as a result of Nazi military defeat and the rise of American English.

Italian has never been widely studied by the Japanese, and contact with it has been primarily through the channel of music, where Italian terms of notation have been transferred—for example, *pianissimo*. Other Italian terms, such as *opera* and *sonata*, entered indirectly through other European languages and are also mainly linked to music. On the other hand, there has been some very limited, culturally specific borrowing for uniquely Italian items of food and culture such as *spaghetti* and *fresco*.

It is worth noting that in the early Meiji period—the 1870s and 1880s— native Japanese university professors fluently lectured and wrote in European languages such as German, French, and English. The reason for this temporary institutional bilingualism among the academic élite was that they had undergone their own education in Western knowledge in these European languages, and the linguistic means for expressing it in Japanese were not yet available. However, by the end of the nineteenth century, many Western concepts had been calqued and the language sufficiently modernized to carry Western learning and information.

Today, the majority of students in higher education, about one third of their entire age-group in Japanese society, are required to study a foreign language in addition to English. This typically involves an introduction to either German, French, or Russian; but Latin or non-European languages may sometimes also be studied during the students' two years of general education. However the levels of achievement in this area are widely acknowledged to be poor, because of insufficient learning-time, low student-motivation, and grammar-oriented teaching. Nevertheless, this institutional situation should be recognized as a potential context for a very low level of contact, or at least familiarization, with European sounds and patterns. Further opportunities for contact are available as student travel to Europe increases and European foreign-language courses are regularly broadcast on television.

Shown in Table 3.1 is the category of other donor-languages, making up 0.52 per cent of the Japanese lexicon and including some small-scale borrowing from European languages, usually transmitted via English or German, in which the borrowed terms have maintained their foreign identity: 'mazurka' (Polish), 'fjord' (Norwegian), 'ego' (Latin), 'Pyrrhonism' (Greek).

Contemporary Euro-Japanese contact is not significant and is restricted mainly to the written channel and mass-media contexts.[8] It is instigated typically in order either to satisfy lexical gaps or to serve as commercial decoration—a topic to be taken up later in this book. Naturally, there exists community resistance to wide-scale borrowing from European resources, because of unfamiliarity with the meaning of such 'exotic' loans.

A Short History of English Contact

The European language which has contributed most to the contemporary Japanese lexicon is obviously English, and it is the development of this interrelationship which constitutes the focus here, considered from three different aspects: human interaction, institutional dissemination, and linguistic responses of the Japanese community. The agents, channels, motivation, and contexts promoting the spread of English contact will receive special attention.

The Early Tokugawa Venture (1613–1623)

In spite of the fact that a tiny group of English-speakers was present in early seventeenth-century Japan as merchants and sailors, one of them even serving the shogun as adviser,[9] there is no record of any contact with English during the limited period between 1613 and 1623, when a British trading company was set up in Hirado. However, intensive competition from the Dutch, and poor profits, rapidly led to the closure of the factory and the departure of the English. The fact that no loans emerged is itself

---

[8] See Haarmann's (1989) extensive analysis concerning the symbolic values of foreign-language use in Japanese commercials.

[9] This was the illustrious William Adams (1564–1620), who arrived in Japan in 1600 as a pilot to a Dutch trading-vessel which had been separated from its fleet. In a relatively short time, Adams established himself as a respected adviser and interpreter to the shogun, Tokugawa Ieyasu, because of his knowledge of shipbuilding and Western science. He married a Japanese woman and, as a reward for his services, received from the shogun an estate near Yokosuka, where he lived as a local lord until his death.

indicative of the social and political insignificance of the minuscule and geographically very limited British presence, which could not match the profound socio-linguistic and cultural impact of Portugal and Spain at their zenith.

The Period of National Seclusion (1633–1853)

British attempts to reopen trade links were blocked for several centuries afterwards, while Japan followed a policy of national seclusion (1633–1853), which was a means of dealing with the fear of Christianity and the accompanying threat of European colonization. However, in 1808, half a century prior to Japan's opening up, the disconcertingly audacious arrival of a British warship in Nagasaki initiated the first study of English by the state interpreters, already engaged in acquiring knowledge of Dutch and French. The ship was called *Phaeton* and deceptively entered Nagasaki under Dutch colours, with the aim of capturing Dutch ships, because Britain was at that time involved in the Napoleonic War with the Netherlands supporting their enemy. The official interpreters were, of course, ignorant of English, and there was some unruliness by the brash British sailors. The governor of Nagasaki committed suicide over his mishandling of the event, and in the same year the government decided that English should become an object of official attention and state security.

The Nagasaki interpreters were a hereditary profession, passing their skills from one generation to the next within the family; they were neither academically nor institutionally trained but self-taught, relying mainly on oral memorization. And they were noted for their possessively mono-polistic attitude towards their 'secret art'. The interpreters, of course, were subjected to official surveillance, and their interaction with the sealed-off community of Dutch 'barbarians' was rigidly circumscribed.

No native English-speakers were available when the interpreters were first required to study English, but they slowly gained access to English written material through the Dutch. Furthermore, in the same year, 1808, they began to take English lessons from a Dutch cook. Remarkably, by 1811 they were able to produce a beginner's textbook of colloquial English and, after another three years, in 1814, an English–Dutch–Japanese dictionary, with over 6,000 entries.[10]

---

[10] The textbook was called *Angeria-kogaku-shosen* ('A Beginning to Studying English') com-piled by Motoki Shozaemon (republished 1982 by Taishukan). The first English–Japanese dic-tionary was called *Angeria-Gorin-taisei* ('The Complete Forest of English') and was also compiled by Shozaemon (reproduced 1982 by Taishukan).

Throughout the first half of the nineteenth century, British and American naval and whaling vessels perservered in their attempts to obtain trade links with Japan, even after a law was decreed in 1825 that all foreign ships should be repelled with force. In 1848 one intrepid American sailor, Ranald MacDonald, actually entered the country; he was captured and forced to instruct the Nagasaki interpreters almost every day in English during his seven-month imprisonment, becoming the first native teacher of the language in Japan. This episode highlights the contemporary obstacles to acquiring English, and the desperation to do so.

From the above, it is obvious that direct Japanese contacts with English before the 1850s were extremely restricted and distant. The few Japanese works pertaining to English culture which appeared were all translations in Dutch—of which the Nagasaki interpreters had a real working knowledge, in contrast to their ability in English. The government maintained an openly hostile attitude towards Western contacts and persecuted Western-oriented scholars. On a popular and academic level, Westerners had for centuries been portrayed and conceived of as 'subhuman'.

It must, however, be mentioned that during the 1830s and 1840s, a few Japanese are recorded as having travelled to America as shipwreck-survivors picked up by American vessels. One of them, Nakahma Manjirō, returned to Japan to take up an important advisory role to the shogunate; others worked as interpreters for Western diplomats and naval staff.

The Opening of Japan to the West (1853–1868)

Japan's two-hundred-year-old, self-imposed isolation could not be maintained in the face of superior Western military technology. This became clear from Japan's capitulation to Commodore Perry's gunboat demands for trade relations in 1853, which was quickly followed by the signing of what the Japanese dubbed the 'uneven' treaties with the United States, England, and Russia in 1855, giving these nations the right to establish settlements with extraterritorial status, engage in trade, and use harbours all along the coast.

This unwilling submission to Western imperialism was accompanied by an emergency programme of defence modernization and dissemination of Western knowledge. The main intention behind this radical turn-about of attitudes was to achieve technological and military parity as soon as possible and avert the chances of becoming subordinated and occupied—as had happened, so the Japanese were shocked to learn, to their millennia-long model, China, after the Opium War with Britain (1840–2). In fact, China's defeat played a decisive role in Japan's drastic promotion of Western learning. That promotion inevitably meant both the adoption of Western values and ways of thinking and the acquisition of practical, scientific knowledge, and it soon led to criticism, notably among those in direct contact with the West, of feudal Oriental practices.

On top of this growing cultural self-doubt and self-denigration, the 1850s and 1860s were marked by acute political crises for the shogunate, which was rapidly losing both the support and trust of its regional lords and of public opinion because of what was regarded as its weak and cowardly yielding to the West. A debate among the Japanese élite over foreign relations began to divide the country and undermine the bonds of power.

It must, however, also be stated that well before the mid-nineteenth-century Western infiltration, dissatisfaction with the *status quo* in Japanese society was already evident in repeated, large-scale rioting and attempts at minor economic reform. Underlying this intensifying domestic malaise was the breakdown of Japan's rigid feudal structure, which had become untenable as a result of socio-economic change: the military class had become impoverished, in contrast to the rich urban merchants, who were officially the lowest class, while the peasants, who were socially classified above the merchants and artisans, faced extreme hardship. Opposition to the shogunal handling of the foreign threat served as a useful cause around which progressive internal political forces could rally in order to plot for a new style of government.

The initial problem with the shogunate's programme of Western education was finding staff qualified enough to teach at the new military and naval institutions it established during the second half of the 1850s; eventually various European expatriate experts had to be hired to lead the drive towards modernization. Dutch, however, remained the principal medium for acquiring Western knowledge during the early post-isolationist decades and was maintained as Japan's offical medium for Western diplomacy into the 1870s, although after a few years English, German, and French also came to be included as subsidiary subjects in the curricula of the training colleges.

However, there was also a growing awareness of the particular significance of the English language, and some scholars turned away from Dutch. One such was Fukuzawa Yukichi (1834–1901), a reformer, educator, and writer. He had begun Dutch studies in 1855 in Nagasaki and later taught himself English. In 1860 and 1867 he accompanied government missions to America, and in 1861 to Europe. He was opposed to the feudalistic shogunate and was one of the most popular leading intellectual forces of the Meiji period. He was a supporter of English utilitarianism and of the modernization of Japan according to the Euro-American model in all areas. In his autobiography he writes how in 1858 he visited a Western settlement and was humiliated by his lack of English knowledge:

Yokohama in those days was a small village, where I saw nothing particular except for a few foreigners. They lived in shabby houses in which they kept their shop. The houses stood scattered in the trading community.

I went into one of such shops and I found myself a perfect stranger: they did not understand me and I could not understand them, either. I could neither read the signboard of the shop, nor could I read the label on the bottles there. I could make out nothing of what they uttered . . . When I got home after midnight I was dead tired and utterly dejected with a deep feeling of frustration. How mortifying! These several years I have used my time and money to study of Dutch, but to no purpose. Ah, I've lost everything . . .

But I couldn't afford to be sad and down-hearted for long. I thought the language I heard and the letters I saw there must have been English or French. Then I remembered I had often heard that English was then widely used abroad. That must be English. My courage had once failed me, but I took heart again to make a second attempt.

With a firm determination to study English, I now turned to concentrate upon mastering it (from Fukuzawa Yukichi's *Autobiography* (1899) quoted from Doi (1983: 64–5).

The beginning of official support for the teaching of English is also evident during this time, with the setting-up of the first state-planned English course in 1857 at the 'Translation Office for Barbarian Literature' in Tokyo. In 1858 the governor of Nagasaki established the first private school of English for local samurai, already familiar with Dutch. Four years later, in 1862, the government English course was expanded and the Office was significantly redesignated the 'Centre for Investigating *Western* Studies'. A second government-run English school was opened nearby in Yokohama, and, for the first time, four American missionary teachers were hired to teach English. Moreover, throughout the 1860s private schools teaching European languages sprang up in great numbers all over the country.

The ban on overseas travel for Japanese citizens was lifted in 1866, but even a few years prior to this the government had sent its own special teams to bring back first-hand information—about America in 1860 and about Europe in 1861. Also, in the early 1860s a few Japanese had clandestinely travelled to the West for education and experience, returning later to assume major political and scholastic roles. Among the best-known samurai who illegally left Japan in 1863 to study at London University was Prince Itō, who later served four times as Prime Minister. Other renegades include Iwasaki Yatarō, founder of the Mitsubishi commercial empire, and Nījima Jō, founder of Dōshisha University in Kyoto.

After Japan opened its doors, various European and American nationals came to the country. Although no exact information is available, it seems that the British were among the most numerous in the early settlements, especially as traders. These pioneering Western communities located in port towns comprised mainly merchants and seamen, soldiers, diplomats and accompanying officials, together with a handful of teachers, advisers, missionaries, and students.

Contact between the two communities was very limited, both sides often being at an extra remove from the other, since interpreters were mandatory for any discussion. English-speakers in the domain of diplomacy had to go through the medium of Dutch, as exemplified by the Dutch interpreter used by the first American consul. Merchants, meanwhile, used Chinese employees, who were more accustomed to Japanese ways of business and could understand the language. The Westerner able to communicate in Japanese in this period was extremely rare, because of the negative attitudes of social distance stemming from notions of cultural and racial superiority prevalent in the Western community.

In contrast, the Japanese in contact with Westerners in Japan demonstrated a high motivation to learn. However, at this stage English was still socio-psychologically too peripheral and unfamiliar to lead to transfers into Japanese, and there is no record of borrowing from English deriving from local interaction, although certain English-derived words do appear in the reports of the government missions and of other travellers who went overseas: *hoteru* 'hotel', *purejiden* 'president', and *konguresu* 'congress'.

In this connection it is important to remember the continuing high status of Dutch as the primary code for gaining access to, and dealing with, Western culture and its representatives. From this outline, it emerges that the last decades of the Tokugawa shogunate still constituted a societally distant, non-bilingual setting with regard to English. However, there was growing, small-scale, institutional support for the acquisition of the language by the bureaucratized samurai class, as a means of gaining access to Western military and technological know-how for competitive purposes. This language-planning was imparting crucial second-language skills that would pay off in the following decades of rapid modernization.

Contemporary attitudes towards the West and its representatives in Japan during the first post-isolationist decades were confusingly ambivalent. On the one hand, there was deep respect for Western scientific and technological capabilities and a fervent desire to emulate them. Many of the Western businessmen, diplomats, and specialists in Japan enjoyed positive, welcoming hospitality. On the other hand, there was resentment that Japan was losing its sovereignty to Western imperialism, and bitterness over its technical and political impotency. During the 1860s anti-foreign agitation, together with economic crises and politically motivated violence, escalated. A few Westerners were attacked and murdered by extremists; the British and American legations in Tokyo were burnt down in 1863, and in the same year Western shipping was shelled in southern Japan. Finally, the shogunate was unable to assert itself against the revolt of young samurai opposing its backwardness and cowardly foreign policy; in 1868 the shogun yielded to their *coup d'état*, carried out under the slogan 'Honour the Emperor and drive out the barbarians'.

Westernization with Japanization (1868–1912)

Those who expected to see a new age of aggressive foreign policy appear with the Meiji Restoration were to be surprisingly disappointed. The young emperor's declaration in the Charter Oath of 1868 that knowledge was to be sought throughout the world proved portentous for at least the first part of this nation-building epoch of 'enlightenment'. Instead of expelling the foreigners, Meiji public and private sectors immediately set about vigorously recruiting hundreds of European and American advisers and teachers; the number of government staff and students officially sent abroad for study also multiplied. The Restoration signified not an end but an intensification of Western-style modernization and industrialization, bringing sweeping social, economic, and political transformation, such as the adoption of the Gregorian calendar, the development of state education, and the abolition of the feudal class-system.

Japan had to catch up with the contemporary world-powers in every sphere, and Western ideas, methods, and materials were rapidly and generally successfully absorbed. As much as 5 per cent of total government expenditure during the Meiji period is supposed to have gone on the exorbitant remuneration of the temporary foreign personnel, almost half of whom came from Britain but which also included American, French, and German nationals. The Japanese were shrewd guardians of their nation's sovereign prerogatives and ensured that they maintained the real policy-making authority, rapidly replacing the foreign experts after the 1880s with their own trained people.

When the modern public education system was established in 1872, along the American model, English became a compulsory subject at the new obligatory elementary schools for six- to eleven-year-olds, and at the optional middle schools for those between 12 and 17; Dutch was not on the curriculum. However, because early Meiji mass education was beset for many decades with such overwhelming problems of staff, material, and attendance, the programme could not be widely implemented in the case of foreign-language teaching. The main social group to experience the benefits were the children of the upper classes, who continued beyond the obligatory school-age of 11 and received what was in many cases a truly bilingual education in the highly academic middle schools. Here English was often the *medium* as well as a subject of instruction, with British and American teachers, for example, giving lessons in mathematics and botany.

The strong influence of English-speaking teachers manifested itself widely in higher-education institutions of the early Meiji decades. Eminent teachers from Britain and America who made succesful careers include Basil Hall Chamberlain and Lafcadio Hearn, who both went on to become professors at Tokyo University.

Furthermore, since Japanese technical terminology for Western concepts was still underdeveloped, it was not uncommon for Japanese university staff to lecture in European languages; certain Japanese academics had taken advantage of the opportunity to study abroad and attained a high level of proficiency in English, German, or French.

The success of the practically oriented English teaching of the early Meiji period can be seen clearly in the bilingualism of Japanese leaders in diverse fields, and of scholars who wrote books in English in the last decades of the nineteenth century: Okakura Kakuzō, author of the *Book of Tea* (1906); Nitobe Inazō, author of *Bushidō—The Soul of Japan*; Uchimura Kanzō, author of *How I Became a Christian*; and Suzuki Daisetsu, author of *Introduction to Zen Buddhism*. The pro-Western mood of the

1870s is nowhere more obvious than in the radical proposal of Mori Arinori, who was to be education minister between 1885 and 1889, for English to replace Japanese as the national language. Arinori was eventually assassinated by an ultranationalist in 1889 for his overliberal education policies, which were in conflict with those of Confucian moralism. The original justifications he gave for making English official included the limited resources of the native Japanese lexicon, the difficulty of absorbing Western culture through Japanese, the inconvenience of writing in characters, and the control of commercial power by English-speaking nations.

However, a host of internal and external developments steadily eroded the initial concept of an English-speaking bicultural élite carrying out the goals of national strength, unity, and independence, and an anti-Western mood took over Japanese society from the 1880s.

One reason for this hostility was an identity crisis created by 'excessive' and overrapid westernization. It led conservatives and reactionaries to produce a nationalistic countermovement in favour of Japanization. This ideology involved the rehabilitation of traditional values found in Confucianism and Shintoism, and it increasingly won over intellectuals and statesmen who were suffering from disappointment and indignation at the fact that Japan had not been accepted into the community of Western nations.

From the 1890s educational reforms inaugurated a return to Japanese 'morality' in contradistinction to Western liberal ethics, the inculcation of reverence for state and emperor and the indoctrination of 'Japanism' (*Nihonshugi*), an ideology stressing Japanese ethnic uniqueness, Confucian ethics, and Shinto statism. Furthermore, Japan's military victories in wars against China (1894–5) and tsarist Russia (1904–5) boosted this ultra-nationalism, which was accompanied by a rapacious imperialism.

On the linguistic level, Japanese was undergoing important processes of written standardization and modernization that were attempting to overcome the diglossic situation of a feudalistic, heavily sinicized High variety and meet the new needs of novelists, scholars, and technocrats. This development of a new style, of course, reduced the reliance on English as a carrier of cultural and scientific progress.

These developments were conscious policies on the part of those in authority. Thus, in 1882 the use of foreign languages in university lectures not connected with European literatures was forbidden. After the 1890s Japanese was established as the main medium of instruction in every educational institution, and many foreign staff were replaced by Japanese. Although European languages, above all English, still featured prominently in curricula, they had been successfully relegated to the status of external languages and were taught principally via grammar-translation methods. Thereby, English acquisition lost its practical character and 'cultivating mission' in Japan towards the end of the nineteenth century and was reduced to a mere instrument for translation purposes; the laments of Japanese university professors belonging to the earlier bilingual generation testify to the decline in the abilities of late Meiji students ignorant of the 'Anglo-Saxon spirit' and 'gentlemanly' values.

A further hindrance to English was the rise of the socialist movement in Britain, since the literature it generated was considered threatening to Japan's contemporary capitalistic course of massive industrialization, which was already confronted with labour unrest and union activity.

However, it is important to realize that the anti-Western feeling which manifested itself in the later Meiji period was not a simple, uniform reaction, but involved diverse political and cultural forces. Some of these were seeking a reassertion of self-confidence and a more realistic view of the West; others were exploiting the issue to manœuvre themselves into positions of power. There was also something conspicuously paradoxical about contemporary attitudes towards westernization on the official level, as is reflected, for example, in the European military dress of the emperor at the inauguration of the Western-style constitution in 1889. In fact, it was during the final nationalistic decades of Meiji that the Japanese widely began to adopt Western hair- and dress-styles. On top of this, it is precisely during this time that the influences and borrowing from Western languages reached hitherto unknown proportions. Also significant is the emergence in the 1880s of a popular movement for the romanization of Japanese, founded to promote literacy, demonstrating the desire for linguistic modelling on a Western basis among progressive forces within the community. From the above, however, it can be seen that the attitudes of the Meiji Japanese towards English were in the long term counteractive and marked by a non-integrative motivation. Although the West and its languages continued to exert a very strong appeal, the approach to it had been rendered more distant and academic.

The native agents of English contact during this period were the same as in the previous phase: merchants, seamen, soldiers, diplomats, teachers, advisers, missionaries, and students. But their numbers were much higher and the quality of their contacts tended to be more intensive and personal, as indicated by the increase in intermarriage on both sides. On the other hand, Japanese able to travel and study abroad, Japanese servants working in European households, Japanese teachers of English in state and private language-schools, translators of European literature, and innovatory Japanese novelists transferring English into their work, contributed to the dissemination of English to varying degrees. The fact that contact with English occurred through the aural as well as the written medium is reflected in the phonetic shape of certain Meiji loans such as *purin* 'pudding', *meriken* 'American', *hankachi* 'handkerchief', *burashi* 'brush', and *wanashi* 'varnish'. Nevertheless, the majority of items were acquired from written sources, since their Japanese representation is based on English orthography and not pronunciation: *airon* 'iron', *konpanī* 'company', *gurobu* 'glove'.

Evidence of close contacts between certain English- and Japanese-speakers during this time is reflected in the appearance of pidginized English varieties in the port communities of Yokohama and Nagasaki and among those serving Westerners. The names of these pidginized English varieties reflect the range of services provided to the Western community—'nurse-talk' (*ama-kotoba*), 'merchant talk' (*shōnin-kotoba*), 'driver-talk' (*kurumaya-kotoba*), 'brothel-talk' (*chabuya-kotoba*)—but little is known of these varieties, because they were not recorded. An English pidgin known as 'sailor-talk' (*madorosu-kotoba*) survived longest and included many English-derived nautical terms. At the same time, a Japanese-based pidgin, which is supposed to have acted as a transmitting agent of early English loans into Japanese, also existed in Yokohama but seems to have been restricted to the domain of trading. Eighty-five per cent of the pidgin's vocabulary was derived from Japanese, but it also included words from various English varieties: *come back, come here* (= 'dog'), *consul, curio, dollar, drunky, hotel, house, Japan, screen, so so* (= 'sew'), *wash, num wun* (= 'no one'), and *sick-sick*.[11]

The dramatic influx of English-derived loans during the late Meiji period is best gauged by considering contemporary efforts at their codification. Thus, the first modern Japanese dictionary, called *Genkai*, for which data was collected by 1886, lists 410 loans, of which 18 per cent originate from English, while the first loan-word dictionary, *Nichiyō-hakuraigo-benran*, which appeared in 1912, contains 1,596 entries, 75 per cent of which are English-derived. Forty-two per cent of the items in the latter were common,

---

[11] Cf. Daniels (1948).

everyday terms mainly connected with food, machines, commerce, fashion, and sport, in that order; the remaining entries were specialist loans related to fields such as science, academic studies, technology, and art.

Furthermore, it should be pointed out that during the Meiji period the term 'high-collar English' (*haikara-eigo*) was popularly employed to refer to prestige borrowing connected with the fashionable adoption of Western paraphernalia and a Western life-style, loans being derived from the following words: *piano, court-dress, ribbon, corset, bonnet, lady,* and so on.

However, the most interesting form of language contact during the latter half of the nineteenth century was the code-mixing with English observable in the interaction of students. This has been recorded in contemporary literature such as the novel *Tosei Shosei Katagi* ('Character of Modern Students') published in 1886 by Tsubōchi Shōyō, from which the following examples were collected by Takahashi (1967: 79–80);

> Wagahai no <u>uocchi</u> [watch] dewa mada <u>ten minyuttsu</u> [ten minutes] gurai.
> *By my watch it is still ten minutes.*

> <u>Webster</u> no daijiten jitsuni korewa <u>yūsufuru</u> [useful] ja.
> *Wesbster's Comprehensive Dictionary is really useful.*

> Chotto sono <u>bukku</u> [book] o misete kurenka.
> *Can I take a look at that book for a moment?*

> Jitsuni Nihonjin no <u>anpankucharu</u> [unpuncutal] ni wa osore iru.
> *I am tired of the Japanese being unpunctual.*

> Kuwashiku ieba <u>neemuri</u> [namely].
> *To say it precisely, namely.*

The explanation for this kind of light-hearted interlinguistic transfer lies in the presence of bilingual diglossia within the upper echelons of education in the early Meiji period, with English as a high-status language. The transferred items in this student code-mixing were bookish and the tone playful, but the style was established enough to serve as a marker of student identity. The code-switching was undoubtedly employed to symbolize in-groupness in that it drew upon in-group resources which were the prestigious object of educational training. Such linguistic mixing was not limited to students, however, since a diarist of the period notes that it also characterized the English of a leading figure of the era, Fukuzawa Yukichi, the founder of Keio University: 'Mr Fukuzawa has a comical way of speaking, using English and Japanese in the utmost confusion, so that it is difficult to understand what he really means. For example, speaking of the Governor: "Mr. Kuriyama is *hontō ni* kind man, *keredomo* he is *taisō* busy *kono setsu*, yes?"' (Mr. Kuri-yama is a very kind man, but he is extremely busy of late, yes?).[12]

From the earliest phases of the opening-up of Japan, both the British and the American models of English were influential. However, statistics show that the greatest number of Western personnel and teachers were British, which suggests that the most intensive oral contact during the Meiji period took place with this variety. Moreover, it is well known that the late nineteenth-century Japanese had a passionate interest in Victorian ethics, trade, and imperialism. The puristic controversy denigrating the status of American English was still strong, and many Japanese were aware of the contemporary normative and social value of British English.

The massive loan-reproduction evident in Meiji Japanese must also be mentioned. This involved the encoding of hundreds of Western abstract and concrete concepts such as 'democracy', '(legal) right', 'bicycle', 'locomotive', 'camera', and was most typically achieved by creating original compounds rather than by literal calquing: 'democracy' > *min* ('people') + *shu* ('primary') + *shugi* ('-ism'); 'right' > *ken* ('power') + *ri* ('profit'); 'locomotive' > *ki* ('steam') + *sha* ('cart'); 'camera' > *sha* ('copy') + *shin* ('reality') + *ki* ('machine').

Americanization through Mass Culture (1912–1930)

The distant non-bilingual setting established in the late Meiji period continued to hold into the next century. Japan's external relations with the English-speaking countries were for the first quarter of the new century mostly cordial: the Anglo-Japanese alliance (1902–23) offered prestige and protection. The First World War, during which Japan fought on the side of Britain and the United States, gave Japan the opportunity to solidify and expand her Asian empire. A mood of Japanese internationalism even manifested itself, as Japan became a founding member of the League of Nations and a permanent representative on its Council. Until the 1930s, Japan continued to co-operate with the West, often under pressure and to its own disadvantage.

However, there were growing causes for tension on both sides. On the one hand, the world economic crisis was causing severe damage to Japan's

[12] The observer was Clara Whitney, whose diary, composed in the 1880s while she was living in Japan, was reprinted in 1981. The quotation appears on p. 221.

industries and agriculture and leading to unemployment and poverty. Furthermore, there was bitter resentment over the racist rejection of Japanese immigration to the USA and to the British dominions during this period. Western powers, on the other hand, were increasingly perturbed by Japan's steady military expansion into the Asian continent.

Inside Japan, growing polarization was observable in politics, in spite of major democratic achievements such as the beginning of party government in 1918 and the institution of universal male suffrage in 1925. Western-style liberalism, encouraged in academic and journalistic circles, was having to confront more radical Western political philosophies such as anarchism and Marxism, popular among students. At the same time, small, ultranationalist groups and patriotic religious sects kept up a virulent anti-Western campaign, promoting the concept of Pan-Asianism and demanding a tougher approach to foreign policy.

From a linguistic stance, the principal agents of contact with English in the Taishō period (1912–26) were new forms of technological mass media such as the radio and cinema, which spread popular American culture and increased the speed and range of transmission. Mass sports events also contributed to the dissemination of English, as a result of their being reported by radio, beginning in 1924. A further technological channel of contact was the gramophone record, which made the reception of oral English an everyday possibility. On the written level, large-circulation newspapers and monthly magazines contributed to the familiarization and dissemination of English, as did the appearance of advertising, which frequently drew upon English resources. In addition, the latest translations of Western books were avidly read, contributing to the acquisition of intellectual and stylistic aspects of the Western world.

Urban daily life during this period was particularly characterized by the enthusiastic following of Western urban trends and fads such as the department store, the ice-cream parlour, the Charleston, and jazz, not to mention fashion, all of which were embraced by Japan's younger, middle-class generations, epitomized by the *sararī-man* (= *salary man*), an English-based nativization of the period meaning 'white-collar worker'. The effects of this physically and mentally Americanizing environment were considerable.

The popularization and proletarianization of Western culture led to an intensification of borrowing that was greater than in the whole of the Meiji period. Continuing industrialization also increased linguistic contact in technical and scientific spheres. In response to new linguistic needs, dictionaries of foreign loan-words proliferated, the most notable being Arakawa's (1931) dictionary of 5,018 entries entitled 'Japanized English'.

The interesting patterns for integrating English which first emerged at this time reveal the socio-psychologically closer and more familiar position of English in Taishō society. Thus, hybridization, where one part of a word is Japanese and the other English, is evident in the composition of Japanese and English-derived stems at that time: *modan-go* (< English: *modern* + Japanese 'words' = 'fashionable use of English-derived items'); *onna-boi* (< Japanese: 'girl' + English *boy* = 'waitress'). Sexual semantics proved a particularly inspiring field for Anglo-Japanese contact, with *ero-* (clipped form of *erotic*) and *-gāru* (< *girl*) very common components in hybrid stems; the latter also involved all-English derived coinages such as *ero-sābisu* (< *erotic service*) and *doa-gāru* (< *door girl*). While the overwhelming majority of lexical innovations were of a compounding type—*sararī-man-shippu* (< *salary man-ship*), *marukusu-boi* (< *Marx boy*), new suffixes were created which diverged from native English patterns: *anākisutikku* (< *anarchistic*), *parashūtā* (< *parachuter*). Morphophonological adaption led to simple clipped forms such as *ripurodakuto* (< *reproduct*) and clipped compositions derived from the first syllable of the stems—*moga* (*mo*[*dern*] *g*[*irl*] = 'flapper'). In fact, well before the wave of Americanization that followed the Second World War, the most typical of Japanese-English lexical patterns had already been established.

The deeper penetration of Western life-styles into society during this period was taken by some as indicative of an inferiority complex *vis-à-vis* the West. Some viewed westernization as positive and necessary for Japan's development, but many opposed it, and these opinions were reflected in the protracted debate on the abolition of English as a compulsory school-subject.

By the beginning of the Taishō period, English was taking up one third of the middle-school timetable and was heavily oriented to grammatical analysis and translation into Japanese; but the abilities of the students were characterized as poor. A number of influential voices expressed highly negative socio-political attitudes towards English teaching, asserting that it made Japan into a British colony, stifled the mind of an independent nation, and cultivated a 'second-class' mentality. In the following decades, the amount of time allotted to the study of English would be steadily reduced.

If it had not been for the introduction of mass media during the Taishō period, this setting would not have registered such an increase in contact phenomena, for on the societal level it continued to remain distant and non-bilingual. Technological innovations, such as the cinema, allowed some narrowing of the distance, but without adequate education and interaction, contact with English was destined to play only an insignificant role in Japanese society.

Purification of the Enemy Language (1930–1945)

The 1930s witnessed an escalation of Japanese militarist expansionism, signalled by the occupation of Manchuria in 1931, and an increased political and economic isolation from Western, English-speaking democracies, starting with Japan's withdrawal from the League of Nations in the same year. In 1937 Japan entered into a full-scale war with China, after which it internally grew more totalitarian. A virulently anti-Western ideology proclaimed bourgeois liberalism and capitalist democracy to be ineffective and commanded the Japanese to repudiate Western values and transform their culture, politics, and economics along purely Japanese lines. A new Asian order was to be created, cleansed of Western colonial vestiges, with Japan as its leader. In 1941 a war against the United States and the British Empire began, proclaimed to be the struggle of Asia to liberate itself from the West. Totally crushed, Japan surrendered in 1945, but, paradoxically, the war experience had in some respects westernized Japan even further in its modernizing requirements for industrialization, scientific development, and mobilization of female workers.

Controlling language contact was on the totalitarian agenda, and even before the start of the Pacific War the English language was attacked as a symbol of the 'enemy within'. As early as 1939 the names of foreign countries appearing in the press reverted to representation in Chinese characters. Borrowing, of course, severely declined, coming almost to a standstill. After 1940 English and romanized Japanese words were removed from Japanese posters, labels, and signs—for example, 'Post' was removed from letter-boxes and 'WC' from public toilets; English-named products were Japanized.

Furthermore, a radical policy of language purification was initiated which attempted to eradicate all Western loans, especially of English origin, from the Japanese language. In public communication many established loans—which were extensive in such fields as music and sport—were painstakingly replaced with new coinages drawing on native lexical stock: 'piano' → *kōkin*; 'clarinet' → *tatebue*; 'record' → *onban*; 'marathon' → *taikyūkyōsō*; 'track' → *kyōsōba*; 'golf' → *dakyū*; 'ski' → *sekkobu*; 'match'

→ *haiyatsukigi*. Most of these purifying substitutes were considered ridiculous by the community, and few survived their war setting.

As for the teaching of English, it had already been reduced in 1931 in response to clamours for its complete removal from the state system. However, a limited amount of English teaching in middle schools continued until 1944, after which time all children who had completed their compulsory education went to work in factories and fields. The war years left a whole generation with no English competence, or very little. Almost every university department of English was closed, and scholars were required to direct their knowledge of the 'enemy language' to the war effort.

In spite of Japanese efforts to promote local South-East Asian languages such as Tagalog in the Philippines, English was frequently unavoidable as a means of communication, often as a pidginized variety, in Japanese-occupied territories. English was, however, removed from schools in Singapore, Malaysia, and the Philippines, and government officials discouraged from employing it.

Since hostility towards westernization has been discernible throughout the history of Anglo-Japanese contact, the war did not reflect particularly new attitudes, although those expressed were of the most extreme in Japanese society. However, Japan's devastating defeat shattered faith in the power of Japanism and paved the way for a further intensification of westernization.

The Occupation (1945–1952)

During the Allied occupation of Japan, the country's politics, society, and economy underwent thoroughgoing reform based on Western institutions and concepts. These transformations were led by the 5,500 American bureaucrats who made up the government of the supreme commander of the Allied powers. Originally, 500,000 mainly American troops were stationed in Japan, which was initially gripped by an 'English fever', with textbooks of conversational English becoming bestsellers and English classes being taught by American soldiers on a broad scale. Knowledge of English was seen as the key to obtaining social advantages, including access to the black market; English was also regarded as the medium through which to learn about democracy, and it regained its social appeal as a code for liberals and internationalists. Although it did not become an obligatory school-subject, and has *never* become one since, its return as a component of university entrance-examinations at this time necessitated that it be studied in school. State media also resumed English-education broadcasts, from 1947, and these drew wide audiences.

Once more, borrowing from English took place, based on the American contact-model and was notable in the areas of political re-education (loans appeared based on 'guidance' and 'purge') and military acronaming (GI, MP, GHQ). Numerous English-based loans associated with Western youth- and media-culture also came into vogue (items derived from *quiz, teenager, mambo style, rock-a-billy, body-building, glamour, elegant, hula hoop,* and *leisure* were common). Of perhaps greater significance was the emergence of English-based pidginized varieties employed in interaction with American military personnel—giving rise to such terms as *pan-gurishu* (< PANsuke 'prostitute' + inGURISHU 'English')—and 'Japanese Bamboo English', as used between American military staff and Japanese labourers and servants.[13] This pidgin operated for trade, amusement (bars), casual interaction, and, occasionally, work.

The post-war switch of attitude towards Western culture, and the accompanying linguistic contact, should not be interpreted as necessarily sudden, insincere, or simply pragmatic. It essentially involved the return of a positive social evaluation of westernization, a viewpoint which went back to the nineteenth century and which had been rejected at various stages in the century-long contact. Admittedly, the immediate post-war years temporarily saw its exaggerated expression—for example, on the linguistic level, in the call to abolish the Japanese language because it impeded cultural development, or to replace Chinese characters with roman script. However, the only innovatory language-planning undertaken, and then mainly under American pressure, was the increased teaching of romanized Japanese in schools and the reduction in the number of characters for everyday use—although more radical reforms were in the offing. America's victory over Japan did not lead to the establishment of official bilingualism but merely re-established a setting in which patterns of Anglo-Japanese contact that had already been constructed in the pre-war period could be extended and intensified. The initial potential for becoming a bilingual nation with English as a High language had been strangled by nationalistic, ethnocentric forces which left English in a socially remote and academicized position. It is a position which English continues to hold today, although contemporary internationalizing developments in media, education, and politics augur a potentially different course in the twenty-first century.

[13] Cf. Norman (1954, 1955) and Goodman (1967).

4

The Contexts of Contemporary Contact

This chapter begins with a look at how contact is instigated and items become established as part of Japanese community resources. Then special consideration is given to the social and ecological dynamics which are leading to the massive linguistic transfer now taking place.

Lexical Absorption (1950–1990)

As Table 2.1 revealed, the main donor of present-day European loans is English. In fact, two items of statistical evidence point to a surge in the absorption of English-based items:

- Between 1955 and 1972 the proportion of English loans increased by a third.[1]
- European-derived single words represented 77 per cent of new vocabulary in 1955, but 82 per cent in 1975.[2]

As for the total number of contemporary Euro-Japanese loans,[3] a recent edition of the most comprehensive European loan-word dictionary, Arakawa's (1977) *Kadokawa Gairaigo jiten*, contained 27,000 entries. More popular loan-word dictionaries, reflecting everyday needs, still list a high number of borrowings—20,000 in the case of Sanseido-Henshū (1979) and 14,000 in the case of Saito (1985).

On the other hand, coinages exploiting indigenous (non-Chinese-based) resources, already low in 1955 at 5 per cent, dropped to 2 per cent in 1975; Chinese-based coinages have also significantly declined.[4]

The Integration Process

Language contact in post-war Japan involves many diverse phenomena, as the next chapter on its formal variation will illustrate. To be honest,

---

[1] This calculation is based on Ozawa's findings (1976), which show that the number of English-derived loan-words, including hybrid compounds, registered in the *Kōjihan* of 1955 totalled 5,632, and in 1972 7,499.   [2] See Tamamura (1981).

[3] These data also come from Tamamura (1981). In fact, single new words derived from Chinese represented 19% in 1955, with compounds standing at 52%, but these figures dropped to 16% and 41% respectively in 1975.   [4] Ozawa (1976).

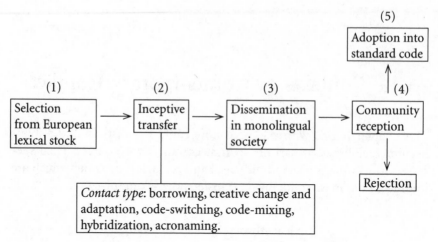

FIG. 4.1. The five stages of lexical innovation and integration in present-day Japanese language-contact.

there are problems with the definition and recognition of contact phenomena which are *not* already codified in loan-word dictionaries but which abound in advertising and other contexts. In such cases, orthographic and phonetic assimilation play an important role in identification, as does the extent of community acceptability. Other factors include the extent of a contact item's community-wide intelligibility and frequency of employment. However, the degree of integration can vary considerably according to social group. Thus, it has been discovered that for certain words there could be a gap of as much as 63 per cent with regard to acceptability as Japanese, depending on the age of the informants.[5] For example, 'live' was considered as Japanese only by 16 out of 100 informants, in their fifties, in contrast to 78 out of 104 university students.

Instigating new language-contact in contemporary Japanese society is a long-term process which can be divided into five basic stages (see Fig. 4.1):

1(a). The selection of European, but principally English, lexical item(s) and/ or

1(b). The selection of items from the already known European loan-stock and their use in an innovatory fashion, as in hybridization: *nama-kon* (Japanese: 'raw' + English: *con*[*crete*][6]).

---

[5] See Ishino (1983).

[6] The square brackets indicate *truncation*, so that the syllable enclosed is not pronounced.

2. The inceptive employment of the selected item(s) in oral and/or written contexts involving various phenomena such as borrowing in assimilated or unassimilated forms, code-switching, code-mixing, or creative changes relating to interference, interlanguage, and pidginization.
3. The dissemination of the new contact-item in the community or subgroup.
4. The reception of the contact item in the speech-community or subgroup.
5. Either integration and acceptance into the community code or rejection and oblivion.

Synchronically viewed, innovatory language-contact includes items that never succeed in joining standard Japanese and which will be rejected in due course. Community members participate in the integration process when they choose to adopt or reject the item(s) they meet. This contact may lead to language change and loss as well as the development of new registers.

The Semantic Impact of Westernization

As for the semantic dimensions of contact with European languages in general, studies show that loans are particularly high in the areas of fashion, cosmetics, food, audio technology, sport, housing, music, art, business management, and engineering. English-based loans have grown conspicuous in a number of Japanese taxonomies: English-derived items make up 52 per cent of flower names, 30 per cent of fruit names, 35 per cent of vegetable names, 24 per cent of animal designations, and 9 per cent of colour names. The European-derived kinship-terms *papa* and *mama* provide a further indication of lexical penetration. Of equal importance is the replacement of previously established Japanese calques of Western items with new loans: *shashinki* → *kamera*; *hyakkaten* 'department store' → *depāto*.

Various types of semantic and morphological adaptation are observable in present-day Euro-Japanese items. The most obvious morphological change is the clipping of the front or back syllable, particularly productive in slang: *baito* 'part-time job' (< German: *Arbeit*), *hōmu* (< [plat]form); *puchiburu* (< French: *petit bourgeois*). Truncated compounding is another assimilatory process: *han-suto* (< *hung*[er] *st*[rike]); *wā-pro* (< *wo*[rd] *pro*[cessor]) which simplifies the pronunciation of the loan and thereby facilitates its integration into Japanese. Hybridization such as *dai-sutoraiku* (< Japanese: 'big' + English: *strike*) and *nouveau-dai*

(< French: *nouveau* 'new' + Japanese: 'era') makes compounds of European and usually Sino-Japanese nominal bases; European bases may also be intercombined: *bakansu-uea* 'holiday clothes' (< French: *vacances* 'holiday' + English: *wear*). Hybrid affixing either way also occurs: *ichigo-ēdo* (< Japanese: 'strawberry' + English: *-ade*); *karuchā-ppoi* (< English: *culture* + Japanese: 'strong').

Of special morpho-semantic interest is the development of lexical coining using European elements, notably pseudo-English, resulting in innovations such as *sukinshippu* (< *skin* + *-ship*) denoting 'intimate, physical closeness'. Most frequently the innovating coinages are compounds: *wan-man-kā* (< *one* + *man* + *car* = 'bus without a conductor') and *hote-shon* (< *hotel* + [*man*]*sion* = 'a rented room in town used for business'). Also related to this is the occurrence of innovating English-based acronyms such as *OL* (< *office lady*); *LDK* (< *living-dining-kitchen*).

Semantic change is another aspect of Euro-Japanese assimilation involving:

1. Semantic restriction: *karute* (< German: *Karte*) refers only to a patient's chart in the medical domain.
2. Semantic shift: *sumāto* (< English: *smart*) 'slim, slender'.
3. Semantic extension: *dorai* (< English: *dry*) 'unsentimental'.

The environment in which these semantic developments are taking place requires careful consideration. What first appears as a simple motivating context—westernization—turns out to elude direct, concrete analysis. Westernization must, of course, be distinguished from modernization, in that it goes beyond the utilization of scientific knowledge for forms of progress. The term is extremely broad and can be understood on many levels: the material, the sociological, and, finally, the ethical and psychological. Then, there are great difficulties in assessing the degree of westernization for each of the latter levels and making generalizations valid for a whole society.

First of all, it must be remembered that Japan's most profound and intensive period of westernization took place during the nineteenth and early twentieth centuries. In fact, it is often maintained that Japanese culture has independently evolved from the initial Western input. From a macro-sociological point of view, Japan undeniably presents itself as a highly industrialized, Western-looking society, but if its institutional and behavioural patterns are closely examined, many socio-cultural differences emerge. Additionally, since the Japanese have succeeded in preserving

TABLE 4.1. Lexical Complementarity through Westernization of Life-Style

Original Japanese word	Western-style, English-based loan
tō/shōji (= sliding door)	*doa* ('door')
futon (= quilted bedding)	*beddo* ('bed')
tatami (= matting)	*kāpetto* ('carpet')
zabuton (= thin cushion)	*kusshon* ('cushion')
hashi (= chopsticks)	*naifu, fōku, supūn* ('knife', 'fork', 'spoon')
kashi (=Japanese cakes)	*kēki, bisuketto* ('cake', 'biscuit')
amedama (= gluten sweets)	*kyandē* ('candy')
ryōriya (= restaurant serving only Japanese food)	*restoran* ('restaurant')
kinoko (= mushrooms)	*masshurūmu* ('champignons')

—admittedly with changes and adaptions—fundamental aspects of their institutions, norms, and values in the face of Western models and pressures throughout the last and this century, it seems likely that they will continue to maintain certain native cultural ways.

When Japan entered into contact with the West, it already had a fully developed, elaborate writing-system, an established tradition of secular literature, and a well-educated group of writers, scholars, and publicists, so that it did not need to import a writing-system wholesale, as had been the case for certain non-Western countries without a unified, national written language in Africa and Asia. In spite of the fact that Japan, unlike India, experienced no colonization, and its geographical position precluded easy access to, and penetration by, Western influences, Western-based language-contact is, surprisingly, extremely pervasive today.

The westernization of Japanese culture is evident in the existence of many pairs in semantic opposition where a word referring to a Western phenomenon is English-based and 'complementary'[7] with a word deriving from (Sino-) Japanese and referring to a related version of the phenomenon belonging to native culture. Thus, all the direct loans in Table 4.1 are semantically marked by the feature [-Japanese].

---

[7] The term 'complementary' refers to 'ungradable opposites like *male* and *female*' (Lyons, 1977: 279). See also Cruse (1986: 198–9): 'Of all the varieties of opposites, complementarity is perhaps the simplest conceptually. The essence of a pair of complementaries is that between them they exhaustively divide some conceptual domain into two mutually exclusive compartments.'

No doubt further complementary pairs could be added to Table 4.1, the scope of which has been restricted to aspects of daily life (housing and food) that can be experienced today by ordinary members of Japanese society. What is significant in the table is that the native and English-based pairs bisect the two cultural worlds. However, in actual life, this material (and lexical) duality definitely operates less in terms of conflict and more in terms of co-existence.

It is also erroneous to attribute this contact-behaviour simply to a need to fill lexical gaps. If one examines the linguistic approach of the Japanese in other instances of westernization, we see that existing native resources have continued to be employed in a way which, though not making calques out of them, incorporates the Western-style version. Thus, through semantic extension, the native lexemes *mado* and *sara*, for instance, cover reference to the Western-style versions of the phenomena 'window' and 'plate'. Similarly, the native term for 'footwear', *kutsu*, has been extended to include Western-style, leather shoes. Obviously, in many cases—for example, that of milk products such as cream and yoghurt, no alternatives existed in Japan which could semantically oppose the Western item.

Indications of culture-change connected with a westernizing context can be observed in the fact that the English-based loan-word is frequently more common than its native counterpart in everyday life: *pen* instead of *fude* ('brush'), *stōbu* ('stove') instead of *hibachi* ('charcoal brazier'). Similarly, traditional Japanese terms for units of measurement have been replaced by English-based metric units: *shaku* (30.3 cm., for measuring cloth), *shō* (1.8 l., for cubic measurement, including that of rice and liquids), *kan* (3.75 kg.), and *ri* (3.93 km.) have yielded to *miri-guramu*, *rittoru*, and *kiromētoru* respectively. A synchronic example is the increasing dominance of *mētoru* (< *metre*) over the traditional unit for counting land: *tsubo* (3.31 m^2). Form these examples, it should be clear that as Japanese cultural styles increasingly orient themselves to a modern, Western model, traditional items from the native vocabulary are phased out along with their disappearing referents.

However, it is extremely important to realize that English contact is not always related to westernization. This can be seen directly in 'Japan-made English', signifying local phenomena. Compounds used in the commercial register—'summer gift', 'bottle keep'—are examples of this. Furthermore, the borrowing of items for referents already encoded in Japanese demonstrates that cultural contact is not the sole motivation for contact with English. Thus, loans based on *fruit, kitchen, couple, pink, fresh, control, power,* and *cost,* to name but a few, all share native encodings, although they are associatively, stylistically, and collocatively different.

This differentiation of transferred items from native terms which share a similar basic sense brings us to the important area of synonymy and how it relates to westernizing trends. At first sight, the existence of loans such as *raisu* (< *rice*), *sutoroberī* (< *strawberry*), *bīfu* (< *beef*), and *uedingu* (< *wedding*) appear quite unnecessary, given the availability from the core (Sino-) Japanese lexicon of the items *gohan, ichigo, hiru-gohan, kekkon,* and *gyūniku* respectively. Yet these loans have been integrated. The linguistic justification for the borrowing suggested here is that their referents are westernized versions, or appear in westernized contexts in Japanese culture. Thus, *raisu* is cooked rice served on a flat, Western-style dinner-plate rather than a bowl, and accompanying a Western-style main course. *Sutoroberī* is used when that fruit appears in Western foods such as ice-cream, cake, or sweets; and similarly *bīfu* is employed in connection with Western-style, but not Japanese, dishes. As for *uedingu,* this too occurs in the context of a materially Western, commercially organized reception which takes place after a traditional Shinto wedding and typically includes the bride's change from a wedding kimono into a Western-style, white wedding-dress and the couple's cutting a Western-style wedding-cake.

A significant linguistic feature of such synonymous borrowings is the tendency for them to be employed in compounds rather than singly: *sutoroberī-shēku* (< *strawberry shake*), *bīfu-shichū* (< *beef stew*), *bīfu-sōsēji* (< *beef sausage*), *uedingu-doresu* (< *wedding-dress*), *uedingu-kēki* (< *wedding-cake*). Once again, the compounds are Western elements. The morphological restriction of the occurrence of such loans to compounds is due to the fact that reference to the fundamental or 'natural' condition of the phenomenon is made with (Sino-)Japanese resources. Thus, raw strawberries and uncooked beef are sold as *ichigo* and *gyūniku*; uncooked rice is called *kome*; when Japanese talk of a marriage ceremony, they always refer to it as *kekkon-shiki,* even if it is not in traditional Japanese style. This folk-linguistic patterning seems to suggest that the westernized referents of such borrowings are interpreted only as modifications of the basic concept, which is natively encoded. In other words, a certain portion of westernization in Japan is regarded as merely material transformation.

Also with regard to these items, the question has to be raised whether the phenomena they represent really constitute westernization, because, in some cases, there has been, not an exact reproduction of Western phenomena, but only a partial adaption of existing local conditions. Thus, even on a flat dinner-plate and with a Western meal, Japanese *raisu* is not boiled and long-grain but steamed and round-grain. A *uedingu-doresu* is not usually worn for the actual ceremony of marriage (unless it takes place in a Christian church, and less than one per cent of the Japanese are Christian) but is most often something for the bride to change into during a Japanese-style reception, as a form of visual entertainment. Even strawberries depart from their Western associations when they are, for example, employed as an essential part of Christmas-cake decoration. The purpose of these examples is to demonstrate the error in equating contemporary contact simplistically with westernization, and believing that the referents of the new loans are culturally identical with their Western counterparts.

In fact, superficial synonymy between an English-based loan and its Japanese lexical complement can be widely observed, but deeper examination often reveals semantic change, of which the most common type is semantic restriction: *kyakusan* 'guest'/*bijitā* (< *visitor*) 'non-member of a golf club'; *bango* 'number'/*nanbā* 'licensed number-plates of a car'; *gyūnyū* 'milk'/*miruku* 'condensed or powdered milk'; *okāsan* 'mother'/*mazā* (< *mother*) 'Catholic nun'; *atsui* 'hot'/*hotto* (< *hot*) used only in compounds relating to the temperature of Western-derived food and drink: for example, *hotto-sandoitchi* (< *hot sandwich*), *hotto-kēki* (< *hot cake*), *hotto-kōhi* (< *hot coffee*) and *hotto-chokorēto* (< *hot chocolate*). Here we can see the convenience of lexical transfer to make new cultural distinctions without requiring the semantic widening of native resources. Again, the referent of the loan is connected with either Western-derived areas such as Christianity and food or Western-inspired, 'modern' phenomena—camera, car, golf-club, food-production processes. A causal link between the transfer of such loans and the process of acculturation, however, cannot be made, since native resources for encoding are readily available in these cases and there is no inherent need for lexical gaps to be filled. The real motivation for such language-contact is the Japanese contemporary preference for English-derived vocabulary as a source of neologizing, a point that is taken up in Chapter 7.

Another common semantic change that can be observed involves shift, often due to truncation: the loan *mōningu* (< *morning*) is not equivalent to the Japanese *asa* 'morning' but is a truncation of *mōningu-sābisu* (< *morning service*), a Western-style breakfast of toast and coffee (instead of traditional rice and fish) in a restaurant. Typically this kind of semantic shift stems from the commercial alteration of existing phenomena, here the restructuring of a breakfast menu.

Inevitably, the lexico-semantic consequences of westernization include the addition of loan-word hyponyms to Japanese taxonomies, as illustrated in Fig. 4.2 with new generic names for shops and shoes. The superordinate terms tend to remain native, while the lower terms are borrowings, although the superordinate term may also appear as an innovative loan in commercial contexts, often in roman script.

It is vital to recognize that not all of the transferred items and referents in the taxonomies follow a 'pure' Western model: formally, *gasorin-sutando* and *rēnshūzu* are Japan-made compounds; semantically, *rēnshūzu* refer to women's ankle-high boots for the rainy season, while *surippā* refer to heel-less and backless lightweight footwear covering only the toes and put on by everyone, including guests, before entering the Western, but not the Japanese-style, rooms of a Japanese home. Thus, the referents of these superficially English words blend Japanese local conditions and customs with Western-derived materials and forms.

It is no coincidence that the type of acculturating lexical transfer so far described does not extend to abstract concepts, being limited to material items such as Western items of food, furniture, and clothing, and Western-derived objects for eating, writing, heating, travel, photography, etc. This is because it is principally on the concrete level of reference that this contact-behaviour operates. In contrast, abstract Western-derived referents are usually calqued with the aid of Sino-Japanese morphology, a pattern set in Meiji times. Examples of some long-established and more recent (Sino-)Japanese contact with abstract intellectual concepts and terms from the West in the domains of politics, law, and Christianity are shown in Table 4.2, which demonstrates that the main process of transferring referents of a non-material type continues through creative translation. This pattern comes from the Japanese tendency to consider representation with characters as carrying more intellectual weight than the syllabic systems, because before the twentieth century nearly all formal and academic texts were written in a heavily sinicized style predominantly composed of Chinese characters. As a result, in spite of post-war language-reforms, the seriousness and scholarliness of Japanese texts is commensurable with the amount of Sino-Japanese compounding it contains. The handful of English-derived loans in Table 4.2 are (like high-level Greek loans in English) semantically opaque to the average

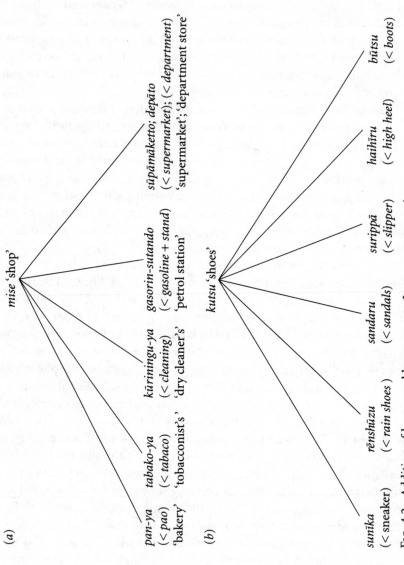

Fig. 4.2. Addition of loan-word hyponyms to Japanese taxonomies.

(a)

mise 'shop'

pan-ya
(< *pao*)
'bakery'

tabako-ya
(< *tabaco*)
'tobacconist's'

kuriningu-ya
(< *cleaning*)
'dry cleaner's'

gasorin-sutando
(< *gasoline + stand*)
'petrol station'

sūpāmāketto; depāto
(< *supermarket*); (< *department*)
'supermarket'; 'department store'

(b)

kutsu 'shoes'

sunīka
(< *sneaker*)

rēnshūzu
(< *rain shoes*)

sandaru
(< *sandals*)

surippā
(< *slipper*)

haihīru
(< *high heel*)

būtsu
(< *boots*)

TABLE 4.2. Japanese Contact with Western-Derived Abstract and Intellectual Terms

English term	Characters	Pronunciation	English loan-word
democracy	民主主義	minshushugi	*demokurashī*
socialism	社会主義	shakaishugi	*soshiarizumu*
communism	共産主義	kyōsanshugi	*komyunizumu*
internationalism	国際主義	kokusaishugi	*intānashonarizumu*
liberalism	自由主義	jiyūshugi	–
individualism	個人主義	kojinshugi	–
feminism	女性尊重論	josei sonchōron	*feminizumu*
developing country	発展途上国	hatten tojōkoku	–
disarmament	軍備縮小	gumbi shukushō	–
fundamental human rights	基本的人権	kihonteki jinken	–
jury system	陪審制度	baihinseidō	–
reprieve	執行猶予	shikkoyūyo	–
hearsay evidence	伝聞証拠	denbunshōko	–
contempt of court	法定侮辱	hōteibujoku	–
sovereignty	統治権	tōchiken	–
right of privacy	プライバシーの	puraibashi	*puraibashi*
	権利	no kenri	
God	神	kami	–
sin	罪	tsumi	–
Holy Communion	聖体拝種	seitai-haijuu	–
salvation	救世	kyūsei	–
Christmas	–	–	*kurisumasu*

Japanese and tend to be avoided. It is difficult to generalize about their usage, but they are normally avoided in official documents or communication intended for the general public. If they appear, it is mainly in the written channel, often in co-occurence with their Japanese counterparts, in academic contexts where they tend to be employed for stylistic variety or with particular reference to non-Japanese situations.

The dividing-line between scientific knowledge and the process of westernization is problematic. Nevertheless, the domains of politics and law, which are also studied as academic disciplines, are featured as examples of contact with Western culture rather than Western-based information because the Japanese apply models from the former to institutional organization and communication. The degree of borrowing in terminology related to these culturally influential fields is dramatically lower than in scientific and technological fields. In a dictionary of contemporary specialist terms (*Gendai-yōgō*, 1985) I could find only 6 per cent of lexical transfer in the field of official politics, and 5 per cent in the field of law, in contrast to, for example, 67 per cent in engineering, 41 per cent in chemistry, and 38 per cent in biology. On top of this, the transferred items belonging to the fields of law and politics consisted almost entirely of hybrid compounds: *puraibashī-hogoseido* ('system for protecting <u>privacy</u>'); *shinjiyū-kurabu* ('new liberal <u>club</u>'), and the majority did not encode abstract Western concepts but had material referents—they included, for example, loans derived from *club*, *centre*, *leader*, and *programme*.

The reason for this low degree of direct English transfer is that Japanese law and politics are not as international as Japanese academia has to be. Although undeniably influenced by, and modelled on, Western patterns, the institutions of politics and law are essentially self-contained and inwardly evolving, as well as being conservative, with a strong awareness of their symbolic role as representatives of the state. A stronger puristic attitude is thus appropriate, as reflected in the preference for Japanese calques over direct transfers from external languages.

This avoidance of Anglicization in institutional officialdom contrasts strikingly with the contact situation in many African and Asian countries, where it is precisely in the domains of government and the judiciary that English is most fully employed. The official terms used in these countries are the same as in English; they are subsequently borrowed into the local languages of these often multilingual states, thereby creating a cultural and linguistic contact fundamentally different from the Japanese one.

Next we turn to the field of religion and the absence of much English-based Christian terminology. It is important to bear in mind that only one per cent of the present Japanese population is Christian and is thus demographically insignificant. Japanese loan-translations relating to religion were established more than a century ago by Protestant missionaries, whose policy was to use the local language for religious texts (unlike Roman Catholics). The only common Christian term in Japanese general usage is the name of the festival 'Christmas', which is not a public holiday and is an entirely commercial event for the vast majority. Nevertheless, it is interesting that the alien character of the festival is symbolized in its loan-word encoding. The purpose of mentioning this area of cultural contact here is to show that, once again, when it comes to non-concrete, and even spiritual, matters of Western origin, a purely Japanese medium is the norm. Furthermore, there are socio-linguistic similarities with the fields discussed above, for Japan's religious domain is a public institution principally involved in serving local needs and purposes through a formal and serious register.

Finally, it is essential to reiterate that the existence of the encoding of a Western cultural item in Japanese, whether through calque or direct transfer, should be taken not as automatically implying that straightforward westernization has taken place but, more often than not, as showing that it has undergone modification and adaptation to the native Japanese cultural context.

Of course, there do exist a limited number of English-based loans without concrete reference which appear at first glance to be cases of westernization: *rabu* (< *love*), *romansu* (< *romance*). Traditional mores tabooed the open declaration and display of affection between couples, but through contact with Western culture, attitudes and behaviour have changed. The acculturation of the notion of romantic love, with its radical values of partner selection on the basis of individual choice, has, like the idealization of women, been gaining ground throughout this century. Today, arranged marriages account for only 60 per cent of the nation's matches.

However, it is interesting to note that *rabu* never occurs by itself in Japanese. On close inspection of the associative range of its compounds, its sense turns out to be primarily physical. The compounds *rabu shin* (< *love scene*) and the local coinages *rabu hoteru* (< *love hotel* = 'rooms rented to couples') and *rabu hanto* (< *love hunt*) reveal its blatantly euphemistic function for 'sex'. Naturally, native terms exist for love—*ai* (愛) or *koi* (恋) 'passion'—and it is significant that the term for a marriage made for love is not English-derived but (Sino-) Japanese: *renai-kekkon* 'pure-love marriage'. Similarly, *romansu* can also signify a 'love affair'.

On the other hand, it could be argued that romantic feelings are universal and have nothing to do with westernizing processes at all. The same could be said of the few adjectives referring to human states or qualities such as *happi* (< *happy*), *chāmingu* (< *charming*), and *furanku* (< *frank*), for which native equivalents exist and which are more readily employed in contexts of sincere and private communication than their English-based synonyms (cf. the function of Germanic words in relation to Latin-based loans in English conversation).

In conclusion to this section on the semantic impact of westernization in borrowing, it can be stated that on the physical level, westernization accompanied by adaption to local cultural conditions is readily observable in areas of domestic interiors, food, dress, and music; the lexico-semantic consequences in these areas are pervasive and self-evident. On the other hand, westernization is far less discernible, both socially and linguistically, in abstract domains which do not form part of factual knowledge in a professional, scientific, or technical field.

In many cases cultural contact with the West has not necessarily entailed the termination or modification of native cultural patterns. These have proven remarkably stable, although many traditional objects have been superseded by Western ones.

Furthermore, it must be remembered that creative Anglicization can equally serve local, non-Western needs on both a physical level (*rēnshūzu* < *rain shoes*, *gūrīn tī shū aisu* < *green-tea choux-ice*—a combination of the flavour of Japanese green tea with ice-cream in choux pastry, *kappu nūdoru* < *cup noodle*—instant Oriental noodles), and on an abstract level (*sukinshippu* < *skinship*—physical intimacy and affection between mother and child reflected in the fact that infants tend to sleep together with their parents, some even into childhood, *shibiru-minimamu* < *civil minimum*—minimum living-conditions to be guaranteed by a municipality). In fact, these local coinages indicate not a westernized but a hybridized culture. The Japanese have not experienced profound Western-based acculturation but live in a state of coexistence with increasingly dominant, selected Western forms while generally adhering to indigenous social and ethical behaviour.

The Context of Internationalization

The construction of a global community is being steadily realized as, each day, through technological progress, the spatial and temporal distance between nations shrinks and their life-styles, pursuits, and even values become homogenized. Language contact with English is obviously greatly promoted by this phenomenon, since English is the principal medium of the spreading international network. As has been seen above, English is the main donor-language in the contact processes taking place in contemporary Japan.

English is the world's most powerful language at this moment in human history. This is evident from the demography of its 600 million users, spread all over the globe. English is an official language in thirty-seven nations and is natively spoken in twelve countries, including leading political and economic forces in the capitalist bloc, such as the USA and the United Kingdom.

The power of English can also be gauged from its diverse applications in the world's activities. It is the medium of the Second Industrial Revolution; and international science and information, international business, world organizations and diplomacy, international tourism, aviation and shipping, entertainment such as sports, cinema, television, and pop music, 60 per cent of the world's radio broadcasts, and 70 per cent of its mail are encoded in English.[8]

On the educational level, English is the most commonly taught second or foreign language in the world, with 115 million studying it at school in Asia (60 million), Africa (20 million), Europe (15 million), and Russia (10 million).[9] These facts about English in the world partly explain why the main contact-language in Japan today is English, but there are also internal, community-specific dynamics that need to be analysed.

Japan has recently launched an offical policy of 'internationalization', in line with the international responsibility which its new-found status as a rich, advanced nation requires it to demonstrate. Whether the policy remains an empty slogan or can fulfil its promise of an improvement in international relations remains to be seen, but the very fact that there arose a need to create such a policy indicates a perceived lack of internationalism by the Japanese themselves. It should also be noted that Japan's massive economic expansion has been the chief factor in this development. As a result, there exists a two-way flow of ever-increasing numbers of Japanese travelling and residing overseas and a growing group of non-Japanese coming to visit, work, and even reside in Japan.

In 1985 nearly 5 million Japanese travelled overseas, but by 1992 this

[8] See Conrad and Fishman (1977), Bailey and Görlach (1982), Platt *et al.* (1984), and Kachru (1986) for statistics on world-wide English users.   [9] According to Kachru (1981: 17).

figure stood close to 12 million.[10] However, 80 per cent of overseas travellers are on sightseeing tours which last an average of nine days, the most
popular destination being the United States (which attracted nearly 4
million in 1992, with many visiting Hawaii and Guam), followed by
the Pacific region, with the following destinations in descending order
of popularity: South Korea, Hong Kong, Taiwan, Singapore, and Australia. Other popular destinations, in descending order, are: Thailand,
France, China, and Britain. Of course, this tourism does not contribute
to language contact in any significant way but does indirectly promote
a favourable environment for its spread and reception.

Japanese residents abroad totalled 679,400 in 1992, with 40 per cent of
this number being settled permanently overseas. As many as half of the
Japanese residing abroad are businessmen sent to branches of their company, and a considerable number of them are accompanied by family
members, with the result that about 50,000 Japanese of predominantly
primary-school age are currently living outside Japan. However, it must
be pointed out that, particularly in the Third World, the children often
attend private Japanese schools. This is not so much the case in the USA,
where, outside of Hawaii, there are only three all-Japanese schools in
operation, and most Japanese expatriate children attend American public
schools. In fact, just over half of overseas Japanese residents are based in
English-speaking countries: in 1992 38 per cent resided in the United
States, while about 8 per cent lived in the United Kingdom, 4 per cent in
Canada, and 3 per cent in Australia. A select group of Japanese also go
abroad for educational purposes; every year about 6,000 researchers go to
the USA, and over 50,000 Japanese students are enrolled there in various
colleges. Emigration, on the other hand, has remained at the very low
level of about 2,000 a year since the 1970s and is restricted mainly to
professionals with special skills.

Internal contact with non-Japanese, although of a much lower intensity, is nevertheless expanding at a dramatic pace and is reflected in diverse spheres such as attitudes towards marriage with non-Japanese: 654
Japanese men applied to marry Filipinas in 1986, but this grew to 4,500
in 1991[11] as a result of the steady rise of the number of Filipinas working
in Japan. In 1992 foreign spouses of Japanese nationals accounted for one
third of permanent residents and totalled 209,269.

---

[10] The figures cited in this section are based on records released by the Immigration Bureau
of the Justice Ministry, Education Ministry, the Foreign Ministry, and the Japan Immigration
Association.   [11] This statistic was quoted in the *Daily Yomiuri*, 22. 1. 92, 2.

Foreign visitors to Japan in 1992 numbered almost 4 million, with more than 90 per cent of these being first-time visitors staying for less than ninety days. More than half of these visitors came for tourism, while 30 per cent were on business; other purposes included education and temporary employment. Americans, who used to constitute 25 per cent of all foreign visitors, have, since 1987, been displaced by South Koreans (28 per cent in 1992), followed by Taiwanese (19 per cent), and in 1992 ranked only third (15 per cent). Officially, there were 1.28 million legally registered foreign residents in Japan in 1992; this figure, when added to that for 'illegals' (see below for statistics) brought the proportion of foreigners living in the country in 1992 to more than one per cent of the overall population of 124 million. Koreans—many of whom were born in Japan, as descendants of those forcibly brought to the country as labourers before and during the Second World War—accounted for 54 per cent of foreign residents; Chinese came second at 15 per cent, closely followed by Latin Americans claiming Japanese descent, with Brazilians at 12 per cent and Peruvians at 2.4 per cent. Other significant groups were Filipinos and Americans, with the latter making up 50 per cent of the expatriate community of executive business and diplomatic staff. The US military and naval bases scattered around Japan employ a staff of about 50,000 Americans.

The number of foreign employees in Japan, particularly those hired for domestic operations—as engineers, managers, and specialists—from foreign research-institutes, has undergone a gradual increase, and since the 1990 liberalization of the immigration law concerning the qualifications of foreigners entering Japan, an increase in non-skilled, Asian labour has been noticeable—the number of 'foreign trainees' almost tripled between 1986 and 1990, when it stood at 37,566. There are numerous signs that there trends will be tolerated, and even encouraged, since, in spite of the recession of the 1990s, Japanese enterprises are suffering from a shortage of young staff willing to carry out hard, dirty, and dangerous work; the shrinking population which is forecast for the next century will make the shortage even more acute. Moreover, at this moment there is a growing pool of illegal migrant labour, which in 1992 officially stood at 278,892. Thais topped this pool at 16 per cent, followed by Iranians and Malaysians (both at 14 per cent) and Koreans (13 per cent); other groups were Bangladeshis and Pakistanis.

As for foreign students at Japanese schools, these numbered 45,000 in 1991, with Asians accounting for 92 per cent. Students from mainland

China were the biggest group, at 44 per cent, followed by South Koreans (29 per cent), Taiwanese (13 per cent), Malaysians (4 per cent), and Americans (3 per cent).

On the other hand, signs of unwillingness to assume international responsibilities persist. For example, currently only 5 per cent of the UN work-force is made up of Japanese, while Japan contributes as much as 10 per cent of the UN budget; Japan ranks thirteenth in the world in the number of boat-people accepted; its overseas development aid in relation to its GNP is much lower than that of certain European nations.

However, it is the lack of acceptance of 'internationalized' Japanese which most of all reveals the community's ingrained insularity and extremely conformist attitudes. Among such Japanese are the above-mentioned children of the business community based overseas, of which 10,000 return to Japan every year. Sixty per cent of the returnees have received education at American public schools.[12] Thus, these children have experienced part of their socialization in a non-Japanese environment and acquired different patterns of cultural and linguistic behaviour that mark them out as targets for bullying and ostracism by classmates, and even by teaching staff. In some extreme cases, returnees have committed suicide, and there is a lack of social awareness of their plight. Teachers are embarrassed by their fluency in English or annoyed by their culturally conflicting style of communication. The government established one special school in Tokyo in 1988 to cater for the needs of such students, but the response has been slow. If the economic and political status quo is maintained, it is very likely that over the next decades an even greater number of Japanese will experience first-hand contact with foreign cultures and languages during their formative years. Japanese companies are increasing the number of their overseas branches and factories, and it is conceivable that, as a result of this interaction, more bilingual and bicultural Japanese will emerge and will, if given positions of responsibility in Japanese society, be able to act as agents of internal internationalization. On the other hand, at the moment, many returnees prefer either to work for foreign companies in Japan or to go abroad again, and they therefore have little effect on the mainstream.

From the above data, the United States emerges as one of Japan's major partners in international exchange today: it is the country where most Japanese businessmen work and most Japanese students and researchers

---

[12] *Daily Yomiuri*, 8. 3. 87, 6.

study; conversely, it is also the country from which many tourists, and even workers, in Japan come. Such migratory dynamics obviously set up positive conditions for English contact. Without doubt, English constitutes the most important language for Japan's external dealings, and this indirectly affects internal contact-processes.

The possibility that the present phase of internationalism will be followed by a new period of inward-looking, retrogressive traditionalism cannot be ruled out, especially when one considers the swings of pro- and anti-Westernness described in Chapter 3. However, the duration of what is essentially trade-induced contact may force upon the community a deeper state of internationalization and concomitant bilingualism in the future.

The Institutional Context

This section looks at institutional contact with English in Japanese society and attempts to answer the question why many students, even after being instructed in English for between six and ten years, still have serious comprehension problems with anything beyond very simple written structures, and also lack a working fluency. In other words, it explores the causes for the creation of a 'distant non-bilingual' language-contact setting.

About 11 million Japanese children in secondary education are currently engaged in the study of English, and about a further million study it at tertiary level, in addition to their major subject.

First of all, it is essential to realize that from the time official contact began 200 years ago, English has never gained any established status, except for its restricted contemporary use in the written channel of the medical profession. Furthermore, Japan has never been colonized or conquered by any foreign group in recorded history, although it was occupied by the American forces for seven years. It has been societally monolingual for nearly a millennium, but from earliest times its educational institutions, including temples, have served as agencies of language contact with, for example, Chinese and Sanskrit and, since the Meiji period, European languages. In the latter case, the institutions were regarded as instruments of modernization and transmitters of useful Western knowledge.

However, with the advent of post-war mass education, the Japanese educational system is facing a functional crisis because of its inherent conservatism, élitism, and over-academic approach, particularly evident in the area of the teaching of English.

It should be noted that English is not a compulsory subject in any state school in Japan, although it is taught in 99 per cent of them—electively. This situation is fundamentally a response to the fact that English is a required subject in university and senior high-school entrance-examinations. The post-war return of English to the curriculum is undeniably also a political consequence of Japan's defeat and the general Japanese socio-cultural pattern of wishing to identify with a perceived source of power. This identification is also reflected in the post-war shift in pedagogic model from British to American English in spelling and pronunciation.

Student motivation for studying English in Japan today, however, has little to do with world-bloc affiliation or the status of English as a world lingua franca. It is primarily concerned with the instrumental access English provides to the country's top universities, which guarantee professional and economic success: English competence is frequently the decisive factor in institutional entrance-tests; it functions as a means of student selection and, ultimately, of social classification in the Japanese meritocracy.

As for the system of education itself, English is available only at the elementary level (between the ages of 6 and 11) at a very few private or university-associated schools situated in the major metropolitan areas. Thus, the number of children under 12 who learn English remains relatively low, and probably less than 10,000. Another small, privileged group of elementary-school children may study English at private tutoring schools (*juku*) which offer after-school tuition. English teaching at this level is outside state control and tends to emphasize the oral/aural aspects.

Secondary education is divided into two stages: junior high school from 12 to 14, and senior high school from 15 to 18. Although school is compulsory only until the last year of junior high, 94 per cent of the students continue into high school. English is not an obligatory subject but is offered at more than 99 per cent of all secondary schools and taken by almost all students because it is a required part of university entrance-tests.

In state junior high schools, attended by nearly 6 million students, English is currently taught for a total of three hours a week made up of forty-five-minute periods, having been reduced from four or five hours in 1981. Many teachers are now claiming this cut in teaching-time has caused a drastic decline in the proficiency of middle-school students in English. At the same time, there is a noticeable tendency for pupils

from well-off families to attend costly private middle schools, which has
supposedly been accelerated by the poor level of English teaching in the
state system. Furthermore, students at state schools are increasingly sup-
plementing their tuition by attending private, after-school crammers. English continues to be taught for four to six periods of 50 minutes a week
to 70 per cent of the fifteen- to eighteen-year-olds who enter senior high
school; many receive extra coaching for the university examinations at
cramming schools in the evening. Low motivation for English at this stage
is prevalent, because of the linguistic level of difficulty and the methodology used. The university entrance-tests, to which senior high-school
education is intensively oriented, hardly demand any active English ability
at all. The typical examination is made up of multiple-choice questions
on reading passages, hair-splitting grammar-points, and a few sentences
of translation into Japanese and English, the latter often emphasizing
the recognition of nuances of Japanese grammar. There is hardly ever
any oral/aural component or any composition in English.

Around one half of all Japanese eighteen-year-olds are enrolled at the
460 four-year universities and 543 two-year colleges,[13] where one period
a week of English is usually required for the first two years. Such lessons
tend to centre around the reading and translating (but rarely discussion)
of literary and academic texts, although opportunities for conversation
classes with native speakers are increasing. In spite of the many years of
institutional focus on reading, university students' passive English competence has been found to be disappointingly poor.

In addition to the standard secondary and tertiary establishments, there
exist a multitude of private language-schools, 800 in Tokyo alone, which
cater for adult learners with time and money to spare, mainly housewives,
college students, and certain white-collar workers needing English at work.
Language schools usually offer a completely different classroom environment from that in other institutions, frequently employing the direct
method, using native speakers and textbooks from abroad, and stressing
practical, productive skills.

In fact, the contemporary teaching of English in Japan has not led to
a working proficiency in the written or spoken channel for the majority
of students. What are the reasons for this failure?

As for system-related deficiencies, the most serious is the heavy emphasis on Japanese translation inherited as part of grammar-translation

[13] Japanese Ministry of Education.

methodology, which has become the end rather than a means of English teaching. Secondly, the university entrance-examinations exert a pernicious influence, with their self-defeating disdain of practical skills.

Teachers, meanwhile, suffer various difficulties, such as limited English proficiency, oversized mixed-ability classes of between forty and fifty students, insufficient time to cover the basics because of pressure to keep up with the syllabus, old-fashioned textbooks strictly controlled by the Ministry of Education, a lack of opportunities for practical training, and, frequently, no overseas experience.

On top of this, there is deep-rooted institutional conservatism, which resents and resists change. The socio-cultural characteristics of local class-room norms such as teacher-centred lecturing, collective conformity, unquestioning rote-learning, and emphasis on absolute correctness, clearly do not provide an environment conducive to successful learning.

As for the learners themselves, many are exhausted already by the need to memorize excessive amounts in their other subjects. Consequently, because of the repressive methodology and frustratingly high demands, English is one of the most unpopular subjects amongst students, who are spurred on only by the instrumental motivation to succeed in the university entrance-tests.

The community's socio-linguistic patterns and attitudes also play a major role. The fact that Japanese and English are linguistically distant, possess different orthographies, and have developed their own culturally specific styles of expression interferes and hinders acquisition. For example, there exist numerous Japanese proverbs extolling the value of staying silent—an attitude which naturally leads to a preference for written texts in the foreign language and avoidance of oral self-expression. On top of this, Japanese polite behaviour puts a premium on modesty and self-control, a fact which tends to inhibit communication. Compounded with this is the comparatively high need for security and reassurance in Japanese interaction, and a proclivity towards perfectionism. The consequence in the classroom is a body of defensive, taciturn students who avoid risk-taking in a foreign tongue.

A further attitudinal aspect of significance is the community's widely noted ethnocentrism, which is closely intertwined with its long-standing experience of monolingualism and racial homogeneity. Japanese ethno-centrism reveals itself in the way the society tends to view its true bilinguals. For example, those who are employed for many years in the foreign service, or spend long periods of their lives abroad, are often considered by community members to be 'contaminated' and no longer 'pure' Japanese (see the previous section on Japanese child-returnees from overseas who suffer discrimination). Thus, some Japanese regard advanced bilingualism and its accompanying biculturalism as subversively threatening.

Japanese non-integrative attitudes may well negatively influence students' chances of attaining basic fluency in English, although it does not seem that they are the principal cause of failure. However, the unavoidable and increasing internationalization of contemporary Japan challenges many conservative attitudes, and challenges the traditional approach to foreign-language learning, with its reductionist concentration on receptive skills for decoding Western texts.

Finally, it must be remembered that there is no immediate need for the majority of Japanese—excepting those in certain professions—to acquire any language other than their mother tongue. An abundance of translations of every major classical and contemporary literary, academic, and technical Western book is usually available but direct interaction with English-speaking people still remains minimal, in spite of increased travel.

As as is the case with all foreign-language learners, the Japanese reveal a pyramid-like variation in their English proficiency, ranging from the few fluent in both spoken and written channels to those who are familiar only with simple words. The majority possess what can be characterized as a basilectal interlanguage variety, which means a low, pidgin-like level covering only the most basic of needs. This is indirectly reflected in the fact that, when all scores were averaged out, Japanese students performing in the 1989–91 sessions of the Test of English as a Foreign Language (TOEFL) managed only one hundred and forty-ninth place in a league-table of 162 countries,[14] behind China, South Korea, and Vietnam, even though it enjoys a higher level of material support for the teaching of English.

For all these diverse educational, socio-cultural, and environmental reasons, it can be concluded that Japan presents a case of a non-bilingual distant contact-setting. Furthermore, as there is usually no social or professional need for English *after* schooling, and little support for its maintenance, it suffers wide-scale attrition. The general level of English ability seems unlikely to rise significantly in the future if the present educational approach is maintained.

---

[14] Report of the Educational Testing Service, New Jersey (1993).

Innovating Forces in the Community: Technology, Commerce, and the Media

Although the present-day Japanese contact-setting has been characterized as 'distant and non-bilingual', certain economic, technological, and socio-cultural forces are initiating changes in communication style which involve an intensive and radical type of language contact.

It is important not to confuse 'modernization' with 'westernization', even though the two processes share common material features, in that Western countries were the first to modernize and are often taken by underdeveloped countries as models of modernization to emulate. However, modernization does not necessarily imply the adoption and integration of Western cultural patterns of behaviour and thought, although it does bring social change with it. In fact, Japan is often presented as a unique case of successful modernization by a non-Western country. Here modernization is understood as economic progress, dependent on the management and exploitation of scientific knowledge. Of course, Japan is no longer involved, as in the Meiji period, in the initial phases of modernization; on the contrary, it is at the forefront of evolving new forms of 'modern' work and life-styles. The relationship between various aspects of Japan's modernized society and language contact are explored in this section—for example, in the fields of science, business, material consumption, advertising, and mass media.

Major features of traditional modernization are industrialization and urbanization, and Japan has reached high levels in both these spheres. Seventy-five per cent of Japan's 124 million citizens live in urban environments with populations of 30,000 or more, and are involved in urban-style occupations. The socio-economic hierarchy is based principally on educational background and place of employment, but job status is also significant. There exists an identification with middle-class status for over two-thirds of Japanese society which has arisen due to the post-war levelling of income and rise of income, intensive urbanization, and increased upward mobility.

Japan's industrialization began in the late nineteenth century and, in spite of destruction in the Second World War, has enjoyed an 'economic miracle' from the 1960s onwards. It has recently reached the position of the world's major creditor-nation and the second most powerful economy in the world, with its GNP accounting for over 10 per cent of the total world GNP. In terms of foreign-exchange reserves, Japan has become the richest nation on earth and is now the world's biggest donor of official development aid to the Third World; most of the world's largest banks are Japanese. This position of economic giant both relies on and promotes language contact.

One of the many factors which supported Japan's economic expansion was its reliance on the translation, transmission, and implementation of knowledge and models from Western science and industry. As far back as the early 1950s, the Japanese government carried out language planning as part of its economic strategy. This involved the government-financed monitoring, translation, storage, and dissemination of basic scientific and technological information under the auspices of JICST (the Japan Information Center for Science and Technology), as well as the training in English of a great many Japanese scientists in the USA.

Thus, the worlds of academic research, big business, and government joined forces to serve economic growth and came to depend heavily upon English as the key language. A large group of engineers, scientists, and technocrats developed a passive English bilingualism and functioned as agents, transferring a great number of specialist English-derived items into Japanese terminologies. Although these professional jargons are limited to the written medium and marked by their formality, this shared encoding constitutes an indispensable and convenient cross-linguistic resource.

In a recent dictionary which lists contemporary technical terms according to specific fields and is intended for use by the general public (*Gendai-yōgō*, 1985), I found that the proportion of borrowing is extremely high in economic and 'high-tech' fields: 75 per cent of marketing terminology, 67 per cent of engineering terminology, and 99 per cent of computer terminology is English-based. Various contact-patterns are evident here: the transfer of complex compounds (*purodakuto-raifu-saikuru* < *product life-cycle*); hybridization (*purasuchikku-hikari faibā* < English: *plastic* + Japanese: 'beam' (optical) + English: *fibre*); truncation (*rimo-kon* < *rimō-kontorōru* < *remo*[*te*] *control*); and local coining (*mai-kon* < *my com*[*puter*] 'personal computer').

Furthermore, certain items from the ever-expanding English-based scientific and technical vocabulary pass into wider employment in the community as the inventions and materials they refer to are integrated into daily life. This is the case with the last two examples above, the abbreviation of which indicates their general currency.

The means by which such forms enter the standard variety also deserve consideration. When writing in Japanese, specialists sense a linguistic need to refer to an object (or more rarely a concept) they have come into contact with while studying material in English, and they make a lexical transfer, which may initially or subsequently involve hybridization, into a Japanese text. In the early phases of transfer, the item may have variant forms, which persist until one form becomes established in the field. The object may eventually be commercially adopted and become available to the ordinary consumer, whose familiarity with the transferred item is strengthened by mass-media advertising and promotion. As the object develops into a household article, community-wide reception of the transfer increases. This process has been observable recently with items typically connected with technological innovations such as the compact-disc player, word processor, and video recorder, to name but a few. Of course, non-commercial English-based scientific terminology also passes into daily usage through mass-media channels such as newspapers, magazines, and television, but its currency tends to be more restricted, and limited to passive understanding, except when used by experts.

The rate of increase in gross national product is often taken as an indication of the degree of modernization. In the period between 1954 and 1971 Japan's GNP rose by the unprecedented figure of 500 per cent but has since sunk to below 4 per cent. Although its dependence on overseas trade as a whole is comparatively low, standing at about 14 per cent for exports and 12 per cent for imports, Japan has succeeded in capturing large shares of the world market in some major industrial fields—80 per cent of video recorders, 40 per cent of semiconductors, 30 per cent of motor vehicles, and 20 per cent of machine tools—to the extent that its foreign trading causes friction and provokes calls for protectionism in the USA and EU. It should be pointed out that for certain Japanese industries such as those producing VTRs, cameras, copiers, and cars, dependence on overseas export is very high. Moroever, 6,000 Japanese-run factories were operating in the world in 1988, 1,500 of them in the USA. Thus, Japan's economic policies and development have a strong influence on the economies of other nations and affect their employment, inflation, and industrial environment.

The consequences of this world-trader scenario are far-reaching: a large pool of internationalized and bilingual Japanese professionals is being built up, since daily business-activities with non-Japanese, in the form of correspondence, telephone/telex calls, face-to-face meetings, contract negotiations, and advertising, are usually conducted in English, both in

Japan and abroad. This bilingual group is steadily growing, and, because of residence abroad, their children are also growing up bilingual. Of course, the younger members of this managerial and office staff are university-educated, but the level of English fluency varies considerably. However, companies rarely employ special interpreters and instead rely on the skills of their general staff. Company-supported foreign-language training and immediate, realistic application help to improve levels of proficiency.

The main effect of this economic activity on linguistic contact is the emergence of a commercial register dominated by English-derived terminology.

Again, in the dictionary of specialist fields explained for the general public (*Gendai-yōgō*, 1985), 80 per cent of trade terms, 69 per cent of the words collected under the 'cost-of-living' entry, 53 per cent of management terms and 34.5 per cent of financial terms involve Anglicization. In many of these areas, hybrid compounding is common, which demonstrates the degree of integration the English elements have attained: *haiteku-bōeki* (< English: *high tech* + Japanese: 'trade'); *yushutsu-doraibu* (< Japanese: 'export' + English: *drive*). Creative coinages are rare, probably because of the strong orientation here to an external linguistic model.

Acronyms are also noticeably preponderant in this economics-based jargon; examples are DSS, PPM, CI, OJT, MRP. Although their meanings are not transparent, acronyms appeal to Japanese with limited English competence, because their brevity and simplicity make them easy to handle and to integrate into Japanese.

However, the most important result of economic expansion from the language-contact perspective is its effect on the Japanese consumer, who is confronted with a deluge of products bearing Anglicized names. Whether this development is connected with increased affluence, accompanied by more intensive Western-oriented desires, or merely with a marketing strategy creating such desires, is debatable; but the fact remains that a heavy dose of English contact constitutes a means of satisfying and appealing to these desires.

The contact agents in the commercial domain need to be recognized; they are copy-writers, advertising agencies, salesmen, and mass-media enterprises. The channel of contact is predominantly written, but in the case of radio and television, advertising is also oral. Here, various linguistic strategies are employed.[15] One style is to write directly and monolingually

---

[15] See Haarman (1989), who discusses certain symbolic values of foreign languages in Japanese advertisements.

SUMMER GIFT	original coinage for Japanese word (seasonal custom: *o-chūgen*)
DRINK MENU	local coinage
fresh meat	direct borrowing
STICK DOG	local coinage for *hot dog*
FAMILY ORANGE PACK	long compound coinage

Fig. 4.3. Anglicization in consumer contexts.

in English; this approach is not limited to commercials but is also typically and frequently used to name a product or a section of a shop. The items in Fig. 4.3, a random selection from a suburban supermarket, exemplify this style. (The original capitalization of the items has been retained; it was obviously carried out to ease decoding for Japanese shoppers.)

These items were on posters, signs, and products, without accompanying Japanese translation. The extent to which they are comprehended by the community is the subject of a survey discussed in Chapter 7. Whole sentences may also be found in monolingual commercial texts, although they are rarer: 'In Kobe the history of Japanese coffee drinking hangs in the air'[16] and 'We wish you to take good care of it, who select the goods just fitted to you at the present.'[17] In a recent weekly mail-order catalogue aimed at housewives[18] that I have analysed, 47 per cent of 206 basic food-products offered included an Anglicized item. As for specific categories, 40 per cent of items relating to fruit and vegetables were English-derived, for ready-made foods the figure was 50 per cent, for meat 54 per cent, and for sweets and cakes 90 per cent. This is hardly surprising, since the last three categories have been strongly influenced by Western eating-patterns. In contrast, only 8 per cent of traditional Japanese food listed in the brochure—pickles for example—and 24 per cent of fish revealed contact with English, and that was mainly due to the addition of words like *pack* and *set*. These results show that housewives of all ages and backgrounds (the brochure was aimed at the entire adult women's market) are expected to understand, accept, and be attracted by, fairly intensive Anglicization, even where the satisfaction of everyday needs is concerned. Contact with English pervades the non-traditional Japanese shopping-world.

[16] This comes from a label on a tin of Japanese-packaged UCC-brand coffee.

[17] This long sentence was printed on a pack of Japanese Bourbon biscuits.

[18] This mail-oder food-delivery service is offered by a nation-wide company called Seikyō. 206 food products in the brochure 'Kyōdō-kōnyū no go-annai' dated for the second week in Feb. 1988 were analysed. Other products such as clothing and utensils were ignored.

COEQUAL
HERE WE GO! ONLY CREATE TIME
TOGETHER
FAVORITE

FIG. 4.4. Roman-script English on a Japanese-made jogging-jumper.

Linked to this Anglicization of the citizen's environment is the extensive employment of English for public signs and posters—'I love Japan' on a Liberal Democratic Party election-poster, for example, or 'Peace of Japan' on a recruitment poster for the Self-Defence Forces. Many shops have English-style names, and most restaurants have bi- and, less frequently, monolingual menus. On many doors, lifts, and vending-machines, words such as 'Push' and 'Exit' may be found. This monolingual English labelling is also applied to buildings ('Community Centre', 'Nishigyō Public Library'), exhibitions ('Osaka Total Living Fair'), shopping-malls ('Whity'[19]), and housing projects ('Port Island'[20]). Interestingly, the last three examples come from government-funded public works and not from the commercial sector.

Furthermore, graffiti involving English are increasingly observable. One example I recently noticed, in children's writing on the back of a bus-seat, read 'SEX したい' (sex *shitai*: 'I want to have sex'). The use of the roman script and the selection of the English phrase are both significant in that they help to upgrade the rebellious, 'deviant' declaration by supplying it with an apparently sophisticated, international identity. This example also reflects the way Japanese youth enjoys exploiting English for anonymous, public expression—just like Japanese copy-writers; such symbolic dimensions will be probed more deeply in Chapter 6.

The extensive display of English in roman script on clothing, primarily items for the young, such as T-shirts, pullovers, caps, and jackets, as well as on bags, pencil-cases, notebook-covers, and writing-paper, is yet another kind of self-asserting, public message, extenuated through the filter of English. For instance, Fig. 4.4 reproduces the text printed on the back of a cheap, made-in Japan jogging-jumper—that is to say, not a fancy designer-brand product (the capitalization and punctuation of the original is retained). What is significant in this example is the preference

[19] This apparently results from the combination of *white* and *city* and is the name of an underground shopping-mall in Umeda, Osaka.

[20] This is the name of a futuristic, man-made residential island stretching out into the Pacific Ocean from Kobe city.

for single, but not always simple, words on three out of the four lines, and the imperative in the longer phrase. That the message should be wholly intelligible to community members is not necessary, since its primary function is decorative.

The affluent youth of a modern society constitutes an important sub-market, whose tastes and values are continually redefined and circumscribed from the mainstream; designers of products targeted at this group utilize English contact, together with other means such as clothes, hair, and accessories, to emphasize and embellish a separate identity.

The decline of native linguistic resources—that is to say, pure Japanese and Sino-Japanese lexis—in the marketing world is clearly illustrated in a survey of changes in cigarette brand-names during this century.[21] Thus, in 1904, 41 per cent of cigarette packs bore names based on pure Japanese lexical stock, while in 1981 this figure had fallen to 17 per cent. Conversely, in 1904, 41 per cent bore non-Japanese (Western) names, but in 1981 this had risen to 75 per cent.

Today over a third of coffee-shops, pubs, and non-Oriental restaurants bears a recognizably Western name.[21] The motivation for the prolific utilization of English items in the naming of programmes and publications in the mass media, and in advertising and product packaging, needs serious analysis. Taking into account the basic criteria of Japanese commercial naming-practices—for example, the 'atmospherics' of the language chosen, the ease with which it can be said and remembered, and the aesthetic quality of the orthography in which it is represented—it is quite remarkable that in so many cases English forms are considered capable of achieving the relevant goals. At first sight it may seem odd that English items should be so frequently drawn upon to fulfil the function of persuasion when they are often not intelligible to the community at large. However, the justification, from the copy-writer's perspective, lies in the symbolic power derived from association with Westernness, which is seen as enhancing the product's value.

It has long been known that advertising language rarely has any direct connection with the material use of a product, essentially aiming at the satisfaction and exploitation of social and psychological needs. In fact, the norms and values of a society can be found reflected in the content of its commercials, the production of which is usually differentiated in relation to age, sex, and socio-economic group. Of course, it must be recognized

---

[21] See Satake (1981).

that Anglicization is only one verbal component among many employed by advertisers. Equally important constituents include visual messages, content or 'story-line', 'hidden' techniques of persuasion, and, in many cases, the primary employment of the Japanese language.

The advertisment in Fig. 4.5 is an appeal to save with a bank: 'bōnusu wa Sanwa e' ('Put your bonus into Sanwa') and thus shows that even such traditionally conservative institutions turn to code-switching today to promote themselves. However, it is not coincidental that the target group are Japanese yuppies in their thirties; the association of English with youthfulness and professionalism has already been pointed out above.

One cannot fail to notice the direct English in spatially separated roman script appearing in the imperative and compound 'Catch the Wave' and 'BEST MIX'. These items seem to be used purely for visual effect, since their semantic relevance is obscure, and they would only really be understood by those with a university education. On top of this, there can be found the nominally based transfer of a few items from English in the angular syllabary—'system engineer', 'Snoopy', 'co-ordinate'—and the repetition of the locally created compound *kuoriti-appu* (> *quality up* 'increase in quality'). Particularly interesting in the latter example is the orthographic representation of the sound *ti* by the combined symbols テ ィ , which is not officially approved but is considered sophisticated in its closeness to English sounds. Middle-class identification is imposed as a somewhat glamorous but attainable model. This comes out: visually, in the images of dress and accompanying objects such as the cello and the basket with wine-bottle and flowers; thematically, in the statusful and very contemporary occupation of system engineer and in the image of the elegant but astute housewife who controls her husband's income and is 'properly' conscious of the value of financial management; and verbally, in the centrally placed key-phrase (the only one to be written vertically), proudly announcing *watashitachi, kuoriti-appu* (literally: 'We, quality up'). Here, Anglicization features as the primary linguistic medium to emphasize the promise of modern, economic success.

The role of mass media in the contact process with English requires some explanation. Although it is generally true that media play the role of gatekeeper, defining social norms but having their radicalism kept in check by the desire to maintain and extend their target audiences, certain types of written media in Japan are characterized by an unusually high degree of neologistic Anglicization (see Figs. 4.6 and 4.7 which are extracts from magazines, *Tarzan* being targeted at male youth and *Focus* at the

Fig. 4.5. Advertisement for Sanwa Bank. (Source: *JAF MATE*, December 1987).

FIG. 4.6. Contents page of the magazine *Tarzan*.

FOCUS

フォーカス　5月16日号
表紙　三尾公三
アートディレクター　柳町恒彦
デザイナー　大塚雅子

FOCUS	中核派「ロケット弾」発射の瞬間―東京サミット警備陣を震撼させたその「威力」	4
party	「リビア」「円高」2連敗―中曽根サミット〝皮算用〟の誤算	8
café	山本陽子プラス沖出浩之プラス？―深夜の六本木で見かけた「三角関係」	10
debut	セツナくもダイナミックな新競技―日本初のウォータージャンプ公式大会	12
ceremony	赤の他人の〝赤い糸〟―山下新郎新婦への素朴な疑問・感想・予感	16
figure	彼女はまだ〝処女〟だった！―日本企業のCMガールになったロック歌手マドンナ	18
game	ベストスコアは77―〝ハンディ〟を克服した37歳のゴルフライフ	20
event	ロンドンを笑わせた「樹座」の珍芸―成功を収めた「蝶々夫人」に狐狸庵晩会心の笑み	22
irony	訪れた代議士はたった二人―田中元首相誕生日の閑散と二階堂副総裁のちょっとした謎	24
couple	筋肉マンの成功物語―故ケネディ大統領の姪と結婚したシュワルツネッガー	30
off limits	高級保養地に「ミサイル」出現―リビアの〝報復〟に怯えるフランスの守り	32
open	県立美術館の目玉「三つの影」―茨城県が1億6150万円で買ったロダン初公開	36
challenge	決死！320メートルのダイビング―地上86階からパラシュート降下した英国人	38
newsmaker	「ダイアナ週間」いよいよ開幕―シンプソン夫人葬儀、カナダ訪問を終えて「来日」	42
underground	「裏ビデオの巨匠」のロックライヴ―学習院卒38歳の趣味ジンセー	44
tradition	「三島由紀夫以来」の格調高さ―松竹90周年記念「新作歌舞伎」作者は財界人	46
dropout	ムショ帰りから一気に主役へ―「大原みどり事件」主人公のライフワーク	48
hero	ボクは「スイッチ投手」―〝左右両刀使い〟米大リーグのリリーフ・エース	50
season	夏には乳房がよく似合う―沖縄で見ィーちゃった「トップレス夫婦」のアイ	52
accident	史上最悪の原子炉事故―放射能より無気味な〝情報汚染〟	54
tour	「大人の歌手」はフンイキで迫る―バラードを歌って人気のシャーデーの来日	56
top	「二人の教主」説まで飛び出して…―ドロ沼化した「世界救世教」の抗争	60
trouble	「モルジブから乾杯！」―エアランカ航空機爆破事件に遭遇した新婚夫婦の「生」と「死」	62
deluxe	これが「俺の最後の女」―塚本「ワコール」社長65歳の女性遍歴	64
parody	狂告の時代　232　マッド・アマノ	66

Fɪɢ. 4.7. Contents page of the magazine *Focus*.

broader public). These kinds of Japanese media reflect a set of linguistic patterns which partly correspond to the consumers' value-system but also alters it as it creates its own styles. Such written media force the community to confront avant-garde language-contact and deal with its decoding. After due exposure and evaluation, these styles may eventually be integrated into established usage.

As well as being disseminators, media can also be educators in regard to English borrowings. For example, when introducing an item considered unknown to the general audience, a translational paraphrase may be given. On a news programme, for instance, an announcer will explain in Japanese that the term *konpūtā gurafikku* (< *computer graphics*) means drawing pictures with a computer, and will then proceed with the topic. For more complex terms, a whole programme or article may be devoted to the explanation. Of course, the agents of media, and indirectly of contemporary language-contact too, are the programme and layout designers, script-writers, journalists, broadcasters, and diverse experts invited to advise or appear in the programmes—and the English competence of all these individuals varies dramatically.

As would be expected of a field that has modelled itself on Western institutions, a high proportion of media jargon is influenced by English. Seventy-five per cent of journalistic and 82 per cent of broadcasting terminology in the dictionary of common technical terms *Gendai-yōgō* are loans deriving from English words such as *quality paper, scoop, deadline, lead, channel, documentary, news, script-writer, mixer, light director, announcer, newscaster,* and *narrator.*

It is, of course, impossible to survey the extent of Anglicization in all written contexts of Japanese society. Research undertaken by the National Language Research Institute in 1956 found that foreign loans accounted for not more than 6 per cent on average of all words within a particular text. However, this was four decades ago, and today there are mass-media texts in which foreign loans clearly surpass this percentage.

First of all, some basic facts about the massive Japanese publishing market need to be known. About 125 newspapers with a combined circulation of 47 million copies are available daily. In 1980 over 3,325 different types of weekly and monthly magazine were published, covering the entire range from science, through literature, the arts, and education to publications for special target-groups such as housewives, teenagers, and children. The Japanese are said to be the world's most voracious readers. In 1980 alone, one billion books were printed, the total number of titles being 27,891, 10 per cent of which comprised translations from major European languages.[22]

Of sixty-eight currently available Japanese weekly and monthly magazines starting with the sound A,[23] as many as 70 per cent have an English-based title. Significantly, ten titles are in purely roman script—*Accounting, Accident, Action Hero, Ad Lib*, etc.—but five of these are accompanied by an equivalent in the angular syllabary. A few titles are made up of hybrid compounds—*aiken-jānaru* (< Japanese: 'dog lovers' + English: *journal*), but the majority are English-derived, presented in the angular script: *akushon-kamera* (< *action camera*); *anime KC* (< animation).

Figs. 4.6 and 4.7 show two contents pages from magazines of national circulation. Even though both weeklies target a low-brow readership, the degree and variation of Anglicization is striking. First of all, note that both titles are English-derived and both are printed in roman letters. Examination of the *Tarzan* contents page reveals that 30 per cent of the titles of articles are presented directly in English—often followed by Japanese back-up:

(iv) Talkin' about	(xiii) BEST 3
(v) TARZAN EXPRESS	(xiv) MEDIA RADAR
(vi) JUNGLE BOOK	(xv) APE CALL
(vii) Here Comes Tarzan	(xvi) Looking Ahead
(ix) Hello Sexy Jane!	

The capitalization of over half of these items is a means of helping the reader to decipher them. Orthographic mixing and code-switching appear together in the opening title (i): 男と女の料理 BOOK (*Otoko to onna no ryōri BOOK* 'Cookbook for Men and Women'), and again in the orthographic switch to Chinese characters for people's names (xii): Fan Letter from 堀越絹衣 to 今中慎二 ('Fan Letter from Horikoshi Kinuoe to Imanaka Shinji'). On the other hand, locally created compounds of mixed elements such as (viii): カラダメンテナンス (Japanese: *karada* 'body' + English: *maintenance*) are instantly transparent to an audience with limited English. Brand-new compounds coined from simple established English loan-words are also utilized to the maximum effect here, in short, catchy phrases such as (x): *omatta zairyō mo muda ni wa shinai, nabe-ryōri no kantan RISAIKURU-MENYŪ* ('a simple stew-pot RECYLE MENU which does not waste the ingredients').

[22] Kasagi (1983).

[23] These magazine titles were listed in a newsagent's guide called *Zasshi no mokuroku*, 1987, published by Tōkyō-shuppan-hanbai-kabushikigaisha.

Now let us consider the magazine *Focus* (Fig. 4.7) which aims at an older, more conventional and conformist readership, a fact reflected in its more restrained level of contact. For instance, the contents page presents no fusion of roman and Japanese scripts in the same phrase, and limits loans to those already codified and established. The only innovation here seems to be the compound *rirīfu-ēsu* (< *relief ace*) in the section under the title 'hero'. However, every article is preceded and headed by one English word spatially and typographically separated from the Japanese body. The psychological implication of this layout is that the Japanese reader is receiving a publication almost identical to an English magazine. Nevertheless, many of the English items in the Japanese headings are not widely known or used outside highly educated groups. In this way, the magazine popularizes high-brow English contact as it diffuses it into the community at large. On the other hand, the monolingual English accompaniment may simply be ignored by those who do not understand it, since it is completely superfluous to the comprehension of the contents. From looking at these two examples we can see how written mass media can prove surprisingly innovative and receptive with regard to English contact.

This section has described and analysed Japanese Anglicizing contexts related to the contemporary setting of modernization and economic expansion—particularly in the spheres of mass consumption and mass media—in order both to illustrate the rich variation in lexical transfer and to identify the agents and channels of dissemination. The phenomenon today differs in intensity and character from that found in earlier phases of Anglo-Japanese contact but resembles in some ways the early stages of integration of Chinese which took place a millennium ago (see Chapter 2): Anglo-Japanese contact includes direct chunks of English; bilingual and code-mixed styles; and massive processes of borrowing, locally adaptive coining, and hybridization.

In the next chapter we will analyse this variation more deeply and study its linguistic outcomes and rules of formation.

5

Japanizing and Westernizing Patterns

The first part of this chapter explores some of the complex and diverse changes undergone by English (and other European languages) when integrated into Japanese. The innovative introduction of sounds unavailable in Japanese, and their written representation, receive special attention here. A systematic account of orthographic variation in this process of adaptation is also offered. Finally, there is an analysis of the morphological patterns involved in Japanizing English. These patterns modify the donor language so radically that the ensuing divergence is often labelled 'deviant'. However, it will be demonstrated that this remodelling of English by the Japanese is not open to sanctions from external normative authorities. It will also be shown how the apparently 'unacceptable' patterns developed by the Japanese have, in fact, rational word-formation correspondences in the English language and thus are morphologically justified on their own terms.

Contact with Non-Japanese Sounds

The transfer of speech habits of the learner's language into that of the second language is technically called 'interference'. Naturally, when the Japanese use English sounds, they adapt them to their native framework and substitute sounds they do not have with those that they do. This Japanese interference has been analysed by numerous researchers, among whom Sonoda (1975: 81–167) and Neustupny (1978: 74–97) offer the most extensive accounts.

European borrowings are 'filtered' not only through the Japanese phonological system but also through the orthographic medium of the angular syllabary (*katakana*), which does not allow the representation of single consonants apart from /n/ (see Table I.1). When transferred into Japanese, the syllabic structure of English is radically altered and new sets of morpho-phonemic and phonotactic patterns are introduced that are not always regular and predictable; this is partly because the loan shapes may be derived either from non-synchronic pronunciation or from spelling; another reason for the irregularity may simply be incorrect

TABLE 5.1. Contemporary Spelling-Innovations for New Sound-Sequences Arising from Contact with European Languages[a]

New sound-sequence	Examples in romanized japanese
ク ワ　ク ィ　　ク ェ　ク ォ kwa　kwi　　*kwe　*kwo	*kwariti* (< *quality*)
シ ェ she	*sherifu* (< *sherrif*)
ジ ェ je	*obuje* (< French: *objet*)
テ ィ　ト ュ　チ ェ *ti　*tu　che	*tisshu* (< *tissue*)
デ ィ　ド ュ　　　　デ ュ *di　*du　　　　*dyu	*paddodu* (< French: *pas de deux*)
ツ ァ　ツ ィ　　ツ ェ　ツ ォ *tsa　*tsi　　*tse　*tso	*kantsōne* (< Ital. *canzone*)
ファ　フ ィ　　フ ェ　フ ォ fa　fi　　fe　fo	*fēn* (< German: *Föhn*)
ヴ ァ　ヴ ィ　ヴ　ヴ ェ　ヴ ォ　ヴ ュ va　vi　vu　ve　vo　*vyu	*viza* (< *visa*)
イ ェ *ye	*yeti* (< *yeti*)
ウ ィ　　ウ ェ　ウ ォ *wi　　*we　*wo	*wōkuman* (< *Walkman*)

[a] The starred items are the least officially acceptable. Compare these patterns with the standard, permissible sound-sequences shown in Table I.1.

dissemination by the original Japanese agent or incorrectness in the contact model. A further complication is the multiple borrowing of the same word from more than one European language, with different semantic specializations: *garasu* 'glass pane' (< Dutch: *glas*) and *gurasu* 'drinking-glass' (< English: *glass*); *karuta* 'card game about Japanese poetry' (< Portuguese: *carta*), *karute* 'medical chart' (< German: *Karte*), and *kādo* 'library card' (< English: *card*). Variant forms used by different generations are an additional source of confusion—*ripōto/repōto* (< *report*); *handobaggu/ handobakku* (< *handbag*)—as is the orthographic variation due to the conflict between different historical donor-models—*uirusu* (< German: *Virus*)/ *bī rusu* (< Latin)/ *bairasu* (< English)—and to phonological innovation (see Table 5.1[1]) *zenerēshon/jenerēshon* 'generation'; *bitamin* ビ タ

---

[1] This table was partly inspired by the work of Tatsuki (1979).

ミン/*vitamin* ヴィタミン. Thus, the acquisition and production of the large proportion of anomalous European borrowings demand laborious and extensive item-by-item rote-learning from the Japanese.

While consonant clusters are numerous in European languages, their occurrence in Japanese is limited, so that many transferred consonant-cluster combinations are intersected with a vowel such as /u/ or /o/.[2] Because Japanese has no equivalents for the English consonant phonemes /f/, /v/, /θ/, /ð/, /l/, they have often been replaced by /ɸ/, /b/, /z/, /z/, /r/ respectively, as in *baraetī* (< *variety*); *sāmosutatto* (< *thermostat*); *on-za-rokku* (< *on the rocks*); *rabā* (< *lover*). As a result of gaps in distribution, the following phonemic sequences are also lacking: /zi/, /dze/, /si/, /ti/, /di/, /hu/, /tu/, /tju/, du/, /dju/; in conservative pronunciation these became /ʤi/, /ze/, /ʃi/, /ʧi/, /ʤi/, /ɸu/, /tsu/, /ʧu/, /ʤu/, and /ʤu/ respectively, as in *zerī* (< *jelly*); *chūbu* (< tube); *goshippu* (< *gossip*); *jiguzagu* (< *zigzag*); *jisutenpā* (< *distemper*); *jūsu* (< *deuce*). Although the English semivowels /y/ and /w/ have corresponding Japanese sounds, their vocalic combinations are limited,[3] with the result that in many loans they are replaced: *īsuto* (< *yeast*); *ierō* (< *yellow*); *ūru* (< *wool*); *ueitoresu* (< *waitress*).

Although from the earliest phase of contact in the mid-nineteenth century, there were diverse attempts to achieve a closer phonetic and orthographic representation of certain European sounds with no Japanese equivalents, these innovations were long thwarted by official planning, which sought to keep within the limits of native phonological resources (see the syllabary chart in Table I.1). However, growing post-war familiarity with, above all, the English sound-system through education and mass media has led to some unorthodox orthographic representations of European sounds and their possible phonetic realization in younger generations. The new phonological innovations and their symbols are shown in Table 5.1; most of them are not officially recognized, but as their use in the community expands, they will become increasingly acceptable to the Establishment. This expansion of the Japanese phonological system may also be interpreted as a form of convergence. In fact, the unorthodox spelling is gaining popularity as a marker of social sophistication, as well as reflecting a greater sensitivity as regards the

---

[2] The CC clusters possible in Japanese are /mb/, /mp/, /my/, /nt/, /nd/, /ng/, /ndz/, /nk/, /nr/, /n/, /ns/, /nt/, /nz/, /kj/, /bj/, /py/, /hj/, /rj/, /gj/, and /ts/. As a rule, /u/ is added to any consonant sound (except /n/) which is not followed by a vowel, creating an open syllable. If the consonant is /t/ or /d/, then /o/ tends to be added instead of /u/.

[3] There are gaps for the combinations /yi/, /ye/, and /wi/, /wu/, /we/, /wo/.

authentic reproduction of donor-model sounds. Of course, it should not be supposed that every young Japanese is either capable or desirous of perfectly pronouncing these patterns; such elocution may be regarded as affected unless executed by presenters of oral media or in other contexts where correctness is a priority. So far there has been no attempt to reproduce the foreign sounds /l/ or /θ, ð/, for which completely new symbols would have to be devised—an innovation still too extreme for the community to stomach.

The Grammar of Integration

The predominant Anglo-Japanese class is the noun: 94 per cent of the 7,045 English loans recorded in the 1972 edition of the *Kōjihan* dictionary were nouns (Ozawa, 1976). The loan noun is grammatically treated in the same way as indigenous nouns and followed by postpositions (case particles) which mark grammatical relations such as subject and object, among other aspects. Consider these romanized examples (the English-derived loans are represented in capital letters to ease recognition):

1. SUPĒSU ['space'] *o* [object marker] *kangaete* ['think'] *okishimashō* ['let's try'].
   Let's try and think about space.
2. KYATTO-FŪDO ['cat-food'] *wa* [subject marker] *eiyō*-BARANSU ['nutrition balance'] *ni* [indirect-object marker] . . .
   As for cat-food [in order to excel] in its balance of nutrition . . .
3. PETTO ['pet'] *no* [possessive marker] *koto* ['thing']
   Things like pets.

Since Japanese does not usually mark plurality, the absence or presence of the English plural morpheme [s] is not significant but occurs arbitrarily, depending on whether the originally transferred model was singular or plural: *surī sutoraiku* 'three strikes'; *shātsu* [< shirt] *ichimai* 'one vest'. Other English-derived loans transferred in their plural form are: *bakettsu* (< *buckets*), *shūzu* (< *shoes*), *donatsu* (< *doughnuts*), while those words which are usually plural in English but have been transferred in the singular include *shizā* (< *scissor*) and *pajama* (< *pyjama*).

The system for employing loans from English and other European languages as adjectives, adverbs, and verbs is exactly the same as that developed for items earlier transferred from Chinese. It must be noted that almost all English and European derived loans in Japanese are grammatically characterized by their nominal status and therefore have to undergo class-conversion. Certain nominal loan-bases modifying nouns assume an adjectival function through copula suffixation with -*na*: *romanchikku-na hito* 'romantic person'.

Conversion to an adverbial function is accomplished with the attachment of the copular infinitive *ni*: *romanchikku ni* 'romantically'. Similarly, a nominal loan-base is predicated by the dummy verb *suru* 'do, make', permitting it to function as a verb: *sain suru* 'to sign'; *appu suru* (< *up*) 'to improve'; *esukēpu suru* (< *escape*) 'to play truant'.

What is remarkable for a synthetic language is that these converting devices, which are uniquely reserved for the grammatical integration of loans, make all morphological change unnecessary in the nominal base. One possible motivation for adopting this system is that the borrowed forms did not and do not conform to the acceptable phonological shapes needed for native-style inflection. Indigenous Japanese adjectives end in -oi, -ai, -ui, or -ii, while verbs end in -ru, -bu, -ku, -nu, -mu, -t(s)u, -gu, -su, and -(w)u. No verbal bases end in -du, -fu, -dzu, or -pu. However, most loans do not conveniently end in any of these native shapes, and even the few which do—for example, *dorai* (< *dry*), *dansu* (< *dance*)— are still integrated through the contact grammar developed for Chinese and do not follow indigenous patterns of inflection.

Exceptionally, however, there are a very small number of European-/ English-derived loans which do follow native inflectional patterns and thereby reveal a deeper degree of integration. Most of these exceptions are verbs taking the indigenous verb-class suffix -*ru*, as in *aji-ru* (< *agitate*), *dabu-ru* (< *double*), and *sabo-ru* (< *sabotage*); this unorthodox suffixation is actually a favourite of non-standard registers such as teenager slang.

Patterns of Assimilation

One way of approaching variation in borrowing is to consider the varying forms in terms of their degree of assimilation in relation to the linguistic system of the transferer. For example, in the case of the variant patterns *bitamin* (ビタミン) and *vitamin* (ヴィミン), the second item is less integrated into Japanese phonology because it employs the /v/ sound, which is not part of the Japanese sound-system. A similar argument could be applied to the truncated variant of *hangā-sutoraiki* (< *hunger strike*), which is *han-suto*, because it reveals a deeper level of integration by conforming more closely to native (Sino-Japanese) morpho-phonology. From such a point of view, different patterns are simply classifiable according to their degree of linguistic assimilation, culminating in complete integration into general usage.

However, the formal (phonological and morphological) characteristics of an item are not the only factors involved in such variation. Contextual appropriateness is a crucial criterion for formal determination. Thus, with reference to the examples just given, *vitamin* (ヴィタミン) is more likely to occur in a technical register and *han-suto* in an informal style. Thus, an analysis in terms of assimilation alone does not present the full reality.

Of course, it is necessary to realize that there exists a phonological cline of nativeness, which depends on the amount of training in pronunciation or exposure to English a community member has experienced. Another way of understanding this is to say that there is a cline of phonological interference in the way borrowings are pronounced, with the majority of the community applying the patterns of the Japanese sound-system to foreign sounds. Furthermore, it must be understood that a high proportion of the English switching and mixing described here occurs in written form, so that readers never need to worry about its oral encoding. Nevertheless, it is true that Japanese singers who code-switch during their songs, or sing entirely in English, do make a special effort to make their English pronunciation sound as native as possible, but they constitute an exceptional case, in which close phonological approximation to the non-Japanese norm is interpreted as highly desirable. A related case would be that of media personnel such as newscasters and disc jockeys, who tend to aim at a closer level of approximation to foreign norms when pronouncing the names of people, places, and songs, for example. Finally, it should be noted that phonological variation in contact with English can also be subgroup specific, with younger members (under 30) more capable of pronouncing certain innovative phonemes and sequences—for example, /f/, /ti/, /va/—because they have had a more oral education in English, and greater exposure to the sounds of English through pop music and other media.

The variation in the use of Japanese and non-Japanese writing-systems for English transfer is a complex area that has so far received hardly any attention. Table 5.2 presents a five-type classificatory scale of this variation within which all patterns of English-based representation can be accommodated. Although the scale indicates the degree of orthographic Anglicization, other European languages such as French or German are sometimes substituted in the same positions by the Japanese.

TABLE 5.2. The Scale of Assimilation: Patterns for Representing English[a]

Classificatory scale		Examples
(Least assimilated) ↑	(5) Roman only (capitals/ lower case)	TARZAN EXPRESS BEST 3 APE CALL Looking Ahead Here Comes Tarzan
	(4) Item in roman letters accompanied by Japanese translation	off limits 立入禁止 ceremony 儀式
	(3) Item in roman letters accompanied by *katakana* version	COUPON CARD クーポンカード NEW MEDIA ニューメディア
	(2) Morphological script-mixing	ゴルフ ING (*gorufu* + *-ing* 'golfing') スーパー JOCKEY (*sūpā* + *JOCKEY* = 'superjockey') 男性 LOGY (*dansei* 'male' + LOGY = 'the art of masculinity')
(Most assimilated) ↓	(1) Japanese script only (usually *katakana*)	バレンタイン生チョコケーキ (*barentain nama choko kēki* 'Valentine cream choco cake')

[a] The examples are drawn from the titles of television programmes, the names of products, and expressions found in popular weekly magazines.

Although from a purely structuralist viewpoint, types 3, 4, and 5 in Table 5.2 are the least assimilated and most innovative, their frequency is so great in commercial and media contexts that they must be considered as conventional patterns. In the case of type 5—where only the roman script is employed—it should be noted that the representation of certain borrowed or made-in-Japan words in capital roman letters is the only form of encoding. Such items tend to be acronyms or abbreviations or short words: *OK, YES, NO, LDK, NHK, OL*,[4] etc. These items show that the roman script has become a fixed component in the already complex

---

[4] LDK stands for the made-in-Japan compound *Living-Dining-Kitchen*, and *NHK* is an abbreviation of *Nippon-hōsō-kyōkai* 'Japan Broadcasting Corporation'; *OL* is an abbreviation for the made-in-Japan derivation from *office lady* or female clerk.

mixture of Japanese orthographic forms. However, the examples presented in the scale next to type 5 differ from acronyms and other integrated, romanized items in their greater length (up to the transfer of entire phrases), their semantic opaqueness to the community, and the fact that they do not occur inside Japanese sentences but are marked off spatially, constituting autonomous units. It should be noted that long, non-integrated English units occasionally appear in Japanese texts as quotations, slogans, titles, or advertising messages.

As for type 4, this is an old, established pattern, often employed in academic and scientific texts, for explaining unfamiliar transferred words by providing a Japanese translation; however, it is currently being exploited as a new stylistic and decorative resource. The examples given in the table show that Japanese alternatives exist and that there is no functional need to resort to the English code; but originally the need for this pattern arose from the lack of cross-linguistic equivalents. Increasingly, this pattern of orthographic bilingualism can be seen on product labels.

Type 3 is similar to type 4 in that a Japanese version of the transfer is provided, but it is different in that the Japanese is not a translation but a phonological adaption of the item into Japanese, thus serving as a guide only to the pronunciation and not to the meaning. In both types 3 and 4, the romanized items are not integrated into the Japanese language but maintain a separate status, requiring special clarification for the reader through Japanese orthographic support. Type 3 can also be found extensively as a labelling and entitling device; it implies that the phenomenon to which it is applied is Western in nature.

The highly innovative, fused script of type 2, employing both the angular syllabary and the roman script for the representation of English words, is rarer than any of the other types and essentially playful in character. It is significant that the two most extreme cases of intra-word mixing—ゴル フ ING (*gorufu* 'golf' + -*ING*) and スーパー JOCKEY (*sūpā* 'super' + *JOCKEY*) come from titles of television programmes which have to do with sport and are thus related to the 'free' world of leisure where the violation of normal patterns can be easily tolerated. The morphological aspects of this fused script deserve attention because it emerges that not only free forms but also suffixes are romanized. Other examples of such romanizable suffixes include -*ism* and -*logy* placed after Chinese characters: 男性 LOGY (*dansei* 'masculinity' + -*LOGY*: 'how to look good as a man'). The fusion of elements on the level of word units is very common and often observable in naming-behaviour (see Figs. 5.1*a* and 5.1*b*).

FIG. 5.1*a*. This example of mixed script (*The* + *tsūhan*, 'mail order') comes from a chain of department stores. The orthographic fusion is facilitated by the existence of the Anglo-Japanese prefix *za-* (< *the*).

FIG. 5.1*b*. This example ('Map of Shin-Tanabe'—the latter is the name of a new town) demonstrates that even the orthography of established Japanese names may be remodelled through romanization. However, this is not particularly radical, since Japanese place-names often appear in romanized form on public signs. The radicalness lies in the combination.

FIG. 5.1*c*. Monolingual English style, accompanied by Japanese transcription and a picture (of sugar) as an aid.

ニューメディアをみんなの手で

F<small>IG</small>. 5.1*d*. The monolingual English style in the cartoon is exploited in a slogan to promote new technology. The English is transcribed in the angular syllabary in the headline: 'New media [to be placed] in the hands of everyone!'

Another increasingly frequently employed pattern belonging in this category is the romanization of the nominal element preceding conjugated forms of the dummy verb *suru* ('to do') in the cursive syllabary: ENJOY する (ENJOY + *suru* 'to enjoy'). A more common version of this involves the use of the angular syllabary to represent the transferred English: エンジョイする (*enjoi suru*). Thus, script substitution (roman letters for native angular syllabary) is yet another orthographic option, which, in fact, is less radical than types 3 to 5 in this scale (in Table 5.2) because the script-switched item is already an established part of the community code.

Type 1 is the most usual style for transfer from any language-source outside Japanese that cannot be rendered in characters, or where the pronunciation of the item is required. It is the most widespread of all orthographic patterns of contact. Nevertheless, recently there has been a marked increase in the occurrence of patterns 3, 4, and 5, and it is highly likely that these innovative script-styles will influence the future development and direction of language-contact behaviour in Japan, easing direct access to the donor language without having it filtered through the angular syllabary (*katakana*).

Code-Switching and Code-Mixing

Code-switching should on the whole be regarded as a controllable strategy, rather than as unavoidable interference, and as differing from ordinary borrowing in that it tends to occur without phonological or morphological adaptation to the recipient language, producing a much higher degree of 'foreign-ness' than borrowing. Furthermore, code-switched items are less stable and systematizable than borrowed ones.

On the other hand, code-mixing is taken here to mean a non-arbitary and stablilized type of code-switching that is recognized as a particular style possible in formal contexts. A distinction between code-switching and -mixing on a purely linguistic basis such as type or length of transferred item(s) is not useful, since researchers have noted variation in transfer from single words to whole sentences for both.

We shall now consider some characteristic patterns of code-switching and -mixing between Japanese and English. First, it should be understood that there often exists a clear boundary between Japanese and the language with which it is switched, although this obviously does not apply to established, non-innovative borrowing. This code-based differentiation is most clearly symbolized in the use of different scripts and the spatial and functional separation of the non-Japanese (usually English) code for labelling purposes, as in headlines, titles, and names (see Figs. 4.6, 4.7, and 5.1). Such use of another code as a labelling device reveals characteristics of both code-switching and code-mixing in that it involves the employment of an external code as a purposeful strategy—labelling—and reveals neither phonological nor morphological adaptation, since the words are often presented only in English orthography. However, this switching constitutes an institutionalized style that can be expected and predicted in specific written contexts such as the mass media and advertising.

Next, an area of mass popular culture which evidences large-scale code-switching will be briefly discussed: pop music. Commercial entertainment has become increasingly important in modern, (post-) industrial societies, but, surprisingly, in spite of its social significance, this type of mass commercial communication is still in need of serious attention by linguists. Apart from its function as provider of relief and escape, such entertainment offers role models for identification and idolization, the former being particularly important for youth. Of course, it is necessary to recognize that pop music itself is an integral part—together with fashion, 'in' ways of speaking, and special articles of consumption—of the subculture of teenagers, embodying and transmitting internationally common values that are often in conflict with those of the older mainstream and traditional culture.

Music plays a central role in Japanese leisure-activities. It is no exaggeration to say that the ability to sing individually in public and to friends in relaxed situations (*karaoke*) is a highly desirable social accomplishment. This may be due to the negative evaluation of expressive, free-style conversation in public situations. One category of popular music which commands a strong following is the modern Japanese ballad known as *enka*. This is differentiated from *wasei-poppusu* 'Japanese-style pop' in its dependence on traditional musical and textual themes, although it has borrowed superficially westernizing tones. In this connection, Satake (1981) has analysed the morphological composition of the lyrics in ten songs from both genres and found that 91 per cent of the lexis employed by *enka* songs was pure Japanese, 6 per cent Sino-Japanese, and 4 per cent hybrid vocabulary (no Anglicization). In contrast, 63 per cent of the lexis of Japanese pop-songs was pure Japanese, 8 per cent Sino-Japanese, and 2 per cent hybrid, with as much as 27 per cent Anglicized. Thus, pure Japanese vocabulary is fundamental to both genres.

The overwhelmingly domestic nature of the Japanese record-market is indicated by the fact that local performers account for 70 per cent of it. Figs. 5.2 and 5.3 present some examples of contemporary Japanese poplyrics: three songs from Miho Nakayama's album *Catch the Nite* (1988) and three songs from the album entitled *Hikaru Genji* (1988) by the group of the same name. The name 'Hikaru Genji' derives from a famous classical work of literature and is extremely traditional. However, the hybrid orthography used to represent the group's name 光GENJI (the first part with a character and the second part romanized) suggests the fusion of the traditional, Oriental and the modern, Western worlds.

By focusing on these examples, one can gain an understanding of characteristics of code-games in such contexts. First of all, the obtrusive presence of the roman script cannot go unnoticed. Two types of orthographic contact are at work here: the monolingual style for song entitling

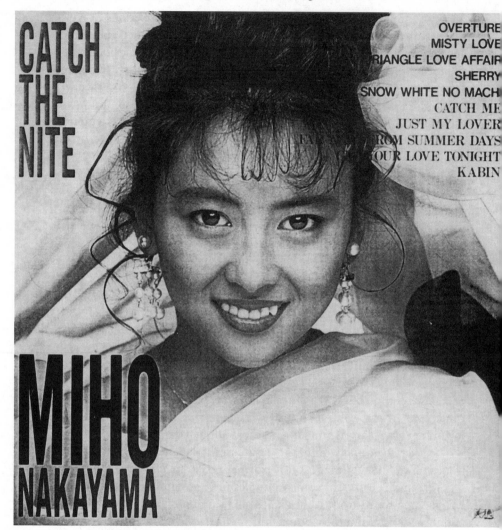

OVERTURE
MISTY LOVE
RIANGLE LOVE AFFAIR
SHERRY
SNOW WHITE NO MACHI
CATCH ME
JUST MY LOVER
ROM SUMMER DAYS
OUR LOVE TONIGHT
KABIN

CATCH
THE
NITE

MIHO
NAKAYAMA

Fig. 5.2a. Album cover, *Catch the Nite*; singer Miho Nakayama. (Lyrics by Kadomatsu Toshiki. © King Records, 1988.)

(cf. the labelling practices discussed above); and code-switching in the fixed position of refrain. Fig. 5.2a presents Nakayama's album cover, which is entirely in roman script, apart from her tiny, seal-like autograph on the right-hand side. It is not coincidental that the singer's name appears in the Western order, with surname last, rather than in the Japanese order, with the surname first. The majority of the song titles in Fig. 5.2a utilize

Misty love いつものように
Midnight call 夜にひびく
Ring my bell 電話の向に
Touch your heart けだるそうに
Lazy talk いまからすぐ
Want see you 会いたいだなんて
Woo darling 今夜も又
Woo darling わがままに負けそう
本気じゃないこと知っていたけど　まだ 迷ってるの
In the night　今夜限りで 終りにして
In the night　ゆくあてのない愛はこれで
Want to be over
Misty Heart あなたの街へ
Drivin' 夜を走る
Highway light 想い出を消して
Woo darling きっと会えば
Woo darling 心が揺れるから
瞳閉じたまま　優しいん言葉さえ聞かないから
In the night　これが最後の愛のかけら
In the night　あなたの部屋においてゆくわ
Good bye love, yes
In the night　霧が晴れれば夜も明ける
In the night　失なうものは何もないわ
Good bye love, yes
In the night　今夜限りで終りにして
In the night　ゆくあてのない愛はこれで
Good bye love

FIG. 5.2*b*. Song 1, 'Misty Love', from the album *Catch the Nite* by Miho Nakayama. (Lyrics by Kadomatsu Toshiki. ©King Records, 1988.)

English vocabulary, but two of them are composed mainly of Japanese elements: SNOW WHITE NO MACHI ('The Town of Snow White') and KABIN ('Flower Vase'); significantly, these songs have no English-based refrain.

Before examining the code alternation occuring in the songs, it is also

踊り疲れたまま みつめてる
Light snow
飾りたてた言葉　聞きたくもないわ
何かが私の中で
変わってゆく気がする
もう流されたくないわ
そのままが一番奇麗だよなんて
それしか言えないのあなたは
　いつでも
うわべのやさしさならば
誰にも言えることなの
もしも信じあえたなら
Don't stop dance とびだす
夜の街が教えてくれるわ
Catch my heart 変わらぬ
もう一人の私に目覚めて
何も考えずに 身をまかせていた
そんな毎日には 今夜でさよなら
大切な日々の中で
Stepを踏んでよ さあ!
素敵な夜の始まり
Don't stop dance 流れる
時の中で 踊り続けるわ
Catch my heart 今なら
あなたにもわかるはずよ
I need you

Just in the dark 真夜中の
扉を開けたままにして
待ってるの 息をひそめ
この退屈な部屋の中から
すぐに連出して どこか遠くへ
You just my lover Can't you see
You just my lover Don't you know
夜明けまで
わずかな時に忘れさせて
I want your love
遠ざかる街燈りみつめる私
写すミラー
決められた毎日に
縛られたまま
ときめくことさえいつか
見失なうのが恐いから
You just my lover Can't you see
You just my lover Don't you know
あぶなげな時に身を委ねてもいいわ
Let's make love
きっとまた ありふれた朝がくる
その前に私を変えて
You just my lover Can't you see
You just my lover Don't you know
アクセルを踏み込んだら
夜空へと Take off I feel the night

FIG. 5.2*c*. Song 2, 'Catch Me'.　　　FIG. 5.2*d*. Song 3, 'Just My Lover'.
Both from the album *Catch the Nite* by Miho Nakayama (Lyrics by
Kadomatsu Toshiki. ©King Records, 1988.)

worth considering the all-English blurb printed underneath the lyrics
(and reproduced in Fig. 5.2*e*), because it offers general insights into code-
switching practices favoured by mass-media professionals. The text is
printed entirely in the roman script, in English, and concerns the production of the record. It cannot be dismissed as purely decorative, since this

PRODUCED BY TOSHIKI KADOMATSU PUB. & BIG APPLE ◆ EXECUTIVE PRODUCER: NORIO HIGUCHI & KIYOKAZU TAKAHASHI ◆ DIRECTOR: AKIRA FUKUZUMI, MASATO ASAMURA ◆ ARTIST MANAGEMENT: MASANORI ENDO ◆ ENGINEER: YOSHIAKI MATSUOKA, KOICHI HIRASE, TATSUO SEKINE ◆ REMIX ENGINEER: YOSHIAKI MATSUOKA ◆ CONTRACTOR: EICHI KOYAMA ◆ SPECIAL THANKS TO MASARU KAJIOKA, HIDETOSHI KOBAYASHI . . . ◆ BACKING VOCALS: TOSHIKI KADOMATSU . . . JACKET: HIROSHI SATO . . . ◆ ARTWORK STAFF PHOTO-GRAPHER: KISHIN SHIMOYAMA ◆ CREATIVE PRODUCER: TAKESHI YAMAGUCHI ◆ STYLIST: HIRO NORIKAWA ◆ HAIR & MAKE UP: HITOSHI TOKIWA ◆ DESIGNER: AKIRA KANAZAWA ◆ COORDINATOR: KIYOMI TAKAHASHI ◆ ARTWORK: CITY HOUSE CO LTD.

FIG. 5.2e. Credits from the album *Catch the Nite* by Miho Nakayama (© King Records, 1988.) The text is reproduced exactly as it appeared on the album cover, in capitals with diamond symbols separating each unit.

information does not appear in Japanese as well. In fact, the text draws upon specialist jargon which may be familiar to those possessing some technical knowledge, but such terms are bound to be unintelligible to the general public: *remix engineer, contractor, executive producer*. Typically, the English units are marked by their brevity and nominal nature, which makes them easier to deal with, since short units do not entail complex syntactic relations and are decodable on the level of lexical equivalents; their heavily nominal nature is connected with the Japanese tendency to internalize and nativize English. Particularly noteworthy is the way an intra-ethnic message is sent in English from one Japanese to another, as in 'special thanks to Masaru Kajioka . . .'. Such code-switching obviously lies outside the patterns of ordinary Japanese communicative behaviour. Given that English is the principal medium of international youth-culture, its appearance in the blurb allows the record company and consumers to set up the fiction of a bilingual Japanese society which can share and reproduce the linguistic, musical, and stylistic patterns of Western pop-culture. Although it is well known that English has become a global resource for pop lyrics, it is important to remember that this text is not a song.

Varying degrees of code-switching are observable in the lyrics of the song-texts in Figs. 5.2b–d and 5.3. English-based transfers, often of one

きのうのどしゃ降りの雨で

倉庫の壁はシミだらけ

接触不良の街灯が

オレの心を照らし出す

あぼ娘はいつもの店で

待ちくたびれてるはずだよ

お前の愛にはお手上げさ

オレにかまわず行けばいい

ハートは泣いてるのに UP SIDE DOWN

意気がってみせる夜 INSIDE OUT

なんだかちぐはぐだね どうかしてる

AH 涙なんて似合わない BAD BOY

あの娘のさびしい瞳を

やさしく見つめてあげろよ

お前の愛なら信じるさ

オレはしげらくここにいる

ハートは泣いてるのに UP SIDE DOWN

強がってみせる夜 INSIDE OUT

ホントにちぐはぐだね どうかしてる

AH 男なんてこんなもの BAD BOY

FIG. 5.3*a*. Song 4, 'Bad Boy,' from the album *Hikaru Genji* by the group Hikaru Genji. (Lyrics by Asuka Ryō. © Pony Canon 1988.) The boxed text is repeated once as a refrain. UP SIDE DOWN is written as separate words in the original.

word, but also of two words, appear integrated into the Japanese body in roman script—'Light snow', 'Step'—as do exclamations such as 'ah'. On top of this, various English loan-words appear in the angular syllabary—*mirā* (< *mirror*), *akuseru* (< *accelerator*), *hāto* (< *heart*), *jōku* (< *joke*)—serving to Anglicize the main Japanese body. The most striking feature, however, is the emergence of English in roman script as an established convention for the refrain, as seen in the songs of the popular group Hikaru Genji (Fig. 5.3).

その時君は奇麗すぎて
遠くの客船を見てるから
'愛しているよ'の言葉さえ
おじけづいてた週末
輝いておくれよ 今は僕の胸で
街中が振り向くほどに
澄んだ瞳抱いて

好きさ YEAH YEAH YEAH
君が WOW WOW WOW
心 YEAH YEAH YEAH
溶けて WOW WOW WOW
ほのかに甘く HOLIDAY

その上ふたりは照れながら
次の台詞をさがすから
真面目なジョークが欲しくなる
返事はいらない only you
はばたいておくれよ
きっと僕の空を
月あかり集めるほどに
罪な笑顔抱いて

——— Section 1 ———

忘れない GRADUATION
また遭えるよ たまらず
CRY CRY
歩き出す GRADUATION
君はいつまでも 君だよ

ほんの少しだけ 息が熱い気がした
心の不安を 誰かに気ずかれるよ
春の曲がり角で
ためらう 君がみえる

——— Section 2 ———

手を振れば GRADUATION
空を滑る鳥になれFLY FLY
つぶやいた GRADUATION
嬉し淋しさの 真ん中

人込の中を 君は泳ぎつづけるよ
古い大人たち いつかうなずくまで
夢をつかむ頃に
針を合わせあおう

FIG. 5.3*b*. Song 5, 'ほのかに甘く HOLIDAY',

FIG. 5.3*c*. Song 6, 'Graduation,'

Both from the album *Hikaru Genji* by the group Hikaru Genji. (Lyrics by Miyaji Takashi. ©Pony Canon 1988.) The second boxed text is repeated and then followed by the first boxed text again.

The Anglicization in the refrains shown in Fig. 5.4 provides a repetitive framework supporting the meaning-loaded, changing Japanese content. It is also a vital rhythmic device: English can be sung more quickly than Japanese, since more than one English syllable may be set on one tone. In contrast, pure Japanese words, many of which are multisyllabic, take longer to sing and thus result in a heavier, slower mood.

However, the code-switches into English in the songs presented here

Song 1 (Fig. 5.2*b*)   Woo darling . . . In the night . . . Good bye love

Song 2 (Fig. 5.2*c*)   Don't stop dance . . . Catch my heart

Song 3 (Fig. 5.2*d*)   You just my lover Can't you see/You just my lover
                           Don't you know

Song 4 (Fig. 5.3*a*)   . . . UP SIDE DOWN . . . INSIDE OUT . . . BAD BOY

Song 5 (Fig. 5.3*b*)   *suki na* YEAH YEAH YEAH (I like yeah yeah yeah)
                           kimi ga WOW WOW WOW (you wow wow wow)
                           kokoro YEAH YEAH YEAH (my heart yeah yeah yeah)
                           tokete WOW WOW WOW (melts wow wow wow)
                           honoka ni amaku HOLIDAY (vaguely sweet holiday)

Song 6 (Fig. 5.3*c*)   . . . GRADUATION . . . CRY CRY (FLY FLY) . . .
                           GRADUATION

FIG. 5.4. Code-switching in pop-song refrains (text encoded in Japanese occurs in the dotted spaces).

(Figs. 5.2*b*–5.3*c*) form autonomous entities, marked off by their roman representation, their semantic non-contiguity with preceding Japanese content, and their distinctly separate musical phrasing. Like the Sino-Japanese component in *enka*, the English is emphatically marked, but, unlike the Sino-Japanese, it is not expected to be entirely decodable by the ordinary Japanese listener and is employed primarily for decorative and rhythmic purposes.

The difference in English sophistication between the texts in Figs. 5.2*b* and 5.3 should be self-evident. The first employs longer phrases, while the second uses shorter, simpler items that are more frequently repeated. This is due to the difference in the singers' markets. The group Hikaru Genji, themselves still schoolchildren, aim at a popular, 'teeny-bopper' audience whose English competence and appreciation is bound to be low. However, just because Nakayama's songs contain a greater amount of code-switching, it should not be presumed that her fans possess a greater comprehension of English. Rather, the high degree of English contact should be interpreted as a symbolic consequence of trying to establish a sophisticated image (in the pop-music sphere), which the associations of the English language are seen to be capable of providing. The low-level acquisition evident in certain cases—'Want see you', 'Don't stop dance', 'You just my lover'—demonstrates the limited bilingualism of the song-writers, as well as their indifference as regards conforming to native norms.

It is important to recognize that the language contact in Japanese pop-music presents a unique case compared with that of most other texts. Although intensive monolingual-style Anglicization as code-switching is usually restricted to naming, headlining, and labelling, in pop music it constitutes a fundamental feature of the entire body of the text which it interpenetrates, albeit maintaining its own cohesion. Its referential value is also different in music, because it is employed as a means of emotional expression. Another very significant difference is that this is an oral medium, while intensive monolingual Anglicization is predominantly a written phenomenon. Furthermore, the Anglicization in this domain stylistically contrasts with much of the contact so far discussed because it draws upon the clichéd lyrics of English pop-music, which originally derive from natural and colloquial speech, while the usual source for English-based contact is written English.

Of course, the strict limitation of the monolingual style to song refrains and labelling is only one, albeit common, pattern of English contact. Other types are observable.

Fig. 5.5 (which includes material from the research questionnaire in Chapter 6) focuses on data[5] in which Japanese elements have been inter-spersed with English, resulting in intra-phrasal mixing. It is not coincidental that the function of examples 1, 3, 4, and 5 is essentially designatory. The order of the examples (1–8) corresponds to an increase in the scale of European contact—mainly with English. Even though some of the examples seem technical, they were all originally intended for the general public and were printed in non-specialist publications. For this reason, code-mixing in contemporary Japanese deserves serious attention.

The data in Fig. 5.5 have been selected because of their radical character

---

[5] The sources of this data are as follows: example 1 comes from the name of a popular comic sports television programme; example 2 is from a restaurant voucher; example 3 comes from a holiday brochure for students called 'Free Way' published in 1987 by Nihon-kyōiku-ryokō; example 4 is from a university-student consumer-magazine entitled *Be5: Campus City Cross Magazine*, 9 (1987), published by Gakusei Engokai-kansaiCo.; example 5 comes from a magazine guide to television programmes called *TV Gaido* (1987) 5/14, published by Tokyo News; example 7 comes from a housing magazine entitled *Homeing News* (1987) 3, from Misawa House; a 1987 holiday brochure called 'Fine Tour' (1151) by Toraberu-hausu company, is the source of examples 6 and 8.

1 ザ・ガマン
za gaman
< the endurance
2 ウエルカムドリンク券をプレゼント
uerukamu dorinku ken o purezento
< welcome < drink ticket (object marker) < present
3 study ゼミ旅行
study zemi-ryokō
< study < (German:) seminar journey
4 スキーのための簡単なストレッチ&トレーニングを紹介。
sukī no tame no kantan na sutorecchi & torēningu o shōkai
for (the) < purpose of < ski(ing) an introduction to simple < stretch(ing)
< & < training
5 2人のパーソナリティと若者たちが一緒にマイ・テレビを創り上げる
ユニークな番組。
futari no pāsonariti to wakamonotachi ga isshō ni mai-terebi o tsukuri-ageru
yūniku na bangumi
two < personalities and youngsters together create < my (= individual)
< unique < television programme
6 4名以上のグループは代金そのままで1ルームOK。
yonme ijō no gurūpu wa daikin sono mama de wan-rūmu OK
(for a) < group of over four the cost is < OK as for < one room
7 天然木のパーッケトフロアーを斜め張りにした2階のロフトスタジオ
を，ギャラリー風にコーディネイトした使用例。
tennenboku no pākketo-furoā o nanimebari ni shita ni-kai no rofuto-sutajio o,
gyararī fū ni kōdineito shita shiō-rei
(an) example of natural wood for < parquet < floor (that) has been
< co-ordinated in the style of (a) < gallery with the panelling of the
second floor < loft < studio
8 ビーチホテルはスーパーデラックス，デラックスリゾート，エグゼクテ
ィプ，クリッパの各クラスから選べます。
bīchi hoteru wa sūpā-derakkusu, derakkusu-rizōto, eguzekutibu, kurippa no
kakukurasu kara erabemasu
as for (the) < beach hotel you can choose from each < class (of either)
< super-deluxe, < de luxe resort, < executive (or) < clipper

Fig. 5.5. Code-mixing in the commercial domain. In each case, the
italicized version is romanized Japanese. < indicates a transfer or Japanese-
made word based on a European language.

—the intensity of the transfer increases with the length of each example. The strongly innovative code-mixing is evident in, for example: the patterns of unusual hybrid compounding, as in (1) *za-gaman* (< *the* 'endurance'); the completion of an utterance with an English transfer because of the ellipsis of the copula, as in (2) *purezento* (< *present*) and (6) OK; the use of the conjunction '&' as a link in (4); a higher concentration of innovative transferred elements, as in *rūmu* (< *room*), *pāsonariti* (< *personality*), and *pākketo-furoā* (< *parquet floor*). A major sign of radicalness in transfer is the high degree of English-derived vocabulary conglomerated into related units through compounding and listing. Examples of the former can be found in (7) *pākketo-furoā* (< *parquet floor*), *rofuto-sutajio* (< *loft studio*), and of the latter in (4) *sutorrechi & torēningu* (< *stretch and training*) and (8) *sūpa-derakkusu, derakkusu-rizōto, eguzekutibu, kurippa* (< *super-deluxe, de luxe resort, executive, clipper*). Another means of heightening the code-mixing is adverbial and adjectival modification derived from English elements: *gyararī fū ni kōdineito* (< *co-ordinate* [like a] *gallery*) (7).

It is worth noting that the primary or matrix code in which this communication occurs always remains Japanese. From such a point of view, it can be argued that the underlying code has, in fact, not been switched, unlike what occurs in the examples from pop songs (Fig. 5.4) and the various labelling phenomena previously discussed (see Figs. 4.7, 5.1). It is noticeable how, in these latter cases of code-switching, the English part tends to be marked off from the Japanese main body both orthographically and spatially, thereby signalling an identity distinct from that of the matrix language.

In conclusion, we shall examine the constraints on code-mixing in Japanese, since certain reccurring characteristics are evident. For instance, the basic verb-forms and grammatical apparatus are invariably drawn from Japanese resources, and the matrix language is fixed as Japanese. No entire intra-sentential switch is observable, although as separate titles, as labels, and as peripheral advertising slogans and messages, total switches into English are frequent, these are spatially and orthographically set apart from the main text and cannot be categorized as code-mixing. Furthermore, it should be pointed out that the English-derived transfers in all the data are predominantly nominal in character, so that even the longest units of code-mixing read more as lists strung together, because they lack a verbal element. However, there are occasional exceptions to this, as illustrated in the following short example from advertising language

TABLE 5.3. Grammatical Constraints in Japanese Contact-Processes

Example[a]	Intra-sentential entry	Japanese grammatical category
1 za-	before noun	adnoun
2 uerukamu-dorinku	before noun	compound noun
3 study-	before noun	compound noun
4 sukī	before noun postposition[b]	noun
4 sutorecchi	following adjective	noun
4 torēningu	and before posposition	noun
4 &	between nouns	English conjunction?/co-ordinating particle
5 pāsonariti	following and before	noun
5 mai-terebi	postpositions	noun
5 yūniku na	before noun	adjectival noun
6 gurūpu	following postposition	noun
6 wan-rūmu	following postposition	noun
6 OK	following English-based noun	adjectival noun[c]
7 pākketo-furoā	before postposition	noun
7 rofuto-sutajio	before postposition	noun
7 gyararī	before adjectivalizing suffix	(adjectival) noun
7 kōdineito	before dummy verb(alizer)	verbal noun
8 ALL TRANSFERS	before postposition	compound/simple nouns

[a] Examples are drawn from Fig. 5.5, and are numbered correspondingly.

[b] Postpositions occur after nouns and have also been termed 'particles'. They serve to show the grammatical relations between the content-words in the utterance and include the following: *ga, wa, ni, o, de, to, kara, made,* and *e.*

[c] OK is classified here as an 'adjectival noun' that does not form an adjective. Note the final copula ellipsis in the utterance, allowing for a more English-like surface-realization.

(reproduced here exactly as it appeared): '*Do Keizai*' ('study economics'). The verbal transfer from English is innovatory, with the nominal element left in Japanese but represented in roman script, which goes to show that the potential for verbal transfer exists—but as yet tends to be avoided.

As for the positions in which the intra-sentential switch may occur, these are the same as for Chinese-derived items and are thus long-established and sanctioned switching-sites of grammatical entry. In all but one of the code-mixed cases in Fig. 5.5 the language contact takes place through nominalization, as shown in Table 5.3. The exception is the transfer of the English conjunction-symbol '&' in example 4, which is a highly innovative but small-scale incursion that is minor enough to be 'tolerated'; it constitutes more of a switch than a mix, in that the symbol does not yet belong to Japanese orthography and stands outside the matrix system but could be reassigned a new value through interference-induced remodelling, making it equivalent to a Japanese co-ordinating particle such as *to* or *ya*. From Table 5.3 it is clear that English-derived items do not usually carry grammatical functions but tend to be restricted to the meaning-bearing components of an utterance, these being encoded within the nominal boundaries of Japanese.

The above discussion shows that a new, English-based style of mass consumer communication revealing characteristics of code-mixing/-switching is establishing itself, and even being imitated by non-commercial subgroups in the community, particularly fashion-conscious youth. In this way, there is some wider penetration of the code-switching and -mixing into other domains of the community and an increase in the potential for its standardization in the future. However, it is difficult to assess how the community evaluates the status of these innovative contact-styles, a topic to be explored in the next chapter. What remains clear is that the code-mixed style has not yet received institutional approval, since it does not appear in formal writing but is restricted mainly to the domains of mass media and advertising. Furthermore, it is also significant that there is no special name for this code-switching/-mixing available in Japanese, which implies that it has not yet reached a level of approved consciousness to warrant specific designation. Nevertheless, this chapter has demonstrated that the occurrence of the style is contextually predictable, as are many of its formal characteristics. The relations between the participants are also fixed: the professional persuaders and media controllers remain anonymous to the pubic receivers of their Anglicized messages, and vice versa.

Remodelling English

> ... the English word looted by the Japanese can expect to be system-
> atically stripped of its national identity after a series of cruel and little
> known initiation rites
>
> (*The Guardian*, 20 March 1976)

The striking and growing divergence from English norms of Japanese
vocabulary derived from the English language has been widely ridiculed,
but in fact such developments warrant careful descriptive treatment
and theoretical consideration for the implications they hold about the
language-contact process in general. In accounting for the changes taking
place, reference to the recipients' linguistic system (here Japanese) through
the concept of interference mentioned above certainly provides part of the
explanation. However, deficiency in learning the second language, caused
by poor models and unsuccessful teaching-methods, is also to blame.

Ultimately, morphological change raises the socio-linguistic question
of norm incompatability (see Bartsch, 1987) in an even more challenging
manner than oral, or even semantic, change, because it leads to conspicuous formal deviation from the donor model in the *written* channel.
This is behaviour which the donor community tends to view with much
less tolerance, because of the long history of the standardization and
codification of the written code; it may seem even less acceptable to the
donor community when it occurs in the monolingual code-switched style
which 'poses' as English.

It is essential to realize, however, that in the Japanese case, normative
control against such innovating change lies beyond the means of the
English donor-community—its networks of authority are still socially
and geographically too distant. In fact, the degree of conformity to the
patterns of the donor model depends on three crucial factors of contact:
the recipients' satisfaction of their socio-linguistic requirements according to the norms of their own system; their competence in the foreign
language; the existence of sanctions for not following donor norms. The
data discussed here present a community-specific solution to these three
variables of language contact.

As we have already seen above, in the basic outline of the morpho-
syntactic patterns for integrating borrowings, in most cases the Japanese
treat loans as uninflected nouns or bound bases that do not belong to a
word class but which are potentially convertible to any class by means of
suffixation. However, it is rare for a loan base to be convertible to the

class of both adjective and verb. The assignment to word class tends to correspond to the original syntactic role played by the transferred word in the donor system: *happy* is adopted as an adjectival noun (> *happī na*); *enjoy* as a verbal noun (> *enjoi suru*), and *bride* as a noun (> *buraido*).

Yet there are exceptions to this basic patterns of transfer. For instance.

- *kanningu suru* 'to cheat' functions as a VERB but the base derives from a NOUN/ADJECTIVE (< *cunning*) in the donor system. It is produced through word-class expansion from its initial integrating allocation as a loan noun.
- *gōru-in suru* 'to score' functions as a VERB but the base derives from a made-in-Japan compound of NOUN plus PREPOSITION (< *goal* + *in*).
- *sūpā* 'subtitle' functions as a NOUN but derives from the truncated past participle/ADJECTIVE (< *superimposed*), itself a compound of PREPOSITION and VERB.
- *yangu* 'youth, young people' functions as a NOUN derived from a donor ADJECTIVE.

The actual restrictions on the class conversion of non-Japanese nominal bases are extremely complex and rather idiosyncratic, and interested readers may wish to consult a reference work such as that of Martin (1975: 176–286). For present purposes, it should suffice to understand that once a base and its word-class allocation have been established, the proliferation of its word-class roles will depend on community innovation and acceptance, as well as on the semantic properties of the base itself. The morpho-syntactic paradigm for integrating foreign loan-words mirrors and derives from those established for Chinese loans a millennium ago. The difference is merely orthographic; the loan base is mostly represented not in characters but in the angular syllabary (*katakana*), with the class-converting suffixes and particles being represented in the cursive syllabary (*hiragana*).

To illustrate the contact paradigm, here is the case of a base derived from the English adjective *private*, which conveniently but also unusually happens to convert to all three major syntactic functions:

1. When the base functions as a NOUN, it is followed by postpositions: プライベートが/を/の *puraibēto ga/o/no*: 'privacy'.
2. *na* is employed for ADJECTIVAL conversion: プライベートな *puraibēto na* 'private'. Its corollary *ni* is suffixed for adverbial conversion: プライベートに *puraibēto ni* 'privately'.
3. *suru* is added for VERBAL conversion: プライベートする *puraibēto suru* 'to use time off for oneself' (radical innovation).

The making of the Anglo-Japanese noun (1) *puraibēto* = 'privacy' from the English adjective 'private' exemplifies the deviation from the donor model necessitated by the setting-up of an uninflecting base for morphological integration. This is not a lone example; there are similar cases, such as *sain* (< *sign*) 'signature' and *puropōzu* (< *propose*) 'proposal'. The etymological development of these items speaks for itself. The Japanese community is forming nouns from either adjectives or verbs without considering the morphological class-distinctions in the original, donor system. Of course, analogous patterning can be found in English in certain cases (e.g. *dance*, *study*, and *glue*, which function both as NOUNS and VERBS); but it is unacceptable in English, as in all speech communities, to innovate a replacement form for an already existing one, above all when the innovation violates existing patterns of class conversion. For example, the existence of forms like *bad* and *small* blocks the formation of **ungood* and **unbig*.

The aim of this section is not to defend or criticize such kinds of development, but instead to look at the possible reasons for their emergence. Here, the recipients obviously value the maintenance of the contact paradigm with an inflexible base much more highly than conformity to external donor-norms of word-class marking.

A major part of the explanation for the patterns described above lies in the morpho-syntactic characteristics of classical Chinese words, which were almost entirely indeclinable and monomorphemic, and for which the Japanese established their contact paradigm of syntactic suffixation with syllabic orthography. Moreover, classical Chinese was 'extremely resistant to any formal word class analysis . . . extraordinary freedom [was enjoyed by] almost any word . . . to enter into what one might call atypical syntactic functions; nouns can function like verbs; verbs and adjectives, likewise, may be used like nouns or adverbs, depending on the syntactic and semantic context . . . most words [could] function as other parts of speech depending on their place in the sentence' (Norman, 1988: 87). The argument posited here is that English loans, not only structurally but also functionally, are currently being assimilated and remodelled in accordance with the patterns of the millennium-old contact-model for Chinese, which managed to maintain some of the properties of the morphologically unmarked flexibility of word-class status in classical Chinese.

Already all the examples above, such as the formation of Anglo-Japanese verbs from *cunning* and *goal* + *in*, and of nouns from *young* and *private*, demonstrate that there can often be a lack of correspondence between the syntactic function of forms in the donor and recipient codes due to remodelling for uninflecting, classical-Chinese-like bases. Another important feature of morphological change in transfers from English which is related to Sino-Japanese modelling is the compounding and clipping of Anglo-Japanese loan-words; both of these processes have been taxonomically classified in Table 5.4. One of the main problems with the classification concerns the class assignment of a particular element in the English donor-system. For example, is 'change' in *imēji-chengi* (< image change) a verb or a noun (cf. *birth control*)?

Even though 70 per cent of these compound subcategories are currently productive in English and therefore 'justifiable' according to English word-formation rules, it is usually the case that members of the donor community react with derision or prescriptive disapproval when encountering them. In fact, for every one of these Japanese innovative formations, English compounds with exactly the same elements or similar class-elements can easily be cited, and they are given in the accompanying Table 5.5. However, even though the examples from English in Table 5.5 may validate Japanese independent adaptation from an English-speaking perspective, compatability with donor word-formation rules is certainly not a condition for loan-word innovation, nor for its subsequent acceptance and adoption. Even those members of the Japanese speech-community possessing a high level of English competence are unlikely to suffer from a norm conflict in the case of perceived deviation, because they will not have to face any sanctions from donor-norm authorities such as 'usage watchers' and codified words which serve as norm-enforcing agencies. In fact, the reverse is true: the Japanese will be subject to criticism, correction, and sanctions that is to say, neglect, ridicule, or even interactional exclusion—if they do not conform to the adaptive patterns of their own speech-community. This is because these forms already constitute part of the Japanese lexicon and are codified and/or employed in colloquial usage. Their 'correctness' is already a *fait accompli* by the community. Consider the perceptive comments of Bartsch (1987: 8) with reference to this matter:

the correctness notion [for lexical items] is very simple: what is in the list i.e. the lexicon, is correct. The lexicon is stored in the 'collective memory' of the speech community. Often it is codified in lexica in the form of books. . . . For the individual speaker, on the other hand, basically what is familiar to him, as a word of his language, is correct.

It must be understood that the loan formations in Table 5.4 are a direct product of Japanese structural and socio-linguistic needs and limits.

TABLE 5.4. A Typology of English-Derived Loan-Morphology

Compounding

1. Noun + noun
   imēji-chengi (< *image change*)
   koin-rokkā (< *coin locker*)
   gasorin-sutando (< *gasoline stand*, 'petrol station')
   shugā-katto (< *sugar + cut*, 'reduction in sugar')
   furonto-gurasu (< *front + glass*, 'windscreen')

2. Noun + preposition
   imēji-appu/-daun (< *image + up/down*, 'image improvement/
                 impairment')
   bēsu-appu/-daun (< *base + up/down*, 'raising/lowering of average salary')
   kosuto-appu/-daun (< *cost + up/down*, 'raising/lowering of costs')
   gōru-in (< *goal + in*, 'scoring a goal')
   shīzun-ofu (< *season + off*, 'off season')

3. Preposition + noun
   ōbā-dokutā (< *over + doctor*, 'surplus of those holding doctorates')
   ōbā-doraggu (< *over + drug*, 'overdose')

4. Noun + verb
   enjin-sutoppu (< *engine + stop*, 'car-engine breakdown')
   dokutā-sutoppu (< *doctor + stop*, 'doctor's orders to stop')
   bebī-sutoppu (< *baby + stop*, 'abortion')
   botoru-kīpu (< *bottle + keep*, 'keeping a bottle of alcohol with one's name
                 on as a regular pub-customer')

5. (Clipped) verb + noun
   engēji-ringu (< *engage + ring*, 'engagement ring')
   purē-gaido (< *play + guide*, 'ticket agency for all entertainment')
   sutāto-rain (< *start[ing] + line*)
   setto-rōshon (< *set[ting] + lotion*)
   furai pan (< *fry[ing] + pan*)
   kōn bīfu (< *corn[ed] beef*)
   sumōku chīzu (< *smok[ed] cheese*)

6. Adjective + noun
   nō-katto (< *no + cut*, 'uncensored')
   nō-tacchi (< *no + touch*, 'nothing to do with')
   nō-airon (< *no + iron*, 'non-iron')
   hai-tīn (< *high + teen*, 'person in late teens')
   hai-misu (< *high + miss*, 'elderly spinster')

Table 5.4. (Cont'd)

---

hai-sensu (< *high* + *sense*, 'stylish')
rō-tīn (< *low* + *teen*, 'person in early teens')
mai-kā (< *my* + *car*, 'private car')
mai-hōmu (< *my* + *home*, 'a home- and family-centred way of life')

7. Verb + verb
    gō-stoppu (< *go stop*, 'traffic lights')

8. Affixation
    misu-kopī (< *mis-* + *copy*, 'failed photocopy')
    semi-hando-mēdo (< *semi-* + *hand-made*)
    miruku-ēdo (< *milk* + -*ade*)
    korekusshonā (< *collection* + -*er*)

9. Adjective + noun + noun
    wan-man-kā (< *one man car*, 'one-man bus')

10. Acronym + noun
    NHK anaunsā (< *N*[*ippon*] *H*[*ōsō*] *K*[*yōkai*], 'Japan Broadcasting
        Association' + *announcer*)

Clipping

(*a*) Clipping of single words
    illustration > *irasuto*
    building > *biru*
    guarantee > *gyara*, 'performance fee'
    cash register > *reji*

(*b*) Compound with one clipped element
    taitoru-bakku (< *title* + *back*[*ground*], 'background scene with titles')
    omu-raisu (< *ome*[*lette*] + *rice*)
    masu-komi (< *mass* + *comm*[*unications*])
    nyū-aka (< *new* + *aca*[*demics*])
    bodi-kon (< *body* + *con*[*scious*])

(*c*) Compounds with both elements clipped
    dan-pa (< *da*[*nce*] + *par*[*ty*])
    han-suto (< hun[*ger*] + *st*[*rike*])
    en-suto (< *en*[*gine*] + *stop*, 'engine breakdown')
    wa-puro (< *wor*[*d*] + *pro*[*cessor*])
    ame-futo (< *Ame*[*rican*] + *foot*[*ball*])
    ka-sute (< *car* + *stel*[*reo*]; first loan usually with a long vowel—*kā*—, but
        this is shortened here)

TABLE 5.5. English Patterns of Word Formation Equivalent to Compounding and Clipping in Japanese Loan-Words Derived from English

1.	Noun + noun	*job change, (news)paper stand, education cut*
2.	Noun + preposition	*press up, put-down, teach-in*
3.	Preposition + noun	*overman, overpay*
4.	Noun + verb	*bee sting, sunburn, godsend* (NOT PRODUCTIVE IN ENGLISH)
5.	Clipped/no suffix verb + noun	*flashlight, stopwatch, hovercraft* (ONLY MARGINALLY PRODUCTIVE)
6.	Adjective + noun	*no-entry, no-ball, high priest, low-class* (*my* as a possessive adjective, does not constitute a compounding element in English, but cf. in exclamations, e.g. *My word!*
7.	Verb + verb	*make-believe, freezedry*, but extremely rare (NOT PRODUCTIVE)
8.	Affixation	*misapply, misprint, orangeade, commuter*
9.	Adjective + noun + noun	*deep structure rule, software program, fast-food chain*
10.	Acronym + noun	*BBC announcer*
(*a*)	Single clipping	*plane* (< [*aero*]*plane*), *porn* (< *porn*[*ography*]), *mike* (< *mic*[*rophone*])
(*b*)	Compound/one clipped element	*op art* (< *op*[*tical*] *art*), *org-man* (< *org*[*anization*] *man*)
(*c*)	Compound/both elements clipped	*sci-fi* (< *sci*[*ence*] *fi*[*ction*]), *sitcom* (< *sit*[*uation*] *com*[*edy*])

Moreover, it is almost inevitable, especially in a contact setting of low-level community bilingualism, that innovators will draw upon their own system for inspirational reference as a restructuring model. These changes arising from interference were identified long ago by Weinreich (1953: 39) as 'replica functions for equivalent morphemes'. Thus, if Japanese and Sino-Japanese patterns of word formation are examined, all the categories of compounding and clipping given in Table 5.4 are attestable, as Table 5.6 demonstrates. Although the correspondence in the word-class status of the elements in Table 5.6 with those in 5.4 and 5.5 cannot always be taken as exactly equivalent, a strong degree of semantico-functional correlation can be assumed. In fact, Table 5.6 proves that the patterns of word formation operating in loan-word innovation all comply with (Sino-) Japanese norms and that it is highly probable that these indigenous processes constitute a model of orientation in lexical integration; whether consciously or not remains open to debate. Of particular interest is the high productivity in the recipient system of the three unproductive patterns in English (see items 4, 5, and 7 in Tables 5.4 and 5.5), which further substantiates the role of the Japanese model in the creation of Anglo-Japanese vocabulary.

Next we shall turn to the morpho-phonological category of clipped forms. The availability of reduced morpho-phonological shapes features extensively in the (Sino-) Japanese system, and it is not surprising to find a desire for parallel patterning in the morphology of loan-words.

In addition to the double compound abbreviation of characters (see Table 5.6, item 10), which is directly comparable to pattern (c) in Table 5.4, the basic morpho-phonological organization of Japanese content-words represented in characters also must be considered as an influencing framework in lexical adaption, although only a simple outline of its principles can be offered.

Most Sino-Japanese characters carry more than one pronunciation. Usually one is the original Chinese reading (*on-yomi*) and the other the Japanese reading acquired after transfer (*kun-yomi*), rather like translation. In some cases a character may have more than one Chinese and/or Japanese reading. Generally, although there are exceptions, the Japanese reading is inflected and not used in compounding with other Chinese characters, while the Chinese reading is non-inflecting and usually occurs only in combination with another Chinese reading—that is to say, it tends to be a bound element reserved for compounding. The phonological shape of the Chinese reading is either of a single or of a double mora,[6] as in *ai* 'love', *aku* 'bad', *ba* 'horse', *ban* 'night', *betsu* 'separation', *gyaku* 'reversal,' *ryō* 'both', etc., while a Japanese reading with its accompanying inflections can reach must greater lengths, as in *naosaserareru* (= 7 morae) 'to have (sth.) mended'.

To illustrate this bi- or multi-morphological realization of Sino-

[6] Cf. Martin (1975: 17): 'In reciting poetry or spelling out the sound of a word, a Japanese will allow an equal amount of time for each vowel, so that a long vowel (marked here with a macron) counts as two timing units or MORAS . . . When a consonant occurs without a following vowel, it is treated as a separate mora: *shinbun* "newspaper" is pronounced si-n-bu-n, and *gakkō* "school" is pronounced ga-k-ko-o. The Japanese term for mora is *onsetsu* and this is often loosely translated as "syllable".' However, as Martin points out, in speech the Japanese may run two moras together to make a single syllable.

TABLE 5.6. Japanese Patterns of Word Formation Equivalent to Loan Compounding[a]

---

1. Noun + noun
   god + wind: 神風 *kami-kaze,* 'suicide plane' (J)[b]
   art + person: 芸者 *gei-sha,* 'traditional hostess' (SJ)[c]

2. Noun + verb ~ prepositional meaning
   value + up: 値上げ *ne-age,* 'price hike' (J)
   value + down: 値下げ *ne-sage,* 'cut in price' (J)

   Noun + relational noun ~ preposition
   direction + up: 向上 *kō-jō,* 'progress' (SJ)

3. Relational noun ~ preposition + noun
   up + person: 上人 *shō-nin,* 'saint' (SJ)
   behind + aid 後援 *kō-en,* 'patronage' (SJ)

4. Noun + verb is a productive indigenous Japanese pattern
   person + kill: 人殺し *hito-goroshi,* 'murder' (J)
   flower + see 花見 *hana-mi,* 'cherry-blossom viewing' (J)

   Cf. SJ compounds of noun + noun (止) for English-based coinages with
   -stop:
   middle + stop: 中止 *chu-shi,* 'calling off' (SJ)

5. (Clipped/no suffix) verb + noun
   live (ike[ru]) + flower (hana): 生花 *ike-bana,* 'flower arrangement' (J)
   sleep (ne[ru]) + saké (sake): 寝酒 *ne-sake,* 'night cap' (J)

   Cf. SJ binomials where the first element contains a monomorphemic
   and non-suffixable base carrying a verbal meaning which is comparable
   to a zero-marked verbal element in compounds:
   see + thing: 見物 *ken-butsu,* 'sightseeing' (SJ)
   enter + hospital: 入院 *nyū-in,* 'hospitalization' (SJ)

6. Adjective (i-stem) + noun
   old + book: 古本 *furu-hon,* 'secondhand book' (J)

   Adjective (*na*) base + noun
   safe + zone: 安全地帯 *anzen-chitai,* 'safety zone' (SJ)

   Pseudo-prefix adjectival noun + noun
   new + constitution: 新憲法 *shin-kempō* (SJ)

7. Verb + verb patterns are indigenous to Japanese, with compound verbs
   derived from two verbs.
   lending and borrowing: kashi-kari
   rising and falling: agari-sagari
   boarding and alighting: nori-ori

TABLE 5.6. (Cont'd)

Cf. Chinese-derived compounding bases with verbal meaning.
fly + go: 飛行 *hi-kō,* 'flight' (SJ)
pour + shoot: 注射 *chū-sha,* 'injection' (SJ)
turn + send: 回送 *kai-sō,* 'out of service' (SJ)

Additionally, in SJ compounding, two antonymous concepts can be combined to express an abstract concept covering their joint meanings.
go away + come: 往来 *ō-rai,* 'coming and going' = 'traffic'
get + throw away: 取捨 *shu-sha,* 'option'

8. Affixation is common in Japanese.
   me-, 'female': *me-buta,* 'sow' (J)
   -tachi (person plural marker): *kodomo-tachi,* 'children' (J)

   There are numerous SJ affixes.

   hi-, 'un-': *hi-kokumin,* 'an unpatriotic person'
   -teki, '-type': *Nihon-teki,* 'typically Japanese'

   The affixes transferred from English in Table 5.4 all share semantically and functionally related SJ bound bases.
   mis-: 不無非 *fu-, mu-, hi-*
   semi-: 判 *han-*
   -er: 者 *sha*

   For the new types of drink denoted by the affix *-ade,* there is, of course, no character equivalent; but there are various drink-denoting compounding bases.
   酒 *-shu,* 'alcohol': *budō-shu* (*grape + alcohol*), 'wine'; *ume-shu* (*plum + alcohol*), 'plum liqueur'

   Cf. 茶 *-cha,* 'tea': *mugi-cha* (*barley + tea*); *ban-cha,* 'coarse green tea'; *kō-cha,* 'black tea'

9. Pseudo-prefix adjectival noun + proper noun + noun
   Bei-Karifōrunia-daigaku, 'University of California in America'

   Pseudo-prefix adjectival noun + noun + noun
   pure + Japanese + person: 純日本人 *jun-nihonjin*

10. The Japanese orthographic systems do not allow acronyms as such, but character compounds can be abbreviated to the first element of the compound. Thus, *Tōkyō* 東京 and 'university' *daigaku* 大学 can be reduced to 東大 *tōdai* 'Tokyo University' and then recompounded: 東大生 *tōdai-sei,* 'student of Tokyo University'.

---

[a] The grammatical classification employed here is that of Martin (1975).
[b] J = Japanese.
[c] SJ = Sino-Japanese.

Japanese words resulting from ancient diglossic language-contact, here is the case of the word for 'east'. This is represented by the character 東, which is pronounced as *higashi* by itself (Japanese reading) but *tō* in compounds (Chinese reading):

東洋 *tō-yō*: 'east' + 'ocean' 'the Orient'
中東 *chū-tō*: 'middle' + 'east' 'the Middle East'
東大 *tō-dai*: 'east' + 'big' 'Tokyo University'

Each of the compounding elements with 東 (tō) of course have their own Japanese readings, as in 中 *naka*, 大 *ōkī*. In the community the Chinese reading is often taken as an abbreviated version of the usually longer Japanese word, which leads to morpho-phonological reduction in compounding. It is important to remember that ordinary members of the community do not possess a diachronic awareness of Japanese language-contact but closely relate the two readings to their single ideographic representation.

Now that these basic principles have been clarifed, it is not difficult to see why the recipients favour the abbreviation of English-derived compounds. As will be shown below, this truncation generally parallels the shorter phonological shapes of Sino-Japanese binomials. Secondly, since loan-words are syntactically integrated through the same system as Sino-Japanese, it becomes convenient and efficient, from a native structural point of view, to Japanize their morpho-phonological shape. Evidence for the convergence of compounds based on clipped loans to Sino-Japanese patterns is not hard to find. In Table 5.4 (*c*), the following English-derived clipped forms of single mora all have more than one Sino-Japanese homonymous equivalent:

dan: 男 'man', 断 'resolution', 団 'group', 談 'talk', 壇 'platform'
h/pa (often voiced in compounds): 葉 'leaf', 羽 'feather', 歯 'tooth'
han: 反 'opposition', 半 'half', 犯 'violation', 阪 'slope', 判 'judge'
en: 円 'round', 炎 'flame', 延 'extension', 園 'garden', 煙 'smoke'
wa: 和 'peace', 話 'talk'

Admittedly, the other English-derived clipped forms of two morae, such as *futo*, *-puro*, and *-suto*, do not have exact Chinese-derived equivalents. However, many characters have individual Chinese readings as *to* and *ro*, and in combination with other bases, not always as compounds, can occur in similar phonological sequences: 不図 *futo* 'suddenly', *sampu rokunin* 'six pregnant women'. The remaining sequence *suto* is often found in native Japanese: *naosu to* 'if it's repaired'. Furthermore, the truncation of *ame-* from 'American' perfectly conforms to an indigenous Japanese pattern:

1. *ame*: 雨 'rain'; 雨風 *ame-kaze* 'rain and wind'; 雨降 *ame-furi* 'rainfall'
2. *ame*: 飴 'wheat gluten'; 飴玉 *ame-dama* 'toffees'

Thus, the formation of English-based elements of double-mora length does not conflict with native phonological sequencing and, more than likely, is actually a direct result of its permitted patterns. Furthermore, since compounds of mixed readings where the first element is pronounced as native Japanese and the second as Chinese, or vice versa, exist as an established morpho-phonological category in the recipient code,[7] the combination of Japanese-like and Chinese-like clipped-loan shapes not only complies with existing morpho-phonological norms but also seems to be purposefully designed so as not to violate them. For instance, the length of a clipped English-based compound element never exceeds more than two morae, which is in accordance with the formal limits of Sino-Japanese binomials. With reference to this issue of phonological length, it is interesting to note that the Japanese have not truncated *processor* as **purose* nor **purosesu*; neither did they clip *strike* as **sutorai*. Additionally, the elimination of the geminate /tt/ in the truncation for *foot* as *-futo*, unlike in the orthodox unclipped borrowing *futto*, provides a striking indication of the desire to maintain English-based compound elements within two-mora limits; the inclusion of the geminate would lengthen the element to three morae.

Finally, it is also worth considering the fact that the English-derived bases have not been further reduced to a single mora such as /su/ or /fu/, even though this would make them correspond exactly to Sino-Japanese forms. It would seem that innovators have opted against such extreme truncation, probably because they view it as semantically ineffective; it would undermine the potential association with the original, unclipped English loan.

The syntactic and phonological adjustments to foreign binomials described above give the transferred elements structural parity with Sino-Japanese nominal bases and must be recognized as systematizations aimed at achieving convergence with the recipient code. This remodelling facilitates reception and assimilation. It has led to the creation of many innovative, hybrid compounds, particularly in the commercial register (see type 3 in Table 5.7).

---

[7] These are: *jūbako-yomi*: compounds comprising Chinese + Japanese readings, e.g. 字引 *ji-biki* 'dictionary'; *yutō-yomi*: compounds comprising Japanese and Chinese readings, e.g. 手本 *te-hon* 'a copy'.

TABLE 5.7. Innovative Patterns of Lexical Contact[a]

1. Innovative nominal patterns in the monolingual style
   (Mainly commercial sources used as titles, headlines)

cafe rest (< *rest*[*aurant*]	*fit love card*
the clean	*wellness pet life*
news up	*yu-me box*
artmodern	*single life basic*
high-grade life	*campus-city cross magazine*
dry and hay	

2. Innovative compounding originally represented in the angular syllabary

   kappu-nūdoru (< *cup* + *noodle* = instant noodles sold in a plastic cup-like container)

   hīrō-intabyū (< *hero* + *interview* = a talk with a sportsman who played successfully)

   dēto-fashon (< *date* + *fashion* = how to dress for a date)

   hea-meiku-ātisto (< *hair* + *make* + *artist* = stylist for hair and make-up)

   moderu-rūmu-ōpun (< *model* + *room* + *open*, 'showroom is now open for viewing')

   maindo-appu-shisutemu (< *mind* + *up* + *system*, 'system for improving your mind')

   mentaru-kontorōru-ikuippumento (< *mental* + *control* + *equipment*)

3. Hybrid compounding character and/or syllabic and/or roman orthographies

   アフダーライン用:
      andārain-yō (*underline* + Japanese: 'use', 'for underlining')
   ブランド商品:
      burando shōhin (< *brand* + Japanese: 'commodity')
   インタビュー中:
      intabyū-chū (< *interview* + Japanese 'in progress')
   リラックス法:
      rirakkusu-hō (< *relax* + Japanese 'method')
   禁煙タイム:
      kin'en-taimu (Japanese: 'no smoking' + *time*)
   錄 TEL:
      roku-TEL: (Japanese: *record* + *TEL*, 'answer-phone')

TABLE 5.7. (Cont'd)

開発コンセプト:
  kaihatsu konseputo (Japanese: 'development' + *concept*)
高校1年生クラス:
  kōkō-ichinen-sei-kurasu (Japanese: 'high-school first-year student + *class*)
オープン記念ツアー:
  ōpun-kinen-tsuā (< *open* + Japanese 'anniversary' + 'tour')
NON 虫シート:
  NON-mushi-shīto (*non-* + Japanese 'insect' + 'sheet')
ノーポイーデー:
  no-poi-de (*no* + Japanese 'butt' + 'day', slogan of rail-station anti-smoking campaign)
ハレンンタイン生チョコケーキ:
  barentain-nama-choko-kēki (< *Valentine* + Japanese 'fresh cream' + *choco*[*late*] *cake*)
レール&レンターカーきつぷ:
  rēru-&-rentākā-kippu (< *rail* + *&* + *rent-a-car* + Japanese 'ticket')
ウエルカムドリンク券:
  uerukumu-dorinku-ken (< *welcome* + *drink* + Japanese 'ticket')

---

[a] The items listed were collected from observed written texts. Many of the patterns are not yet established and thus are likely to be considered radical, or even deviant, by certain community members.

So far nothing has been said about the clipping of single words— category (*a*) in Table 5.4. Deletion processes are, in fact, common and extensive in Japanese and are especially favoured in casual speech. It is not surprising to discover that this kind of truncation also leads to closer conformity to native Japanese patterns in terms of mora length and phonology:

sassato 'quickly' ~ *irasuto* (< *illustration*)
jara 'jingle' ~ *gyara* (< *guarantee*)
kiru 'kill' ~ *biru* (< *building*)
meji 'wall joint' ~ *reji* (< *register*)

Next, the innovating patterns of lexical contact as illustrated in Table 5.7 will be discussed, particularly in their relation to the issue of normativeness. Table 5.7 has been divided into three sections: type 1 was written in the monolingual style, while the English-based types 2 and 3 were encoded in the angular syllabary. Because the monolingual-style compounds and phrases occurred in Japanese texts, often placed next to Japanese words, their designation is problematic. Should they be interpreted as English or as Japanese—or as something in between, as denoted by the derogatory lay term 'Japlish'? The term 'monolingual style' is employed but its role in creating a bilingual, code-mixed text must not be forgotten. The term 'Japanese English' is not used here and is best reserved for situations where: Japanese are communicating (or attempting to communicate) entirely in English contexts, without recourse to the Japanese language; and Japanese are not uniquely addressing their own community, that is to say, when they employ English for *inter*national purposes and not *intra*national ones.

In fact, the monolingual examples in Table 5.7(1) have been specifically selected because of their deviation from English normative patterns. However, it is erroneous to believe that only deviant monolingual patterns exist, since items which conform perfectly to donor norms may also be observed in Japanese texts. Although no study of comparative frequency was undertaken, it is my subjective judgement that Japanese concern for compatibility with donor norms tends to increase with the expense of the product or commercial. Before I enter into the controversy surrounding non-native remodelling, certain characteristiscs of the monolingual style warrant comment. Of course, it is not the aim here to witch-hunt all possible 'corruptions' of the donor model. The table is meant only to serve as a non-stigmatizing illustration of the reality of this linguistic divergence, and as an analytic inspiration.

It should be evident that the patterns of type 1 in Table 5.7 spotlight many of the aspects of morphological remodelling treated above, in addition to raising some new dimensions such as:

- *Truncation* here leading to semantic confusion because of homonymy: *rest* < *restaurant*
- *Creative formation* arising from original suffixing of orthodox loan-elements —*za-* (< *the*), -*appu* (< *up*) (cf. Table 5.4(2)) appearing in titles of magazines and television programmes (*The Clean, News Up*).
- *Reversal of word order* or linear sequencing different from donor norms: *artmodern* (modern art), *single life basic* (basic single life), *campus-city cross magazine* (cross campus-city magazine), *wellness pet life* (pet life wellness).
- *Word-class parity* between adjectives, verbs with nouns (cf. the discussion above on the absence of word-class marking in Sino-Japanese and English-

derived bases): *Dry and Hay* is the name of a product; *fit love card* is 'a questionnaire card that will fit (match) your love (requirements) by computer'.
- *Radically innovative compounding: yu-me box* (title of a section of a magazine devoted to answering readers' questions).

This kind of monolingual Anglicization cannot be explained solely in terms of interference from, and convergence with, the (Sino-)Japanese substratum. It is also necessary to relate its production to the generally low level of community competence in English. The institutional setting for the acquisition of English has been outlined in detail in the previous chapter, in which it was concluded that in the last decade of the twentieth century Japan still presented a 'negative' learning situation because of social factors such as:

- Predominantly instrumental motivation.
- A disdain for practical, active skills fostered by a conservative grammar-translation approach providing for only a passive, reading ability.
- A lack of access to native second-language models.

Given such acquisitional parameters, it is to be expected that many Japanese learners will not advance to higher levels of active proficiency but remain at a restricted, underdeveloped, and not necessarily stable, stage of English competence, at which their output constitutes an *approximative system* or interlanguage. Of course, there is bound to be heterogeneity in the mastery of the donor language, and, although a cline of interlingual varieties of English exists in the Japanese community, the most typical level of active, performing ability is essentially *basilectal*.

Various linguistic processes have been found to operate in such non-developmental models of second-language proficiency. These include over-simplification, over-generalization, regularization, ignorance of rule restrictions, false analogy, error fossilization, incomplete application of rules, and false concept-hypothesization (see Richards, 1985; Ellis, 1985). Furthermore, all kinds of categories of mistake-making in a foreign language have been identified: there are 'developmental errors' reflecting built-in stages of acquisition, and 'communication-based errors' resulting from strategies of getting the message across, and so on. However, no attempt will be made here to interpret the data in terms of individually categorizable errors, for such an effort is not only theoretically questionable but also problematic to carry out in practical terms, because of the possibility of multiple explanations. Instead, it is more profitable to consider the data comprehensively in relation to the characteristics displayed by Japanese society in its learning of English. In fact, there are some striking correspondences between the socio-linguistic ecology of Japanese language-contact with English and what has been termed pidginization. The latter can refer to second-language learning in formal institutional settings (see Schumann, 1978). For example, both the Japanese and pidginizing settings share the following features:

- A lack of direct access to, or contact with, an input model (the typical model is a Japanese teacher, often with a limited command of the language).
- Non-integrative motivation.
- The absence of authorities and sanctions to enforce conformity to the norms of the second-language community when it comes to the employment of the code outside the classroom—for example, in the commercial domain.
- An output characterized by linguistic reductionism and invariance—that is to say, there is no derivational, inflectional, declensional, or conjugational variation in the transferred forms (this particularly applies to loan-word bases here).
- Extensive borrowing and syntactic convergence.
- Phonological and syntactic interference from the recipient group.
- Imperfect learning and simplification strategies.

From the above it should be clear that the causes of the diverging modifications from the donor model found in English loan-patterns are complex; they are simultaneously connected with: influences from the recipient's first language-system; environmental, acquisitional, and individual constraints in second-language competence.

Data-type 1 in Table 5.7 also raises the controversial issue of the validity of communication in a foreign language which does not conform to native-speaker norms. This question has received much attention in the literature; the most articulate defender of this adaptation of English in the multilingual, multiethnic, and multicultural states of Asia and Africa has been Kachru (1982, 1983b, 1986). As for Japanese contact with English today, we have seen here how it involves similar processes of interference, convergence on phonological and syntactic levels, and hybridization; the latter is exemplified in the Japanese data collected in Table 5.7(3).

In spite of there being a fundamental difference between the status of English in multilingual societies such as India and Nigeria, on the one hand, and Japan, on the other, where English does not constitute a locally institutionalized variety, some of Kachru's arguments are still applicable, in that the Japanese are communicating creatively with their own community through the monolingual style, in order to satisfy internal, local needs. If the mere documentation of the socio-linguistic reality of monolingual Anglicization does not supply sufficient ontological legitimacy, then it is surely its operation by and for members of the Japanese community that can and does validate what is perceived by English natives as 'deviancy'. The Japanese see no need to justify this divergence; unlike 'New Englishes', it has no polemic defenders.

It should be clear from the above discussion that monolingual stylists operate without according the criterion of correctness a supreme position: appropriateness, effectiveness, and intra-ethnic intelligibility are the principles which serve the highest criterion of successful message-transmission. Here it is taken for granted that perfect conformity with donor norms is neither practical nor especially desirable.

The geographical and social distance between the recipient output and donor model leads not to a norm conflict, as in the case of institutionalized second-language societies, but to norm incompatibility. Above all, there is no community-recognized authority in Japan to control or punish the lack of compliance with donor norms in monolingual Anglicization. There is, of course, no reason to believe that this will always be so. With increased proficiency, donor norms may come to be perceived more acutely.

Certainly when it comes to remodelling English parts inside the Japanese language, as in types 2 and 3 in Table 5.7, donor norms are totally irrelevant. However, the fact that the community has so far avoided the codification of these now prevalent hybridized compounds in its loan-word dictionaries indirectly indicates the radicalness of the patterns, as well as prescriptive disapproval. The frequency of such hybridization in slogans and commercial catch-phrases is steadily growing. The phenomenon simultaneously symbolizes the extent of English penetration and serves as a pointer to future morphological developments between the two languages that are likely to become orthodox eventually.

Type 2 includes examples of an increasingly popular, trinomial, type of compounding. The data in type 2 also firmly prove that English-based contact cannot be interpreted solely in terms of a structural response to gaps, but involves the independent, creative, evolutionary reworking of transferred elements in order to meet local needs. New compounding patterns emerging here and not classified in the typology of Table 5.4 include:

1. N + TRUNCATED N + N: ⁾hair_make [up] artist
2. N + PREP. + N: ⁾mind_up system
3. N + N + V: ⁾model room_open

The hybridization in type 3 demonstrates the true interchangeability of loan-word bases with Sino-Japanese bases, and their mutual bond-ability testifies to the deep integration of English into contemporary Japan-ese. Monosyllabic units in roman orthography can be combined with a Chinese character (as well as syllabic script) to form new compounds: 録TEL (answerphone); NON 虫シート (sheet for catching insects). The compounding position of the English base is very flexible—preceding, following, or encapsulating the Sino-Japanese.

As a conclusion it can be said that English-derived loan-words are being morpho-phonologically made to converge with Sino-Japanese character-bases through the zero marking of word class, through trunca-tion in binomial formation, and through the replication of native Japan-ese patterns of mora length and compounding. An attempt has been made here to understand the morphology of English contact within its own terms and dynamics. The analysis reveals that contact-makers manipulate their English knowledge with differing degrees of awareness, sophistication, and legitimization. In this way they develop new linguistic systematizations and models that diverge from the original donor-norms. Furthermore, this Japanese remodelling contradicts the expectations for a distant non-bilingual contact-setting as defined in the typology of Table 1.1. Instead of the language-contact phenomena observed here—code-switching/-mixing, interference, interlanguage—only small-scale bor-rowing and some institutionally restricted pidginization would normally be expected. Thus, the study of the contemporary Japanese assimilation of English challenges and extends traditional conceptions of language-contact settings in general.

6

The Social Reception of Contact with English Now

In this chapter the focus shifts from texts to the variation among community members in their interpretation and evaluation of the language contact taking place around them. Conclusions from the last chapter already indicate that intensive Anglicization is a predominantly orthographic phenomenon associated with the public spheres of marketing and media and does not extend to ordinary interaction in the speech community. It was also pointed out that the main types of foreign transfers in daily conversation, unlike those in the commercial domain, arose from the need to fill lexical gaps for mainly concrete, material referents; sinification, on the other hand, appears to be the preferred method for encoding abstract Western concepts. These findings suggest that the active creation and dissemination of contact vocabulary across the entire community is still extremely limited.

The study of non-broadcast, daily interaction has not been attempted, because the collection and analysis of such data is fraught with innumerable methodological problems such as comparability in number of subjects, rates of speech, and context, and cannot lead to definitive conclusions. Instead, a discussion of the social reception of contemporary contact with English is offered based on the findings of a questionnaire answered by 461 informants (see Appendix 1). Before discussing these data, some general findings and comments concerning subgroup and attitudinal variation in Japanese society in relation to Anglicizing processes are set out. However, it must be pointed out that information in this area is scanty and that the following is based on personal observation combined with the limited material available.

The principal group innovatively and enthusiastically involved in Anglicization in a non-commercial way is undeniably Japanese youth, whose slang and in-group styles repeatedly draw upon it as a resource whereby young people can distinguish themselves from the mainstream and older generations. The favourable attitude towards Anglicization among young

Japanese is reflected in the findings of a survey of 2,639 people conducted by the state broadcasting corporation (NHK) in 1979,[1] in which twenty-year-olds scored an average of 72 per cent for loan-word preference, while the average for all age-groups was 47 per cent. In marked contrast, only 14 per cent of seventy-year-olds were found to favour loan-words. This spotlights the wide age-based range in the acceptability of foreignisms.

Furthermore, it should be pointed out that many loan-words already constitute part of the active vocabulary of young Japanese children today, some already well integrated into children's talk: *OK, toire* (< *toilet*), the clipped form *gū* from *gūddo* (< *good*).[2] Equally significant is the fact that the European-derived kinship terms *mama* and *papa* are employed in certain families which correlate with white-collar and nuclear types;[3] children in such families tend to switch to Japanese forms after adolescence. Additionally, the farewell routine *baibai* (< *bye bye*) is the most common form of parting among children today, and the first taught to babies.

Although no study has yet shown this to be the case,[4] it seems reasonable to expect that women, because of their universally more conformist style, adopted for the sake of a decorative, feminine image, will avoid unorthodox loan-words, English-based slang,[5] and high-brow foreignisms. Of course, there are certain semantic areas—such as sex (to be discussed in Chapter 7), sport, and technology—which are stereotypically considered male topics and which draw profusely upon Anglicization; but then there also exist semantic categories, such as food, fashion, and cosmetics, particularly associated with women which are equally rich in loan-words from English.

In spite of the recent concern with attitudinal behaviour, it is widely acknowledged that there is a general lack of theory in this field. Although the correlation between attitude and behaviour is not necessarily high, attitudinal investigation still provides a framework for understanding and predicting behaviour towards an object.

---

[1] This research is described in Ishino and Tsutsumi (1979: 6).

[2] See Hirosue (1984).   [3] According to Peng (1975*b*).

[4] Stanlaw's loan-word-frequency study of male and female students' conversations (1982) does not, unfortunately, permit comparison between the sexes, because of differences in length of time recorded, number of informants from each sex-group, and, above all, contextual content.

[5] e.g. *panku suru* (< punc [ture] 'to give birth'); *poteto* (< potato 'a pregnant woman'); *tanku* (< tank 'a physically strong man'); *antena* (< antenna 'a tall person'); *basu* (< bus 'a loose woman').

The primary focus of most socio-linguistic research into language attitudes up to now has been the perception of minority regional, ethnic, or non-standard varieties, or of completely different languages. Most research concentrates on describing and explaining community support for, and prejudices against, particular varieties and their users. There has been hardly any exploration of the social evaluation of borrowing and code-switching/-mixing involving the behaviour of an entire society.

A community's attitudes towards language contact can be shaped by many factors, including: the level and intensity of the contact; the degree of social distance from, and ideological position *vis-à-vis*, users of the donor language; the perceived ability of the community to satisfy linguistic needs from its own lexical resources. According to Fishman (1971: 228–31), the three most significant socio-cultural determinants of social judgements about different varieties are: the extent of their standardization; their autonomous status as unique and independent systems; their vitality— meaning 'the interaction networks that actually employ them natively for one or more vital functions' (ibid. 230). The contact process taking place in Japan obviously does not constitute a separate variety, although, as shown in the last chapter, it has led to the emergence of distinctive, code-mixed or purely monolingual English-based styles in mass-media and commercial contexts serving specific functions. Some of these styles have become expected patterns of language-use and standard practice within certain contexts, but they cannot be considered as established within the community as a whole.

As for Japanese attitudes towards present-day Anglicization, the re-action which receives the most publicity is one of puristic alarm at the lack of national pride and respect for the Japanese language and culture, accompanied by a plea for the curbing of innovative, obscure, and opaque transfers.

A typical comment belonging to this ethno-linguistically defensive position is that of Takao Suzuki, a renowned authority on the Japanese language, who recommended a process of linguistic purification similar to the politically supported limitation of contact with English recently imposed in France to resist the influx of foreign words.

Related to this hostile reaction is the complaint about the surfeit of English words in current plans for government-sponsored projects and budget statements. Nevertheless, it should be pointed out that not all government agencies are in favour of foreignisms. For example, in November 1987, the then Minister of Transport, Shintarō Ishihara, blocked the plan of the Japanese national railway to use the letter E as an abbreviated prefix for express trains, as in E 電 (*E-den*) 'E-train', because he found such terming 'thoughtless' and believed that, if allowed to continue, it would turn into a 'nightmare'. Similarly, in 1989 the Health and Welfare Minister, Junichiro Koizumi, irritated by the profusion of English-derived technical terms in ministerial reports, ordered the establishment of a Terminology Rationalization Committee to deal with the problem. (Examples of terms to which he took exception are *tāminaru-keya* (< *terminal care*) and nōmaraizēshon (< *normalization*), meaning the integration of patients into society after long stays in nursing institutions.) The minister stated that the elderly, as well as other beneficiaries of welfare programmes, could not possibly understand the language used by ministry bureaucrats. Such actions reveal that active resistance towards Anglicization by certain individuals with power in Japanese society can be effective, even if it is small-scale.

In 1990 two lawyers filed a petition against the Shimane Prefectural Assembly demanding that it stop using 'Japanese English' in its official documents and project titles. The lawyers stated their purpose as 'promoting the preservation and distribution of correct, beautiful, and elegant Japanese and English' and went on to attack the sense of local-government coinages such as *Rifuresshu Rizoto Shimane* (Refresh Resort Shimane) and *Shimanesuku Shimane* (Shimane-esque Shimane).

The general policy of the NHK (Japan Broadcasting Corporation) is to avoid unfamiliar and opaque foreignisms in the language of its own announcers, and, where necessary, to accompany loan-word terminology with a Japanese explanatory paraphrase. However, the media observe no absolutist rules in the matter. They leave it to the discretion of the individual programme-writers and producers to guarantee maximum, community-wide comprehension, unless the programme is clearly limited to a circumscribed audience with presumed specialist understanding of the jargon, as in music or sport.

As for established official policy towards Anglicization, there exist specific guide-lines promulgated as a 'Declaration on Foreignisms' (*Gairaigo no Hyōki*) by the Japanese Language Council (Kokugo Shingi-kai) in 1954 and subsequently adopted for public dissemination by the Ministry of Education. Recently, a Committee on Foreign Loan-Word Writing-Styles, a section of the latter ministry's seventeenth Council on National Language was assembled to update the pronouncements so that they correspond more closely to the changed *status quo*, as official patterns are now frequently unheeded in technical, commercial, and mass communication. In the last three decades it would seem that the average Japanese citizen has, by way of education and exposure through mass media, dramatically improved their oral ability to reproduce certain English sounds. This is revealed in the unorthodox, innovative spelling currently in vogue. For example, a common, non-standard variant spelling for *telephone* today is テレフォン (*terefon*), instead of the official テレホン (*terehon*), in which the /f/ sound is represented not by the prescribed h- symbol but by the innovative combination of the symbol フ (fu) accompanied by a small-size vowel;[6] another case is the contemporary disregard for the rule that words ending in *-er*, *-or*, and *-ar* should be written with a final long dash: *konpyūtā* (コンピューター) versus *konpyūta* (コンピュータ). Explanation of such radical revisions requires considerable familiarity with the complexities of encoding non-Japanese sounds via the syllabic medium (see Table 5.1 for more orthographic innovations).

The principal significance of these innovations is as an indication of the desire among certain innovating members of the community for a more accurate reproduction of foreign (usually English) sounds. This striving for greater phonological authenticity is a consequence of an important increase in contact with the oral channel by certain sections of the recipient community—in contrast to past relations, which were predominantly established through writing. In its interim progress-report of December 1988, the Council declared that loose rules were necessary for katakana spellings of foreign words, and that orthographic variations for one word should be accepted, although the committee would select one 'representative' pattern. There was little support for the symbolic recognition of the sound /1/, but strong support for the official approval of the /v/ sound. These conservative deliberations come as no surprise, since the 1954 prescriptions were also dominated by orthographic concerns, giving phonological advice to borrowers and innovators that reflected a stabilizing, non-élitist, and non-extremist attitude aimed at keeping within Japanese phonological limits.

From most of the above reactions and approaches to the question of

---

[6] There is no /f/ phoneme in Japanese, but the bilabial fricative /Φ/ is usually taken as the closest approximation to it, and this occurs in the first part of the syllable フ (fu). However, the official prescription is to represent /f/ sounds such as /fa/, /fi/, /fe/, and /fo/ with the symbols for /ha/, /hi/, /he/, and /ho/, which are respectively ハ, ヒ, ヘ, and ホ. The unorthodox innovation involves putting a small-size vowel next to the フ symbol, e.g. ファ (fa), フィ (fi), フェ (fe), and フォ (fo).

language contact, it is clear how strongly Japan remains a 'script-oriented culture' (*moji-bunka*), language issues being interpreted primarily within the framework of the written channel.

So far only negative and official attitudes towards foreignisms have received mention. Favourable attitudes tend not to be directly expressed, because those who hold them obviously do not feel it necessary to publicize their satisfaction with the situation; but they are indirectly reflected in certain linguistic behaviour. Two often-cited cases of the profound penetration of socio-cultural and aesthetic barriers are the 1965 inclusion of the loan-word based on the English term 'conveyor belt' in a poem by Prince Mikasa (as he then was) for the annual court ceremony of haiku poetry,[7] and the use, by the now deceased Emperor Showa himself, of the loan-word *damu* (< *dam*) in a 1976 poem;[8] usually not even Chinese-derived vocabulary is permitted in this type of text. The breaking of enshrined language-rules in this year-end ritual celebration of Japanese nationhood, by those very persons who, as symbolic embodiments and guardians of Japanese values, are expected to uphold them most of all, is an extremely significant indication of the intimate acceptance of English transfers.

The favourable attitudes of the young towards contact has already been stressed above. Hirosue (1984) found that children seemed to prefer vocabulary presented in the katakana syllabary to characters which were more difficult to read and memorize. However, nearly half the children supported the view that only intelligible loan-words should be permitted to increase, which suggests that a considerable number of youngsters have serious problems understanding such words. In fact, it would seem that it is this lack of comprehension, rather than notions of preserving linguistic purity, that constitutes the main factor in resistance.

The Survey

In order to explore the relationship between social factors and the intelligibility of, preference for, and attitudes towards, Japanese contact with English, a questionnaire was administered to 461 informants by exclusively Japanese assistants. An English translation of the questionnaire is provided in Appendix 1.

---

[7] 'The *conveyor belt* that brings in the feed revolves and thousands of young birds cluster about it to eat.'

[8] 'Having reached the top of a slope through the forest so dark and gloomy, I am now here to command a fine view of the broad *dam*.'

Before the results are discussed, the methodological procedures and aims of the investigation will be briefly outlined. First of all, the selection of the questionnaire as a method of investigation requires explanation. The principal justification for its choice was that it seemed to offer the most efficient means of collecting data about large-scale patterns in a controlled manner and in a form that would be relatively quick and reliable to process.

Open-style interviewing of a large number of informants would have been very time-consuming, and the results difficult to systematize. Furthermore, such interviewing could not be conducted by the investigator, who, as a non-Japanese asking about attitudes towards the West and English, would have had a nullifying effect on the validity of the responses. On the other hand, the alternative approach of candidly or surreptitiously tape-recording informants' speech would have been fraught with the problems of gaining suitable access to the interaction of diverse social groups, assuring the continual technical reproduction of their discourse during the interaction, sifting through lots of data without, or with only very limited, contact-features, and tackling the impossible task of trying to compare the occurrence of contact features in different contexts in relation to multiple social variables. Additionally, because the primary focus of the research was the community evaluation and understanding of contact behaviour, rather than the provision of a descriptive model of it, the questionnaire was more appropriate than the recording method. Moreover, the questionnaire approach does not rule out the possibility of making inferences about informants' real-life linguistic behaviour.

In fact, the development of the questionnaire as a linguistic tool dates back to the nineteenth-century methodology of traditional dialectologists and has today widely come to be accepted as a method of collecting socio-linguistic data, especially in the area of language contact and attitudes towards language.[9]

---

[9] The first significant language-contact study in which it was utilized was that of Haugen (1953) in the seminal work on Norwegian–English bilingualism. In recent research on language maintenance and shift, the questionnaire method features prominently: see Lieberson and McCabe (1982); Veltman (1983); Clyne (1988); and Sridhar (1988). It also figures in studies of code-switching and mixing: Parasher (1980); Amuda (1986); Holmquist (1987). The implementation of the questionnaire in the investigation of the community's understanding, employment, and acceptability of words transferred from English into German also deserves mention for its similarities with some of the research objectives and methods here: see Viereck (1980) and Hannah (1986). On top of this, the questionnaire has emerged as the most popular

Obviously the questionnaire as a research instrument has numerous deficiencies that cannot be ignored. The possibility of error from the inaccurate self-reporting of the informants is probably the major threat to its reliability. An established relationship between the assistant interviewers and the informants for most cases in this study was intended to provide a minimal guarantee of the sincerity of the responses obtained, in that the informants were likely to feel a sense of responsibility to report honestly to their relative, friend, or teacher. A further attempt to ensure consistency in informant response was made through the repetition of certain questions with similar content. Possible inconsistencies in the physical conditions or the assistants' style of administering the questionnaire are, of course, uncontrollable variables which could have distorted the responses in some way, although the assistants were asked to follow exactly the same procedure of not revealing any position or showing any kind of negative reaction to responses. Although no independent set of values exists against which the survey results can be compared, the general observations and analyses of language behaviour described in this book should provide some sort of corroboration or refutation. Additionally, the possibility of subjective biases in the design and interpretation of the questionnaire cannot be ruled out, but I believe that worthwhile quantitative research must ultimately draw upon perceptions from ethnographic-style participant-observation. In my case this consists in fourteen years of living in the community.

As for the design of the questionnaire itself, a pilot version was first drawn up and tested, after which it was shortened and revised. Initial considerations were: the determination of potentially significant social variables in language contact; and the amount of personal information that could be expected from informants without causing offence and losing willingness to co-operate. A mixture of thirteen direct open and closed questions on the background of the informants was decided upon, including information on sex, age, region of longest residence, urban/

research-method for studying linguistic attitudes: see Cooper and Fishman (1974); Trudgill and Tzavaras (1977); Zughoul and Taminian (1984). Of particular note is the widespread popularity, in attitude studies, of the matched-guise technique for eliciting judgements on oral input: Lambert *et al.* (1960); Lambert (1967); Giles and Powesland (1975). However, the matched-guise approach did not seem appropriate for this study, which centres on diverse forms in texts and not on the social assessment of a circumscribed variety, i.e. the delivery of a text in a particular code or accent. Furthermore, as has been demonstrated above, the most common encoding of intensive contact in Japan is in the *written* channel, particularly as code-mixing.

rural identification, occupation, education, extent of foreign-language study, experience of living abroad, knowledge and use of other languages; this data is summarized in Tables 6.1–6.2.

Next, six question-boxes, each examining different facets of contact with English, were drawn up. Question-box 1 offers variant orthographic representations of transferred items and aims at finding out the degree of acceptance of innovative forms over established ones by asking informants to mark their preference. Indirectly, this question also reflects the degree of conservatism towards orthographic innovation within the community.

Question-box 2 contains a list of ten signs and labels in the monolingual English style noted and collected from a suburban store/supermarket in Kyoto (Izumiya) somewhat comparable to the British Woolworths. The reason for choosing items from this store was that its target market seems to be the average, not necessarily sophisticated, consumer engaged in shopping in a basic and economical manner, with the linguistic ramifications such an ordinary market-setting implies. Some items appeared on large signs on the wall or on posters above the shopper's heads; others were printed on products such as a tin of coffee, a pack of oranges, biscuits, and a paper bag. The original capitalization and small lettering have been retained. The aim of this section was to test the degree of intelligibility of the monolingual texts by asking informants to provide a Japanese version or translation. In cases where the items are local coinages—for example, SUMMER GIFT (which refers to the custom of sending presents to relatives and others to whom one feels indebted)—the equivalent (*chūgen*) is not directly derivable from the English.

The purpose of question-box 3 was to see if there existed any significant differences in the degree of self-reported usage of foreignisms in terms of age, sex, occupation, etc., and also to compare these results with the degree of loan-word favouritism indicated in question 6. The diverse twenty-five contemporary borrowings for this box were selected on the basis of their high frequency in the mass media, the purpose being to discover to what extent the community associates with, and thus indirectly favours, them. The encircling of the item is, of course, not taken as a true indicator of the informants' usage but merely as signalling their positive identification with the item and their acceptance of it. The words range from a few initial items which are very familiar—(1) *chansu* (< *chance*) and (2) *baibai* (< *bye bye*)—to those which are hardly ever

TABLE 6.1. Informants' Social Background

(a) Sex of informants

	No.	% of all informants
Male	210	46
Female	251	54
Total	461	100

(b) Residential identity of informants

	Male	Female	Total	% of all informants
Urban	186	237	423	92
Rural	24	14	38	8

(d) Occupation of informants

	Male	% of males	Female	% of females	Total	% of all informants
Student	92	44	106	42	198	43
White-collar	72	34	49	20	121	26
Housewife	0		55	22	55	12
Professional	21	10	22	9	43	9
Independent	12	6	6	2	18	4
Skilled manual	9	4	1	0.3	10	2
Part-time/unemployed	2	1	8	3	10	2
Service	0		3	1	3	0.6
Unskilled manual	2	1	1	0.3	3	0.6

(e) Educational background of informants

Attending/completed	Male	% of males	Female	% of females	Total	% of all informants
Primary school	9	4	4	1.5	13	3
Junior high school	16	8	34	13	50	11
Senior high school	44	22	87	34	131	28
University	134	63	125	50	259	56
Postgraduate level	7	3	1	0.3	8	2

(c) Regional identity of informants

Region	No. of informants	% of all informants
Hokkaido	3	1
Tōhoku	0	0
Kantō	50	11
Tōkai	9	2
Hokuriku	5	1
Kinki	309	67
Chūgoku	13	3
Shikoku	45	9
Kyūshū	27	6
Other	0	0

(f) Age of informants

Age band	No. of informants	% of all informants
80–92	5	1.08
70–79	13	2.82
60–69	18	3.90
50–59	63	13.67
40–49	56	12.15
30–39	33	7.16
20–29	183	39.70
25–29*	43	9.33
18–24	173	37.53
13–17	56	12.15
9	1	0.21

* This age-band was included separately in order to discover whether the responses of university students change after graduation.

TABLE 6.2. Informants' Linguistic Background

(a) Number of years of formal English study completed by informants

Years	Male	% of males	Female	% of females	Total	% of all informants
0	17	8	12	5	29	6
1	5	2	2	1	7	1
2	7	3	9	4	16	4
3	15	7	23	9	38	8
4	6	3	10	4	16	4
5	4	2	8	3	12	3
6	33	16	78	31	111	24
7	7	3	11	4	18	4
8	36	17	53	21	89	19
9	16	8	13	5	29	6
10	56	27	26	10	82	18
11	3	1	1	0.3	4	0.8
12	5	2	4	2	9	2
13	0		0		0	
14	0		1	0.3	1	0.2

(e) Self-rated English ability of informants in relation to educational background (1 = none, 2 = fair, 3 = good)

Educational level	L2 rating	Female	Male	Total	% of all informants
Primary	1	3	9	12	3
	2	1	0	2	0.2
	3	0	0	0	
Junior	1	17	8	25	5
	2	17	7	24	5
	3	0	1	1	0.2
Senior	1	60	31	91	20
	2	26	11	37	8
	3	1	2	3	0.7
University	1	58	60	118	26
	2	58	58	116	25
	3	9	16	25	5
Postgraduate	1	0	2	2	0.4
	2	1	1	2	0.4
	3	0	4	4	0.8
Ratings totalled	1	138	109	247	54
	2	103	78	181	39
	3	10	23	33	7

(b) Informants having attended private language-schools (Age range 20–29)

	No.	% of all informants
Male	5	2
Female	22	9
Total	27	6

(c) Number of informants with experience of living overseas (Age range 16–80)

	No.
USA	18
SE Asia	12
Australia	3
UK	3
Italy	1
Kenya	1
France	1
Total	39 (9% of all informants)

(d) Informants using English at work (Age range 21–80)

Sex	No.	Informants using particular skills (as a % of this subgroup)			
		Speaking	Reading	Writing	Listening
Male	27	52	82	63	33
Female	13	69	39	39	23
Total	40	58	68	55	28
As % of all respondents	9				

(f) Informants citing other uses of L2

	No.	% of all informants
At home	2	0.4
With friends	23	5
For travel	2	0.4

(g) Informants having contact with languages other than English

	Male	Female	Total	% of all respondents
German	50	28	78	17
French	25	34	59	13
Chinese	19	5	24	5
Russian	7	0	7	1.5
Spanish	3	3	6	1
Italian	0	3	3	0.6
Manchurian	0	1	1	0.2
Pilipino	1	0	1	0.2
As % of this subgroup	58.7	41.3	39	

heard in daily discourse, although they all derive from texts aimed at the general public.[10]

Question-box 4 presents respondents with five contexts in which to choose between a foreignism and a (Sino-)Japanese alternative—for example, *raisu* (< *rice*) or *gohan* 'cooked rice'. In sentences (1) and (2) the context might trigger the selection of the foreignism by association with the restaurant and the television studio. However, in the remaining three sentences there are not meant to be any suggestions which favour any particular form. Again, the purpose of the box is to determine whether there are any significant correlations between the choices made and social variables, and to provide a means of checking the results with declared attitudes towards language contact in general.

Question-box 5 requires informants to judge ten texts, arranged in order of length, which may also heighten the degree of code-mixing radicalness. The objective is to examine the community's levels of tolerance and acceptance of innovative and, in some cases, quite unorthodox contact-behaviour in advertising and see if these can be correlated with social variables. Texts (2) and (10) are examples of code-switching into the monolingual style which maintain the katakana syllabary as the orthographic medium; the remaining texts are examples of code-mixing. Informants were asked to rate the texts in terms of five reactions, the usual range in the Likert approach. The texts also remind the informants of extreme patterns of contact produced around them and may raise their sensitivity to their attitudes.

Question-box 6 consists of twenty statements for each of which respondents are asked to express a degree of endorsement or rejection. Ten statements concern the topic of language transfer, and the remaining ten relate to ethnocentrism, but the statements are mixed. The rationale behind asking the same basic question ten times is to maximize the chances of a faithful and consistent representation of informants' attitudes. The aim is to compare these scores and correlate them with social variables. The

---

[10] Some are associated with certain age-groups, e.g. (3) *sankyū* (< *thank you*) with children; (20) *ekisaito* (< *excite*) and (21) *yangu* (< *young*) with teenagers; some are dependent on a high level of education and possibly knowledge of English, e.g. (10) *ekizochikku* (< *exotic*), (15) *puraibashī* (< *privacy*), and (19) *dorasutiku* (< *drastic*). There is one locally created abbreviation: (6) *OL* (office lady), and some local coinages, e.g. (9) *purēgaido* (< *play guide* 'ticket agency for entertainment'). Certain items belong to special registers such as sport, e.g. (12) *gōruin* (< *goal in*), and others are still at the innnovative stage and not yet codified, e.g. (24) *furīwākā* (< *free worker*) and (25) *shinseritī* (< *sincerity*). An abbreviated monolingual title is also listed: (8) *Q & A*.

statements are worded in a simple, unambiguous, and direct manner, and their length is intentionally kept short.

The advantages of this correlational approach is that it makes straightforward demands on respondents and is relatively easy to conduct, score, and make inferences from. Seeing the demands clearly set out before them also reassures informants about the structured content of the interaction, and this is an important factor in the Japanese speech-community, where the unknown and the unpredictable are often interpreted as particularly threatening.

Sampling and Questioning

As has been widely documented and analysed, the Japanese do not generally express themselves directly and openly in public, non-intimate settings, where their behaviour tends to be characterized (from a Western perspective) as introverted, circumspect, shy, and uncommitted, as a result of classifying situations and people in terms of insider and outsider frameworks (see Lebra, 1976: ch. 7; Barnlund, 1975). As Lebra (1976: 122) states, one way around the problem of achieving self-disclosure in such situations in Japanese culture is to use 'mediated communication', which involves the use of a mediator who is skilful in manipulating the exchange of messages between *ego* and *alter* in a way that ensures neither loses face. The strategy adopted here in order to get informants to reveal their personal details and viewpoints was to have 'insiders' mediate for the researcher. That is to say, individuals conducted the questionnaire among their own relatives, pupils, co-members of shared interest-groups (political, religious), and other internal networks. A total of thirty-six assistants were recruited among my own Japanese relatives and among final-year undergraduate students of my linguistics seminar at Doshisha University in Kyoto, some of whom were engaged in teaching-practice; they were all given the same precise instructions about how to conduct the questionnaire. This method clearly resolved the invalidating effects of the polite but not necessarily honest responses that might be given to a non-Japanese, or even to a Japanese 'outsider'. At the same time, however, it meant that random sampling was out of the question. The validity of random sampling could not have been guaranteed because of the doubtful sincerity of informant responses. Finally, it should be pointed out that none of the informants were preselected by the researcher; their participation depended on their affiliation with the assistant interviewers alone.

As for the administration of the questionnaire itself, this took place in various settings—predominantly homes, schools, and university campuses, but also temple grounds. All interviewers were told to avoid steering informants towards any preconceivable answer. The anonymity of the questionnaire was one measure to minimize the social desirability effect while the affiliation with the interviewer set up obligations of response honesty. Many of the interviewers reported that their informants reacted as if they were being tested. Younger informants, used to filling out forms and written questions, appeared in general to finish the questionnaire quickly and without much fuss; this may also be related to their greater familiarity with English.

The sample population in this study consisted of 461 informants. This number was determined by various practical limitations: the amount of time which each assistant had available for interviewing; the time required to process the data; and the final number of fully completed questionnaires to be analysed. The sample size of 461 appears large enough to allow for generalizations when one compares it with the numbers involved in other surveys.

General social information about the sample population is summarized in the tables. The ages of the 461 participating informants ranged between 92 and 9. Females made up slightly more than half the total number (54 per cent). This is most probably a reflection of the fact that the assistants who interviewed the greatest number of informants were themselves female. A large number of informants (67 per cent) identified the Kinki region of western Japan as that of longest residence, which is not surprising since this is the principal area in which the interviews were conducted. Furthermore, most informants (92 per cent) claimed to be living in an urban environment, which is to be expected, as the majority of the interviews were carried out in urban settings.[11]

Nine basic classifications were worked out[12] in which to accommodate

---

[11] There is a certain amount of stigma attached to identification with 'ruralness', but this high proportion does not seem unlikely, because the majority of the respondents were interviewed in urban areas and also because 75 per cent of Japan's 121 million citizens live in urban environments of 30,000 inhabitants or more (Yano Tsuneta Kinenkai: 1986). The original wording in the questionnaire sought euphemistically to avoid the directly negative association with *inaka* 'countryside' by referring to either *jinkōmisshūchi* 'a densely built-up area' or *kasochi* 'a depopulated area'. However, this category is not calculated as a factor in the attitudinal correlations.

[12] Cf. Steven (1983), who establishes five basic categories in his analysis of classes in contemporary Japan: bourgeoisie, petty bourgeoisie, peasantry, middle class, and working class.

informants' occupational background as indicated in the questionnaire. This information was then ordered into Table 6.1(*d*). The category *professional* includes those who identified themselves as, for example, teachers, doctors, dentists, priests, or engineers. This group made up only 9 per cent of the total sample and included respondents who had undergone a long period of training before taking up the sorts of employment that are generally associated with high social status in Japanese society.[13]

The category *independent* includes those informants who described themselves as, for instance, shopkeepers, farmers, or fishermen—that is to say, small entrepreneurs;[14] they made up only 4 per cent of the total sample. In the few cases where the decision as to whether informants belonged in this category or in that of *skilled manual* was problematic (no detailed description of employment was required on the questionnaire), the final classification was reached on the basis of the interviewers' additional comments and evaluation of the nature of the occupation; however, this group is underrepresented here.[15]

The category *white-collar worker* generally includes those who declared themselves to be office workers, banking staff, or civil servants. In fact, this category highlights the problems of applying Western conceptions of class to Japanese society, for included here are those with high-ranking white-collar positions, particularly among those over 40, with a university education, who should be considered part of the bourgeoisie (see Steven, 1983). On the other hand, also according to Steven (1983: 171), the appropriate classification of almost all women between 35 and 54 and certain males under 35 employed by non-major companies[16] involved in white-collar work should be as working class, because of their comparatively limited conditions. Of course, it is not possible within the confines of this book, to enter into a discussion of the value and validity of the concept of class in Japan and the West; nor would it serve our direct

[13] Steven (1983) calls this group 'middle class' and estimates their size at 6.9 per cent of the national population.

[14] This category includes groups which are considered separately in Steven's analysis (1983) because it includes both the 'petty bourgeoisie' and the 'peasantry'.

[15] Cf. Steven's estimation (1983: 319) of the size of the petty bourgeoisie at 17.3 per cent of the national population and of the peasantry at 9.5 per cent, making up 26.8 per cent of the active work-force.

[16] Cf. Steven (1983: 162): 'The educational background of a company's workers . . . seems to justify it as a first-, second-, or third-rate company, just as education seems to lie behind distinctions among members of a company . . . the fundamental basis of one's livelihood appears to be the type of company one works in.'

purpose. Instead, it should just be borne in mind that class conscious-ness in Japan today is relatively weak, with the great majority of people sharing middle-class incomes, ambitions, attitudes, and life-styles. This middle-class identification is amply illustrated in annual government public-opinion surveys, in which as many as 90 per cent of respondents unfailingly place themselves in the broad middle-class.

As for other occupational categories in the survey, the fourth group was that of *skilled manual* workers, who made up only 2 per cent of the total; respondents who designated themselves as craftsmen or carpenters are represented here. However, it is highly likely that these are also self-employed and could be considered in conjunction with the *independent* category. *Unskilled manual* workers, the fifth category, constituted only 0.6 per cent of the total sample. Both these categories are obviously underrepresented here, since about 30 per cent of the national work-force are employed in factories or workshops.

Similarly, the sixth category, which grouped together those involved in the *service* sector, was also underrepresented, with only 0.6 per cent appearing in the sample whereas 14 per cent of the national work-force are involved in selling.

The seventh category, of *part-time* workers, may also include the un-employed, since this is often how working people designate themselves because of the stigma associated with the term 'unemployed'. It is not coincidental that 80 per cent of this category is female. The sample pro-portion of 2 per cent is also very low, since as much as 25 per cent of the active work-force probably belongs to this category, at least two-thirds of which is female. This underrepresentation is almost certainly a reflection of the middle-level socio-economic background of the interviewers and their corresponding networks; connected with this is the figure of 38 per cent for adult women respondents identifying themselves as *housewives* (the eighth category), in other words classifying themselves as not involved in work outside the home.

The final category, *student*, is clearly overrepresented at 43 per cent, which is nearly double the national number of those attending institu-tions of education (23 per cent). The highly educated are also over-represented, with 56 per cent of the sample attending, or having attended, university; but this appears less inflated when one considers that 42 per cent of high-school students now go on to higher education. Of course, these overrepresentations are a direct consequence of the fact that the majority of the interviewers themselves were university students or graduates. As a result, the attitudes of young, educated Japanese under 22 receive considerable weighting in this sample. However, this should not necessarily be viewed as a deficiency, because it is precisely these generations who are most in touch with developments in linguistic contact and are most likely to exert influences on its future socio-linguistic course.[17]

From the tables it emerges that the size of the different groupings in the sample reflects the sex, socio-economic background, and networks of the interviewers. Thus, it turned out that the greatest number of questionnaires were conducted under the supervision of female, university-educated assistants. It is unfortunate, in this affiliation-based data-collection, that the proportion of skilled and unskilled manual, part-time, and service workers (totalling 5.2 per cent) was so low, and, with hindsight, it is clear that interviewers from less educated and lower socio-economic groups should have been recruited, even though they were outside the range of the researcher's own network. The implication for the present sample is that it offers a predominantly middle-class set of attitudes. Nevertheless, this is not such a distortion, because it is precisely this social group which is particularly concerned with the maintenance and control of linguistic forms, especially when it comes to the written channel.

Next, certain important aspects of the informants' linguistic background will be briefly discussed, with reference to the data shown in Tables 6.2 (*a–g*)). Although nearly three-quarters of the informants had received as much as six years of instruction in English, one has to allow for the effects of attrition over time, and for the generally low levels of proficiency attained in the school system. None the less, the sample includes a substantial proportion of informants (21 per cent) with ten or more years of instruction in English.

The results for self-rated English ability shown in Table 6.2(*e*) are not surprising, given the local, cultural pressures for modesty and under-statement in self-presentation. The table shows that 54 per cent judge themselves as having no competence in English at all; women seem to have less confidence than men.

Of the entire sample, only 6 per cent have sought to improve their foreign language at a private language-school, and these have been mainly young females under 29. Equally few (9 per cent) need English at work, and the skill in most demand there is, predictably, reading. The overall

---

[17] It is important to remember with regard to Table 6.1*d* that age is not indicated, so that e.g. those whose education finished at primary school and those currently attending primary school appear together.

picture of a monolingual society is reinforced by the minute percentage who use a language other than Japanese outside work or school, which stands at 6 per cent. The low level of contact with non-Japanese is reflected in the fact that only 5 per cent use English to communicate with 'friends'; the 0.4 per cent who use a language other than Japanese at home were children who had grown up overseas and maintained it as a private language with siblings. On the other hand, although the proportion with experience of living abroad, for periods ranging from 1 month to 8 years, was as high as 9 per cent, it must not be forgotten that Japanese abroad often tend to confine their interaction to their own ethnic network, often establishing microcosmic communities overseas. Interestingly enough, however, nearly half of those who had resided overseas had done so in the USA, reflecting the strong Japanese connections with the latter and supporting the view of the USA as the main external source of direct contact.

As for exposure to languages other than English, the next most commonly studied language was German, listed by as many as 17 per cent of informants, particularly among well-educated males of middle age or older. In most cases, the third language was a European one—German, French, Russian, Spanish, or Italian—and was learnt in an institutional setting for, typically, two years, so that only very low levels of competence, if any, can be expected in most cases. The acquisition of Chinese as a third language either follows the latter institutional pattern or, exceptionally, occurs during residence overseas.[18]

A final and important observation is that since no radical or unaccountable divergences[19] between the male and female data concerning social and linguistic background are detectable, a certain degree of consistency in the sample can be inferred.

Results of the Survey

Before an analysis of the results is undertaken, the scoring and processing of the data will be briefly described. The questionnaire is divided into six

[18] This also applies to the acquisition of Manchurian and Pilipino.

[19] e.g. the lower number of females in white-collar work or with/in university and postgraduate education, in spite of their greater numbers in the sample, is, of course, connected to the role-expectations and socio-economic opportunities for women, which are traditionally below those for men; the latter also explains why fewer females use English at work and fewer study a third language at university level; similarly, far fewer females have overseas experience. The sexual divergence in self-rated ability in English may be attributable to conformity to cultural expectations concerning the gender role of a modest, unassuming female.

sections, the last section being split into two parts: Language Contact (questions 1, 4, 6, 8, 11, 12, 14, 15, 16, and 19) and Ethnocentrism (questions 2, 3, 5, 7, 9, 10, 13, 17, 18, and 20), resulting in seven scores:

Question-box	Score
1	8
2	70
3	25
4	5
5	50
6: Language contact	50
6: Ethnocentrism	50

Each of the eight innovative orthographic variants in question-box 1 scores one point; these are *rēnkōto, vitamin, ripōto, tyūristo, terefon, bīrisu/bairasu, handobaggu,* and *jenerēshon*; the established forms score zero. In box 2 successful renderings in Japanese of the first six compound-nouns (from 'summer gift' to 'family orange pack') score a maximum of 5 points, while the four longer phrases each score a maximum of 10. The scoring was carried out only by the investigator, so that judgements of the rendering were consistent. In question-box 3, informants scored one point for each of the twenty-five loan-words they selected as part of their usage. The scoring for box 4 is similar to that for box 1, in that informants receive one point for a foreignism and zero for a Japanese equivalent. Box 5 offers five attitudinal labels and these are scored as follows: (*a*) 5, (*i*) 4, (*u*) 3, (*e*) 2, and (*o*) 1, so when these are applied to the ten texts, the maximum score possible is 50 and the minimum 10. The sixth and last section involves a more complicated scheme of scoring depending on the selection from the five ranges of opinions. If informants strongly support language contact and are strongly in favour of contact with the West, they score 5 points for each statement. If they are strongly against both these issues, they score only one point, while those who neither agree nor disagree score 3. Those who somewhat agree or disagree score 2 or 4, obtaining a higher score if they support borrowing and Western contacts.

The questionnaires were scored by the investigator, and the responses were put into tabular form according to age and sex, with details of social and linguistic background included. Next, with the assistance of a computer programmer and using an NEC (Nippon Electronics Corporation) computer N5200/05, this information was first entered into a data base (LANFILE 4), after which histograms were obtained by applying an

NEC software program entitled LANSTAT 3, which can carry out simple descriptive statistical analysis.

A general homogeneity in the responses across the majority of inform- ant categories (for all but question 2) is instantly observable in Tables 6.3–6.9. This corroborates with the widespread characterization of Japan- ese society as one with a high degree of shared values and suggests that such consensus extends to language behaviour. Furthermore, the attitu- dinal similarity across most question-categories points to an internal logic that validates the findings. The inferences to be drawn from the tables are, of course, limited to the psychological levels of awareness and evalu- ation, but these are essential stages preceding and predicting the adoption of innovations.

Before the most salient aspects of the results are discussed, certain categories in the tables require explanation:

- 'Total' refers to the total 461 informants in the sample.
- 'Basic Eng. (> 40 Q. 2)' refers to those informants who scored more than 40 in question 2, which tests understanding of the monolingual English style; this score is taken as an indicator of a basic level of passive English competence.
- The difference between the category 'Student' and the age-group '18–24' is that the latter includes those who now engaged in the work-force.

Table 6.3 clearly demonstrates that the favouring of radical loan-word orthography increases with the length of the informants' education; those with postgraduate status are the most progressive, while those of primary background are the most conservative. Occupationally, a similar tendency is observable, with professionals and white-collar workers the least con- formist; the latter categories, of course, correlate with higher levels of education. Acceptability is higher among those in their twenties than among older groups, but this radicalness is not found among those in their early teens, probably because they are more sensitive to norm adherence. Basic English comprehension correlates with a slightly higher tolerance of orthographic innovation than average. The table suggests that the potential adopters and disseminators of the innovative repres- entation of foreignisms are: those who experience higher education; and those in their twenties. These groups are the least hostile to the norm changes necessary in order to narrow phonological differences between English and Japanese.

Table 6.4 presents the greatest heterogeneity among the findings: wide divergence (over 1,000 per cent) between different informant-categories

TABLE 6.3. Community Acceptance of Innovative Orthography for Transferring English (Question 1)

Informant category	Average score[a]	
		0 5 10 15 20 25 30
Total	1.9	s = 1.2
Male	2.0	s = 1.3
Female	1.8	s = 1.2
Primary	1.2	s = 1.1
Junior	1.4	s = 0.9
Senior	1.9	s = 1.2
University	2.1	s = 1.3
Postgraduate	3.1	s = 1.2
Basic Eng. (> 40 Q. 2)	2.2	s = 1.3
Professional	1.9	s = 1.4
Independent	1.1	s = 0.8
White-collar	2.1	s = 1.3
Skilled manual	1.2	s = 1.1
Unskilled	1.6	s = 0.6
Service	1.3	s = 0.6
Part-time	2.4	s = 1.0
Housewife	1.4	s = 1.0
Student	2.1	s = 1.2
80–92	1.6	s = 2.0
70–79	1.3	s = 1.0
60–69	1.2	s = 1.1
50–59	2.0	s = 1.2
40–49	1.7	s = 1.1
30–39	1.6	s = 1.3
20–29	2.2	s = 1.3
25–29	2.2	s = 1.3
18–24	2.2	s = 1.3
13–17	1.7	s = 1.1

[a] Maximum points = 8.

TABLE 6.4. Community Comprehension of Commercial Contact with English (Question 2)

Informant category	Average score[a]		
		0 5 10 15 20 25 30 35 40 45	
Total	33.7		s = 20.6
Male	34.5		s = 21.7
Female	33.0		s = 19.5
Primary	3.5		s = 4.7
Junior	17.7		s = 15.1
Senior	28.4		s = 18.3
University	40.8		s = 19.3
Postgraduate	40.1		s = 16.7
Professional	32.1		s = 20.7
Independent	13.9		s = 13.4
White-collar	34.9		s = 19.9
Skilled manual	13.3		s = 22.8
Unskilled	3.7		s = 6.4
Service	39.3		s = 4.0
Part-time	35.9		s = 19.7
Housewife	25.7		s = 19.4
Student	38.5		s = 19.6
80–92	16.0		s = 30.3
70–79	9.2		s = 10.0
60–69	14.3		s = 12.3
50–59	26.0		s = 20.5
40–49	29.2		s = 20.1
30–39	35.1		s = 15.0
20–29	43.7		s = 18.6
25–29	41.7		s = 19.0
18–24	42.9		s = 18.2
13–17	25.1		s = 16.6

[a] Maximum points = 70.

in the comprehension of commercial Anglicization is visible. Nevertheless, certain trends already observed in Table 6.3 re-emerge, together with new patterns:

- A pronounced and steady increase in comprehension occurs with each level of education until university.
- The 'upper' professions, apart from 'independents', evidence distinctly more competence in English than blue-collar informants, but they are surpassed by those categorized as 'service' and 'part-time', who, in this sample, reveal high levels of English comprehension.
- English understanding markedly decreases with age, and consequently those over 60 are bound to suffer from decoding frustration; even those who attended university show signs of attrition. Interestingly, comprehension among young teenagers is comparable to that of those in their fifties, suggesting no significant rise in the level of community bilingualism in the near future.
- Females' understanding of the monolingual style is only minimally less than that of males, and the difference is most probably due to the fact that fewer enter higher education.
- A very interesting finding is that the total average level of comprehension lies only at 33.7 per cent of the monolingual items in Box 2 (App. 2), with even the highest still only at 43.7 per cent. This indicates that certainly more than half of the monolingual English style must remain semantically opaque and unknown to community members. This indirectly suggests that the message in commercial Anglicization tends to be less valued than mere form; such an interpretation would also account for the lack of concern for norm adherence and lexical 'meaningfulness' by contact agents in media and marketing.

Table 6.5 shows that there may be variation of up to 85 per cent in the degree of community identification with foreignisms, again noticeably rising with length of education and grade of occupation, being particularly marked in those with backgrounds in higher education. As for age bands, those between 25 and 29 demonstrate the highest level of identification; their pronounced favouring of loan-words provides the basis for the future expansion of English transfer into the community. Significantly, after 50 there is a steady decrease in loan-word identification, reinforcing the association of borrowing-behaviour with youth. Although over-reporting among informants may have taken place here, the conclusion that seems to emerge, namely that the most ready adopters and disseminators of foreignisms are to be found among young people and those with higher educational and occupational backgrounds does not seem unreasonable, given that these groups are the most exposed to

TABLE 6.5. Community Identification with English-based Foreignisms (Question 3)

Informant category	Average score[a]	
Total	12.7	s = 5.1
Male	12.2	s = 5.3
Female	13.2	s = 4.9
Primary	9.2	s = 6.3
Junior	11.8	s = 5.5
Senior	13.0	s = 4.9
University	13.0	s = 4.9
Postgraduate	11.3	s = 6.3
Basic Eng. (> 40 Q. 2)	13.1	s = 4.7
Professional	13.6	s = 5.4
Independent	10.7	s = 5.7
White-collar	13.5	s = 5.2
Skilled manual	11.3	s = 6.8
Unskilled	12.0	s = 2.6
Service	13.7	s = 4.2
Part-time	11.8	s = 4.6
Housewife	14.1	s = 4.4
Student	12.0	s = 5.0
80–92	8.0	s = 6.4
70–79	12.5	s = 6.2
60–69	13.7	s = 5.5
50–59	14.1	s = 4.8
40–49	13.5	s = 5.1
30–39	12.2	s = 6.4
20–29	12.8	s = 4.5
25–29	14.8	s = 3.7
18–24	12.1	s = 4.6
13–17	11.4	s = 5.8

[a] Maximum points = 25.

English. Finally, it should be noted that a basic competence in English does not significantly alter the degree of loan-word identification.

In Table 6.6 extreme variation occurs in only three categories: the lowest community preference for foreignisms is found among those in skilled manual and unskilled occupations, and the highest among service workers. The variation across other categories does not appear dramatically significant, although a small but steadily increasing avoidance or disfavouring of foreignisms is observable as informants age; all those under 24 evidence higher levels of preference than the total average.

Table 6.7 reveals only small-scale divergence (35 per cent) across the social categories in the evaluation of radical code-mixing, implying mild approval on a community-wide basis. However, the most severe in their judgement are those with the highest educational background: postgraduates. Could this be because they are more puristic and prescriptive with regard to Japanese, or more sensitive to donor norms? Serious decoding problems, which are likely among the elderly, do not seem to affect approval ratings; surprisingly, those between 60 and 79 present the highest evaluations of code-mixing. This remarkable tolerance for a radically Anglicized style across diverse categories, averaging at 56 per cent, challenges the stereotype of the Japanese speech-community as ultra-conservative, and also explains why such styles can come into existence. The slightly higher approval of code-mixing by females than males may be attributed to social constraints on the former to restrain their expression of disapproval.

The measurement of positive attitude towards contact with English in Table 6.8 similarly reveals a distinct consistency in responses expressing reserved support for the phenomenon, averaging at 63 per cent. Only one out of the twenty-seven categories presents a value under 29: unskilled workers (25). In Table 6.4 this group was seen to have one of the lowest levels of comprehension of English, comparable to that of individuals in primary education, who can also be seen, in Table 6.8, to be the next least-favourably disposed to Western borrowing. A common characteristic of both these groups, in addition to lack of ability in English, is a limited span of education. The most positive evaluation of borrowing comes from the service and independent category. The reaction of the former group is understandable, given that English transfers are an essential component of service communication. Also of note is the fact that the most positive responses in the age categories are to be found among the youngest and oldest. In fact, respondents between 80 and 92 show

TABLE 6.6. Community Preference for Established Foreignisms over Japanese Alternatives (Question 4)

Informant category	Average score[a]	
		0 5 10 15 20 25 30 35
Total	3.0	s = 1.3
Male	2.9	s = 1.3
Female	3.1	s = 1.3
Primary	2.4	s = 1.2
Junior	3.0	s = 1.1
Senior	3.1	s = 1.3
University	3.0	s = 1.3
Postgraduate	2.5	s = 1.5
Basic Eng. (> 40 Q. 2)	3.1	s = 1.3
Professional	2.8	s = 1.4
Independent	2.4	s = 1.2
White-collar	2.4	s = 0.8
Skilled manual	1.3	s = 1.5
Unskilled	1.3	s = 1.5
Service	3.7	s = 1.5
Part-time	2.6	s = 1.5
Housewife	2.6	s = 1.3
Student	3.3	s = 1.2
80–92	2.8	s = 1.3
70–79	2.5	s = 1.2
60–69	2.9	s = 1.6
50–59	2.7	s = 1.4
40–49	2.5	s = 1.3
30–39	2.8	s = 1.3
20–29	3.1	s = 1.3
25–29	2.8	s = 1.3
18–24	3.3	s = 1.3
13–17	3.4	s = 1.0

[a] Maximum points = 5.

TABLE 6.7. Community Evaluation of Radical and Innovative Code-Mixing
(Question 5)

Informant category	Average score[a]		
Total	28.0		s = 5.3
Male	27.0		s = 5.4
Female	28.8		s = 5.2
Primary	26.8		s = 8.4
Junior	28.4		s = 4.9
Senior	29.0		s = 4.8
University	27.6		s = 5.4
Postgraduate	23.4		s = 6.2
Basic Eng. (> 40 Q. 2)	27.0		s = 5.0
Professional	28.2		s = 5.7
Independent	29.7		s = 5.4
White-collar	28.3		s = 5.3
Skilled manual	31.0		s = 5.0
Unskilled	27.3		s = 3.8
Service	32.0		s = 6.1
Part-time	28.5		s = 4.1
Housewife	28.9		s = 4.0
Student	27.3		s = 5.3
80–92	26.6		s = 4.4
70–79	31.5		s = 4.2
60–69	30.2		s = 3.1
50–59	27.9		s = 5.4
40–49	27.8		s = 4.4
30–39	27.9		s = 5.6
20–29	28.1		s = 5.1
25–29	28.4		s = 5.2
18–24	27.5		s = 5.4
13–17	28.6		s = 5.4

[a] Maximum points = 50.

TABLE 6.8. Positive Attitude towards Language Contact in the Community (Question 6a)

Informant category	Average score[a]	s
Total	31.5	s = 5.5
Male	31.7	s = 5.6
Female	31.3	s = 5.4
Primary	29.2	s = 6.3
Junior	32.0	s = 6.6
Senior	32.1	s = 4.5
University	31.3	s = 5.6
Postgraduate	29.8	s = 3.2
Basic Eng. (> 40 Q. 2)	31.0	s = 5.4
Professional	30.7	s = 5.9
Independent	33.2	s = 5.2
White-collar	32.0	s = 4.3
Skilled manual	30.7	s = 4.4
Unskilled	25.0	s = 2.8
Service	34.0	s = 7.6
Part-time	32.3	s = 4.9
Housewife	30.5	s = 4.2
Student	31.8	s = 5.5
80–92	33.0	s = 2.2
70–79	31.9	s = 4.2
60–69	30.6	s = 5.8
50–59	31.5	s = 5.4
40–49	30.9	s = 4.3
30–39	31.7	s = 4.6
20–29	31.7	s = 5.2
25–29	31.6	s = 4.8
18–24	31.5	s = 5.3
13–17	33.1	s = 5.2

[a] Maximum points = 50.

a noticeable tendency, throughout the survey, to be more supportive of borrowing-behaviour than are individuals between 60 and 79. Could there be some connection with the fact that the former did not experience their education during the totalitarian period prior to, and during, the Second World War; or is the octogenarian sample unrepresentatively liberal? Sex does not appear a significant variable here. The general inference from Table 6.8 is that informants feel neither saturated by, nor hostile towards, current levels of contact, even though they were directly confronted with its most radical manifestations in the questionnaire.

In spite of the characterization of the Japanese as strongly ethnocentric, Table 6.9 demonstrates that there is a strong level of support (70 per cent as a total average) for external cultural models, which are generally equated with Western, or simply American, ones by the community. Since the cross-category variation in response, constituting only 16 per cent, is the lowest of all in the survey, broad community consensus on this matter is evident. Again, it is worth observing the steady increase in positive attitude, saliently rising by one point at each stage of education, with postgraduates the most favourable. Those in higher professions are much less ethnocentric than those in lower professions, and slightly less so than students. It is also clear that all those over 25 show greater support than do teenagers and those in their early twenties, suggesting that full adulthood brings a more positive evaluation of external models.

When conclusions are drawn from the survey as a whole, it must be remembered that the results can offer implications only for written, not for oral contact with English.

As a first conclusion, one can say that sex appears not to be a significant variable. On the other hand, informants with higher educational backgrounds and higher occupations, and those aged between 18 and 29, do indicate a stronger tendency to accept and adopt English-based innovations, indirectly pointing to members of these groups as the agents for dissemination of such innovations into everyday communication-styles. Generally, a broad level of tolerance and reserved approval for language contact with English is observable in the community, even though older and less educated members often fail to comprehend it adequately. This community approbation signifies that from now on the chances that such Anglicization will intensify are high, provided future socio-political conditions coincide with those prevailing today. Attitudinal disparity does not feature prominently in the survey, and this results in an impression of a community with highly shared values and understandings.

TABLE 6.9. Positive Attitude towards External (Western) Cultural Models (Question 6*b*)

Informant category	Average score[a]	
Total	34.8	s = 5.0
Male	34.8	s = 5.4
Female	34.9	s = 4.6
Primary	32.2	s = 4.6
Junior	33.4	s = 6.1
Senior	34.8	s = 3.9
University	35.2	s = 5.2
Postgraduate	36.9	s = 2.5
Basic Eng. (> 40 Q. 2)	35.3	s = 4.9
Professional	36.0	s = 5.2
Independent	35.1	s = 4.3
White-collar	35.6	s = 3.9
Skilled manual	31.7	s = 4.3
Unskilled	32.5	s = 0.7
Service	36.0	s = 6.6
Part-time	32.0	s = 5.3
Housewife	34.9	s = 3.8
Student	34.7	s = 4.7
80–92	36.6	s = 4.4
70–79	33.7	s = 5.1
60–69	33.1	s = 5.2
50–59	35.5	s = 4.2
40–49	34.9	s = 4.5
30–39	36.4	s = 3.5
20–29	35.4	s = 4.5
25–29	36.1	s = 3.6
18–24	34.7	s = 4.8
13–17	34.6	s = 4.4

[a] Maximum points = 50.

7

The Functions of Language Contact
in Japan Today

The diverse purposes behind Japanese contact with the English language constitute the final topic to be dealt with in this work. Certain functions of Anglicization in media contexts can already be discerned from the description presented in Chapter 5, particularly as regards the switching and mixing of codes. Now it is necessary to shift the focus from the transferred items themselves to their producers, and to ponder why people choose to lexify with foreignisms. Such a functional perspective requires consideration of the stylistic and symbolic dimensions of contact behaviour, but because neither of these fields as yet offers a widely accepted, ready-made paradigm for approaching the problem, a novel, exploratory framework will be suggested.

The most common factors cited as motives for language contact are collected in Table 7.1[1,2] in an effort to clarify the extent to which they relate to the Japanese setting. Of course, most investigators have treated the motivations for borrowing and for code-switching/-mixing as separate matters. However, in our description of the contact processes taking place in Japan today, it should by now be obvious that borrowing constitutes only one type of contact among many others, such as hybridization, monolingual Anglicization, creative coining, acronaming, code-mixing, so that a complete functional explanation of the Japanese case must treat all these phenomena as a coherent whole. Furthermore, research into the motivational aspects of language contact has been fragmented, and no unified model or theory has emerged beyond the Weinreichian foundations established in the early 1950s.

If a rational conception of social behaviour is adopted, many of the

---

[1] This inventory is a summary of the findings of various researchers. For borrowing, see Weinreich (1953: 56–61); Appel and Muysken (1987); Mosha (1971). For code-switching or mixing, Gumperz (1964, 1982); Hatch (1976); Scotton and Ury (1977); Gal (1979); Brown and Levinson (1979); Saville-Troike (1982); Breitborde (1983); and Fasold (1984: 200–9).

[2] The motivations listed under (11) derive from Pfitzner's (1978) analysis of English loans in German newspaper language.

TABLE 7.1. An Inventory of Language-Contact Functions

Observed motivations for borrowing-behaviour

1. To fill lexical gaps economically through donor transfer rather than recipient resources.
2. To display knowledge of a second or foreign language for social prestige or status.
3. To respond to cultural influences from outside the community.
4. To replace words that are rare in one language.
5. To resolve homophony in one language.
6. To provide synonyms, especially affective vocabulary.
7. To create new semantic distinctions.
8. To produce new pejorative and/or humorous vocabulary.
9. As 'accidental' transfer through intensive biligualism.
10. To entertain—as a piece of adventure, fun, glamour.
11. To achieve stylistic effects such as:
    i. A particular, local, technical, or social flavour.
    ii. Emphasis or vividness; attracting attention.
    iii. Linguistic economy or precision.
    iv. Marking a tone such as humour, parody, or irony.
    v. Enhancing or depreciating semantic/stylistic value, as well as providing euphemisms and pejorative connotations (cf. nos. 6 and 8).

Observed motivations for code-switching/code-mixing

12. To discuss a topic more appropriately.
13. To mark a particular identity, role relation, or status, and, related to this, to symbolize solidarity or the degree of social distance.
14. To redefine the situation or its tone ('metaphoric switching').
15. As a rhetorical device to soften, emphasize, or intensify communication (cf. no. 11).
16. To quote, make asides, reiterate, or summarize.
17. To express or assert expertise (cf. no. 2).
18. To cater for affection, humour, swearing (cf. nos. 8 and 10).
19. To include, exclude, or identify an interactant.
20. To avoid unfamiliar or tabooed items (cf. no. 6).
21. To repair discourse.

motivations listed in Table 7.1 can be taken as goal-directed strategies carried out by people when communicating. This strategic notion is readily applicable to function types (2), (6), (8), (10), and (11), while types (4) and (9) turn out to be only indirect, or even arbitrary, consequences— but not functions—of language contact. As for types (1) and (3), these may also be understood as strategies of encoding, because in these cases agents of language contact decided not to seek for an equivalent in native lexical resources.

The term 'strategy' itself is undeniably problematic, and it will receive fuller treatment below; but the following quotation should serve as sufficient introductory clarification of the concept.

We do not mean to imply that what we dub *strategies* are necessarily conscious. For the most part they do not seem to be, but when interactional mistakes occur, or actors try to manipulate others, they may very well emerge into awareness. And they are open to introspection . . . We cannot pretend to have any special insight into what is probably the biggest single stumbling block to theory throughout the social sciences: the nature of the unconscious and preconscious where all the most important determinants of action seem to lie. We continue to used the word strategy, despite its connotations of conscious deliberation, because we can think of no other word that will imply a rational element while covering both (a) innovative plans of action, which may still be (but need not be) unconscious, and (b) routines—that is, previously constructed plans whose original rational origin is still preserved in their construction, despite their present automatic application as ready-made programmes. (Brown and Levinson, 1979: 90)

Table 7.1 demonstrates the multifunctionality of contact behaviour and the inadequacy of any monocausal approach. Although many researchers have made disparaging comments on the assignability of a functional value to code-alternating phenomena,[3] many of the purposes mentioned

---

[3] e.g. Scotton (1983: 122) finds that code-switching 'has no single motivation. It may be unmarked, a marked, or an exploratory choice'. Sankoff (1971) does not believe in a 'predictive approach' because, although variables such as participants, topic, context, channel, message-form—including 'trigger words' (Clyne: 1967, 1978)—mood, tone, and intentions may each motivate switching, certain cases defy explanation. On the other hand, Gumperz (1982: 70) strongly disputes the arbitrariness of code-alternation, declaring that 'if members can agree on interpretations of switching in context and on categorizing others on the basis of their switching, there must be some regularities and shared perceptions on which these judgements can be based', not deriving from the grammatical but the stylistic or symbolic level. Gibbons (1987: 129) also states: 'the nature of the influence upon code choice appears to be probabilistic rather than absolute', and he identifies three major factors as correlating with code choice: topic, social situation (time, place), and identity (characteristics).

in Table 7.1 can be, and have been, shown to apply to the case of present-day contact in Japan:

- The case of filling lexical gaps (function 1) has been identified earlier, in Chapter 4, in connection with modernization and non-abstract referencing.
- Function 2, concerning prestige, has been repeatedly illustrated in the discussion on the monolingual style of marketing and consumer-oriented product-labelling and packaging in the texts appearing in Chapter 4.
- The section on semantics in Chapter 4 also clearly demonstrated the lexical response to westernizing cultural influences listed as a very broad type of cause (function 3).
- Function 4 revealed itself in the cases of relexification mentioned in the early part of Chapter 4 and the survey described in Chapter 6. Of course, speakers do not initially set out to replace native words, but wave-like forces within the community eventually lead to such results.
- No example of function 5 could be discerned in the data under study.
- Function 6 will be discussed in depth below, particularly with regard to the use of English-based resources for slang and euphemism in Japanese, but the widespread occurrence of English-derived synonymy should already be obvious from the preceding presentation.
- Synonyms as mentioned under function 6 are associatively and collocatively different from those referred to under function 7: the former are differentiated from their Japanese equivalents by their altered defining components as a result of Western acculturation: *gyūnyū* 'fresh milk' ~ *miruku* 'condensed milk'.
- Function 8 will be treated fully below, under the use of foreign resources for slang and euphemism, but has already been mentioned in Chapter 4, when the use of English vocabulary in commercial reference to the sexual sphere was discussed.
- Function 9 has probably occurred in Japanese contact-processes but conclusive identification would require direct observation. Such cases have been anecdotally recorded when Japanese journalists working abroad come under pressure to report back quickly on overseas news in Japanese and as a result unconsciously introduce hitherto unknown foreign words into their articles because they are totally familiar with them and do not think about their problematic decodability; despite the novelty, their compatriots back home take to the new terms, which then enter the community's lexical inventory.
- Finally, when it comes to the style-linked motivations mentioned in (10) and (11), the code-switching in pop songs and advertising has been shown to conjure up a world that is geographically and socially exotic. Morphological script-mixing such as THE 通販 (cf. Table 5.2 (2)) provides an element of fun as well as attracting attention. In fact, it is easy to see how most of the

monolingual or code-mixed styles used by advertisers in the texts are both an attempt to attract attention and a means of emphasizing or establishing notions of glamour. They may also provide entertainment, either by serving as a kind of 'puzzle', to be decoded by interested receivers in the community with limited English competence, or by constituting provocative, and even humorous, acts of Japanese norm-breaking creativity.

Although the distinction between borrowing and code-switching/-mixing is far from clear-cut, speaker consciousness of the foreignness of the transfer, which is dependent on the degree of assimilation, is often taken as a significant factor in contact behaviour. In fact, all of the general motivations for code alternation in Table 7.1 (12–21) can be interpreted as strategies of people involved in language contact. Although these functions should not necessarily be expected to occur in every contact-setting, only one type (5) was not instantly identifiable in the material we have seen so far.

For instance, most technical, scientific, and commercial topics (function 12) depend on extensive English-based terminologies, as do the modern fields of sport, fashion, cosmetics, food, and music, and this results in a high frequency of English loans in related texts, often producing code-mixing

It is definitely not coincidental that in a great many of the contexts of contact with English discussed above the social relations between interactants (function 13) are characterized by their distant, anonymous, public, and semi-formal nature. As for the occurrence of Anglicization in intimate, casual relations, this will be dealt with below, in connection with English-based slang, humour (function 18), and taboo terms (function 20).

The Western-intensifying and Western-emphasizing effects of Anglicization (function 15) should be self-evident from the above description of the occurrence of monolingual, bilingual, and code-mixed styles in marketing, advertising, titles, and other forms of labels.

The graphic layout of the monolingual style, marking it off as spatially separate from the rest of the text—for example, as a headline or label (cf. Chapter 4, and Chapter 5)—corresponds closely to strategy 16, where code-switching functions as an aside or quotation. Additionally, it should be noted that, because of low levels of bilingualism, for a considerable number of community members the English word(s) really constitute only a peripheral text, since the reader focuses primarily on what is instantly decodable—that is, the Japanese text.

The value of Anglicization as a marker of expertise has not been directly treated but is reflected in the prevalence of technical terms in, for instance, the short, commercial code-mixing in Chapter 5, Fig. 5.5 especially examples 6, 7, and 8, which incorporate many English-derived terms to stress the professional and specialist qualities of their services. Of course, all technical terms carry the implication of expertise in that they require specialist understanding from both user and decoder. Furthermore, this aspect of expertise is closely related to the prestige value of the source language mentioned above as function 2, and to the perceived need to handle technical topics more appropriately through borrowing (cf. function 12).

The use of Anglicization to mark off an identifiable decoder (function 20) has frequently been seen in the setting under study, with particular reference to (would-be) youthful and 'trendy' consumers. This targeting of English lexis at a specific audience is demonstrated in the way that consumer settings specifically aimed at teenaged customers and those in their twenties—fast-food shops, discotheques, specific restaurants or boutiques—rely heavily on written English resources for describing, naming, and labelling products. Of course, this linguistic behaviour is not intended deliberately to exclude customers of older generations, who are often not interested in the particular products offered anyway; but it does lead to the restrictive association of much consumer Anglicization exclusively with the 'young marker'. This is evidenced in the favouring of the monolingual style to adorn apparel and other goods for the young, to serve in the titles and contents of their magazines (cf. Chapter 4, Fig. 4.7), and to figure on their album covers (Chapter 5, Fig. 5.2) and in their pop-song refrains (Chapter 5, Fig. 5.3). This exploitation of English lexification for the targeting of specific audiences is obviously bound to its semiotic potential as an identity marker (function 13).

Code-mixing is rarely observable as a repair strategy (21) in Japanese contact with English but may occur when speakers realize they have made a mistake with, or are confused about, a foreignism and revert to their own language in order to maintain communication. The low frequency of this strategy is due to the fact that most Anglicized texts are carefully preplanned and, if oral, often rehearsed or memorized in advance; the low level of community bilingualism precludes the implementation of the spontaneous monolingual style in the oral channel for intra-ethnic purposes.

Towards a Strategic Understanding of English Contact Behaviour

For the remainder of this chapter, further characteristic functions of Anglicization will be identified, illustrated, and integrated into a broader, unifying model that sets out to capture underlying principles providing for a certain measure of predictability and causal explanation.

As already stated above, one important area of English contact in Japan that has yet to be explored is its occurrence in intimate, in-group relations, for informal, non-standard communication either as slang or even as anti-language.[4] In fact, the 'in' talk of teenager and university student subculture reveals a high proportion of extremely creative English-based vocabulary involving typical patterns such as

1. *Nativizing and hybrid suffixation: -chikku* (< *-tic*[5]), as in *poteto-chikku* (< *potato* + *-tic*, 'peasant-like'); *okama-chikku* (< Japanese: 'effeminate man' + *-tic*, 'camp') and *-resu* (< *less*) as in *shūchi-resu* (< Japanese: 'shame' + *less*); *konjō-resu* (< Japanese: 'spirit' + *less*)

2. *Innovative formation of new verbs* with the attachment of a dummy verb to a nominal lexical base: *adaruto suru* (< *adult* + Japanese: 'to do', 'to act and dress in a sophisticated style'); *puraibēto suru* (< *private* + Japanese: 'to do', 'to go on a date')

3. *Avant-garde coining of English-based verbs* following the native-style, inflectional paradigm, often with truncation, constitutes an extremely radical type of contact because of the degree of integration it assumes; it is rare in the evolution of Japanese contact with other languages: *paroru* (< *paro[dy]*, 'to parody'); *konparu* (< *com[panion]*, 'to hold a student party'); *bideoru* (< *video*, 'to record on video')

4. *Metaphoric transfer*, often with a pejorative and comic connotation: *panku suru* (< *punc[ture]*, 'to give birth'); *poteto* (< *potato*, 'pregnant woman'); *tanku* (< *tank*, 'physically strong man'); *antena* (< *antenna*, 'a tall person'); *basu* (< *bus*, 'a promiscuous woman'); *supagetti* (< *spaghetti*, 'mixed up, unintelligible'); *manē tōku* (< *money talk*, 'bribery').

The above data, as well as that presented in the discussion of the teenager magazine *Tarzan* (Chapter 4, Fig. 4.6) and local pop-music lyrics (Chapter 5), demonstrate that this teenager jargon not only includes standard English borrowings of international youth—for example, items

---

[4] Cf. Halliday (1978: 164–82). 'An antisociety is a society that is set up within another society as a conscious alternative to it. It is a mode of resistance, resistance which may take the form either of passive symbiosis or of active hostility and even destruction. An antilanguage is not only parallel to an antisociety; it is in fact generated by it' (ibid. 164).

[5] As in *roman*TIC and *exo*TIC.

derived from *hit, star, rock,* etc.—but also involves distinctly local, innovating patterns in the creation of slang. Whether some of these unorthodox, socially restricted forms will ultimately join the established set of community foreignisms or fade into oblivion cannot be predicted; however, certain innovations originating from student styles have already become acceptable, orthodox usage—for example, *saboru* (< *sabo*[*tage*], 'to miss class').

It is not only the in-group language of youth that exploits Anglicization; the Japanese underworld also draws upon it as one means of achieving external unintelligibility for its cant. For example, transferred items from English undergo various kinds of morphological and/or semantic change:

1. Restriction: *pēpā* (< *paper*, 'forged money'); *ado* (< *ad*[*dress*], 'hidden location').
2. Metaphoric transfer: *aisu* (< *ice*, 'usurer'); *anaunsā* (< *announcer*, 'informer').
3. Syllabic exchange or truncation: *sugara* (< standard Japanese: *garasu* < *glass*); *pai* (< standard Japanese: *supai* < *spy*, 'detective').

Contact with English for anti-language purposes such as criminal codes, slang, and obscene graffiti may initially seem surprising because of the usually dominant prestige-symbol function of English in commercial contexts. However, the underlying link between these apparently opposed applications is their mutual interest in the manipulation of reality through creative encoding:

They are both products of the urban scene, both are creative, innovative and audacious, lacking in reverence and deference. On the other hand, advertising language is not meant to be imitated or repeated by the recipient, and it is not meant as a protest in any conceivable sense. Slang to a vast extent is protest and criticism of a world which is far from the near-paradise which advertising promises it to become in the nearest of near futures, but rather the filthy place slang speakers know they inhabit. . . . Both variants of creative and innovative language use, advertising and colloquialism, are dedicated to the same creed: to change reality by changing its names. (Sornig, 1981: 64).

Another point to bear in mind is that when novel, English-based resources are employed in commercial contexts and in slang, they require a special effort of decoding, or almost deciphering, on the part of the consumer/listener. The English not only up- or downgrades the value of a product or person but also contributes to its *semantic opacity*. Furthermore, covert insider prestige may also emerge from the transgression of standard linguistic norms by slang innovators—although this happens not directly from the English-based word itself but through the social relations of its employers and their creative en-/decoding sensitivity for 'deviant' language.

Clearly related to this obscuring potential of Anglicization is its function in supplying the Japanese with euphemisms for taboo topics. This exploitation of mainly English resources is far from new and can be observed as far back as the Meiji period. Today, it is notably in reference to the sexual sphere that locally created Anglicization is resorted to: 'massage parlour' is *sōpu-rando* (< *soap land*); 'hotel for sexual liasons' *rabu-hoteru* (< *love hotel*); *abekku* (< French: *avec*, 'young, unmarried couple'); *shisutā-bōi* (< *sister boy*, 'gay young male'); *pinku-mūdo* (< *pink mood*, 'erotic atmosphere'). In a 1993 advertisement (distributed to the public through post boxes in Kyoto) offering to introduce lonely women to male hosts, the following romanticizing English-based euphemisms were employed, each serving to label a different degree of financial commitment: *dēto kōsu* (< *date course*); *rabu kōsu* (< *love course*); *torai kōsu* (< *try course*), and *abanchūru kōsu* (< *adventure course*).

Not only the sex industry, but also moneylending companies take advantage of the indirect vagueness of Anglicization. Thus, the following phrases in the monolingual style gathered from the commercials of such companies do not sound as harsh and embarrassing as they would in Japanese: 'money-loan', 'family lease', 'money plan', and 'fresh start'; of course, this obfuscatory English is also related to the general prestige of English resources in the language of advertising.

Physical needs and states are further semantic domains for which Anglicization is preferred over the potential offensiveness of the instant transparency of Japanese: *toire* (< *toilet*, instead of *benjō*); *chibi* (< TB> tuberculosis, instead of *kekkakubyō*); *X-dē* (< *X-day*, 'day of the Emperor's death'; used in media when it was expected at the end of 1988/ beginning of 1989.)

Finally, the employment of socio-linguistically unsuccessful or inappropriate innovative English contact, and the incorrect use of the established set of foreignisms for humorous effect, must be mentioned. For example, the English-derived word *o-jūsu* (< *juice*, preceded by the Japanese honorific prefix: *o-*, 'respectful') provoked laughter in a studio audience watching a comic drama[6] because of the attachment of the honorific prefix to

---

[6] Source: NHK 'Comedy Theatre', broadcast on 26. 3. 88, 19.30.

a drink considered to be ordinary and associated with young people (who do not warrant special respect). However, the addition of an honorific prefix to foreignisms is not always deemed odd by the community, although it is admittedly rare: for example, *o-toire* (< *toilet*) and *o-bīru* (< *beer*) can be employed by women or service staff without causing mirth. Mishonorification resulting from ignorance of the community's linguistic conventions is, in fact, a traditional target of Japanese humour.

A different type of—usually unintentional—humour arises when foreign phrases appear ridiculous to community members either because of their morphological length (tongue-twister effect), or their exaggeratedly aggrandizing qualities (cf. Appendix 1, no. 7), under negative community attitudes towards contact with English. Such aspects may be exploited by professional comedians or ordinary members of the community for humorous effects.

In contrast, items in 'straight' written texts that is, texts not aiming at entertainment—do not tend to evoke humour, because of the community's high respect for communication via that channel. Clearly, the balance between the degree of integration and the innovativeness of a foreignism has a considerable bearing on the extent to which the community finds it appropriate or not—their reaction of humour ultimately constituting an expression of rejection.

It is obviously very difficult to try and accommodate the multiple functions served by Anglicization (as listed above) into one unifying model; no such system has ever been suggested for this type of contact behaviour. In spite of the problems of synthesis, Fig. 7.1 offers a framework which tries to account for and predict the fundamental strategies adopted by the Japanese speech-community when its members implement Anglicization. The framework is constructed from the active perspective of the creators and producers of the language contact. The model focuses on the innovative processes of language contact in the making, and not the end-products which may eventually be authorized as part of the community code, although an instrumental etymology of items listed in loan dictionaries can be indirectly inferred.

The model in Fig. 7.1 covers all the data described above by subsuming it under four Contact Strategies;[7] these work with External Language Resources such as borrowing, creative adaption, hybridization, code-mixing, monolingual Anglicization, and acronaming. First of all, it must

[7] Strategies are understood here as connected to the *plans* which steer, monitor, or control speech-execution: cf. Faerch and Kasper (1983*b*: 23).

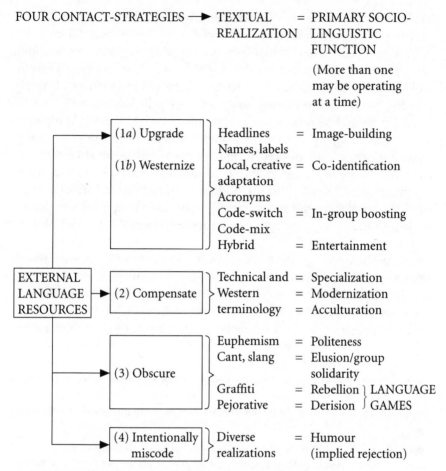

FIG. 7.1. A socio-functional model of contact-strategies.

be admitted that the theoretical concept of a linguistic 'strategy' is far from precise. The term has been applied to a wide spectrum of linguistic processes,[8] including the following:

- The ways advertisers exploit and target language.
- The approaches second-language learners adopt to overcome their communication problems, and their methods of learning a foreign language.
- The underlying principles of social interaction.

[8] In fact, there exist numerous defining labels for all kinds of strategies, e.g. 'message adjustment' and 'resource expansion' strategies (Corder, 1983), 'politeness strategies' (Brown and Levinson, 1978), and 'discourse strategies' (Gumperz, 1982), to list but a few.

The theoretical appeal of the term *strategy* and the popularity of the functional perspective it represents explains why many researchers have used it in different ways. How then are linguistic strategies understood here? Their meaning in this work closely follows the conceptions of Faerch and Kasper (1983*b*), who view strategies as part of the 'language planning process',[9] steering, monitoring, and controlling the execution of speech. Strategies should be recognized as the utilization of language knowledge as a means of satisfying specific, contextual needs. The strategies in my contact model are the devices by which community members put to use their knowledge of foreign resources to satisfy varying needs in Japanese communication. Needless to say, additional pragmatic and stylistic strategies for employing the native language are usually applied simultaneously with the contact strategies, for Japanese remains the matrix language in this contact setting.

The problematic question concerning the degree of consciousness of a strategy has already been raised in this section. It arises from the implications of active decision-making included in the everyday sense of the term 'strategy'. Even though it is normally the case that language-planning processes in one's native language are subconscious and highly automatic, it has been argued that in the planning and execution of 'high level' elements like vocabulary, the degree of consciousness is greater than for other components of communication such as articulatory features.[10]

---

[9] The psycho-mechanics of the operations involved in language-production lie outside the parameters of this book. Of course, it is important to remember that in a first language, planning processes are normally subconscious. It is not possible to enter here into the measurement of the degree of consciousness in the mind of Japanese using foreign resources, but it can be safely supposed that those involved in its creative, innovating application operate on a higher level of consciousness than those who opt for established, codified loans. For Faerch and Kasper (1983*b*), 'language planning processess' retrieve items from the linguistic system which then become part of a plan leading to a communicative goal. As Brown and Levinson (1978: 90) state: 'We do not mean to imply that what we dub "strategies" are necessarily conscious. For the most part they do not seem to be, but when interactional mistakes occur, or actors try to manipulate others, they may very well emerge into awareness. And they are open to introspection, at least in part. But the general unconscious nature of such strategies raises fundamental methodological problems that we simply skirt. We cannot pretend to have any special insight into what is probably the biggest single stumbling block to theory throughout the social sciences: the nature of the unconscious and preconscious where all the most important determinants of action seem to lie. We continue to use the word "strategy", despite its connotations of conscious deliberation, because we can think of no other word that will imply a rational element while covering both (a) innovative plans of action, which may still be (but need not be) unconscious, and (b) routines—that is, previously constructed plans whose original rational origin is still preserved in their construction, despite their present automatic application as ready-made programmes.'   [10] Cf. Jordens (1977: 16).

Furthermore, because Anglicization involves the selection and production of markedly alien lexical phenomena, it does not seem unreasonable to expect that the level of metalinguistic awareness is even further heightened. On the other hand, awareness of internal mental operations varies among individuals, so that different contact-producers will, of course, experience different degrees of awareness of their selected strategies. In fact, it seems unlikely that ordinary members of the Japanese speech-community would be able, without special pre-sensitization, to identify and classify the functional categories that have been abstractly formulated here in the model. It is reasonable to assume that some contact-makers such as copy-writers, journalists, technical translators, and contributors of innovatory slang possess a higher degree of strategic awareness than community members who do not actively engage in the inceptive and disseminating stages of language contact (see Fig. 4.1).

Furthermore, over time a strategy can become so automatic that it turns into a mere routine, its functional value comes to be taken for granted, and its implementation no matter for reflection. Anyway, the aim here is not to enter into a psychological analysis of the planning processes used by agents of language contact but principally to emphasize that the term *strategy* should not be taken as necessarily implying a particularly high degree of metalinguistic competence. However, it does seem probable that such competence is held by contact-producers, since they are operating on the more conscious level of the lexicon, and the material they handle derives from an external code.

Returning to the model, it can be seen that heterogeneous linguistic and stylistic phenomena which result from contact strategies such as those at work in advertising texts, the specialist terminologies of science and technology, substandard varieties of youth culture, slang and underworld cant, connotatively rich expressions such as euphemisms and pejoratives, code-mixed pop-lyrics, etc., are all here gathered together under the term 'textual realization'.

Finally, in the last column on the right the primary socio-linguistic functions of the strategy are suggested. Apart from the first two functions of *image-building* and *co-identification* (to be treated below), all the other strategies have been explicated and illustrated at length above (although not always directly referred to).

Of course, also from the opening discussion of this section, it is evident that more than one motivation at a time may be assignable to a textual realization at a time, but these additional functions often turn out to be secondary and concomitant interpretations or consequences. Thus, in code-mixed texts such as pop songs and articles for teenagers, we find the simultaneous operation of co-identification (the increased sense of sharing in English-speaking and international culture) together with other functions such as entertainment, the boosting and marking of in-group solidarity, and image-building. Acculturation and modernization may also be regarded as motivations for such code-mixing, but they do not form part of the direct plans of the text-producers and are not primary functions.

As for the meaning of the labels describing the four contact-strategies, a certain amount of explanation is necessary. A brief description of each strategy and of its primary functions will now be given.

The first strategy, *upgrading*, refers to the production of foreignisms for the purpose of socio-stylistic profit, or, in Goffman's terms, (1967) 'impression management'; so the main focus is not on denotation but on connotational value. Resources from an external language are chosen instead of native ones because they are deemed more 'estimable' in a particular context. The 'estimable' quality of English-based resources, on which the upgrading strategy relies, is closely bound to the high status attributed to the source of the donor model (which tends to be equated in the Japanese consciousness with the United States or the English-speaking West). It is also important to bear in mind that items which originally started with an upgraded status can, over time, lose their positive semantic charging and end up connotatively neutral, or even negative. This process is ongoing and comes into operation as initially new and statusful phenomena come to be taken for granted, especially in an affluent, post-industrial society. As an example, consider the widespread negative evaluation of the locally created compound *sararīman* (< *salary* + *man*, 'white-collar worker') by younger Japanese.

The strategy of *Westernizing* is intimately connected with the strategy of *upgrading*, but it does not work for the imposition of a 'better' Japanese reality. Instead it seeks to fuse and blend foreign derivations into the native matrix in order to express and symbolize a new, internationalized Japanese identity that superficially appears to have much in common with the admired and idealized aspects of the prestigious, external model-culture and its members. The most extreme realization of this strategy is monolingual encoding in the foreign language, which, if not merely cosmetic, tends to be limited to short and decipherable linguistic units such as headlines and labels because of the low level of comprehension amongst the Japanese general public. Since *upgrading* and *Westernizing* are so intertwined, they must be regarded as two sides of the same coin.

As for the four primary social functions of this double-sided strategy, the nature of entertainment and in-group boosting emerges quite clearly from much of the above discussion. Entertainment here also includes the visually decorative function of Anglicization in cases where a text with English words has no referential intention. Both these functions are particularly associated with code-mixed texts such as pop-song lyrics and hybridization—consider the radical innovations of youth subculture, and the monolingual English style so popular in youth-oriented communication. The identity and solidarity of young people is affirmed and boosted through the sharing of socially restricted vocabulary based on unfamiliar linguistic resources older people cannot understand.

Image-building, on the other hand, is related to that oft-cited motive for language contact: prestige. The term refers to the enhancing of the social evaluation and status of a product, person, or concept through its representation, which may consist entirely or partly or not at all of language (see Goffman, 1967). For our purposes, however, image-building will refer to the social effects of strategically planned and implemented language in texts and discourse. Of course, upgrading through foreignisms is only one of the multitude of verbal and non-verbal strategies available to community members for their management of prestige-inducing impressions. On the lexical level, for instance, Chinese-based resources can produce an erudite, classical effect, and purely native vocabulary (*wago*) can also achieve a traditionally respected image in certain contexts. However, the community obviously deems such native resources either inappropriate, inadequate, or unappealing in constructing a modern, Westernized image.

Image-building in this model is achieved through the symbolic exploitation of the associational value of the donor code as a carrier of an imputed 'worldliness', 'modernity', and/or 'sophistication'. Image-building depends on the upgrading potential of external linguistic resources, which, in turn, is based on the currently high evaluation of the donor code in the recipient community. The function will cease to be realized through external resources if and when the external contact-language loses its social attraction and worth. The function is undoubtedly connected with Japanese admissions of an 'inferiority complex' *vis-à-vis* the West, and with Westerners' accusations in regard to a Japanese propensity for 'imitation'. Although the realization of this function through foreignisms is frequently the object of criticism, it must be stressed that image-building is employed without any value judgement here—it is a need that every society seeks to satisfy in its own ways.

Image-building is one of the most readily identifiable functions of language contact in Japan today, and many examples have been catalogued above. Especially prominent in this regard is its realization in the monolingual English style, as in the consumer-targeted labelling of food products, in names of shop departments, in public signs, on posters and buildings, in government projects, in slogans, on clothing, in advertising, in magazine format, and on album covers. One particularly illuminating demonstration of this function can be found in the current fad for upgrading job designations through foreignisms: *guzzu-puropōzā* (< *goods proposer*, 'salesperson'); *terehon-kondakutā* (< *telephone conductor*, 'assistant conducting market research by telephone'). The following anecdote should suffice as a final illustration of this function:

A Canadian friend told me that he knew of a Japanese doctor who displayed English encyclopedias in the living room as one part of his 'interior decoration' scheme. It should be mentioned that nobody in his family could read English well.[11]

A corollary function of image-building is co-identification: the desire of certain community members, particularly youth, to partake of the predominantly material aspects of the external model, as embodied in its language. This sharing in, and aligning with, Western patterns is achieved by exploiting the symbolic value of the donor code, usually through English monolingualism and code-mixing—that is, in unadapted or non-integrated transfer; it is less associated with the processes of hybridization and local coining, which result more from specific signifying needs of the Japanese community. Instead, the realization of this function provides a symbolic demonstration of the Japanese acquisition of the socio-cultural forms of the external model. It takes place without users relinquishing their native identity and sense of ethnic belonging, operating within the parameters of Japanese society and only serving Japanese needs. Generally,

---

[11] T. Iwabuchi and M. Okada, 'Cultural Barriers Q & A', *Daily Yomiuri*, 11. 10. 84, 6.

no conflict is perceived when material, Westernizing features are added to, or superimposed on, a Japanese identity,[12] because co-identification is not usually accompanied by any profound, permanent, or strongly emotional association with the external model-society; it can be evoked even when there is very little knowledge of, or familiarity with, the donor culture and language. Furthermore, the linguistic realization of co-identification is often conventionalized, for, as previously described, it constitutes almost expected behaviour in many contexts such as monolingual naming in the mass media (for example, titles of television programmes), magazines and their contents pages, pop-song album-covers and lyrics, and the majority of commercials. As with image-building, co-identification is not realized through linguistic means alone but equally often through non-verbal channels such as dress and kinesics. Even though from a very broad perspective it is possible to view all contact behaviour as a kind of 'co-identification' with an external model, since native lexical resources are renounced in favour of external ones, it must be pointed out that co-identification here refers to a context-dependent function—that is to say, it is not the primary motivation behind all contact phenomena found in Japan today but is especially associated with commercial and youth-oriented communication.

The second strategy, *compensation*, consists in the offsetting of a lexical deficiency perceived in the native language through contact with material in the donor language—in other words, filling lexical gaps by means of

---

[12] However, deeper identification on a socio-psychological level is much more threatening —cf. the discrimination against Japanese children returning from abroad. Also, particularly proficient speakers of a foreign language who are ethnically Japanese may also appear suspect, but this reaction can be found in many other communities. The question of an *identity crisis* caused by westernization for the Japanese is, of course, a frequently expressed concern among intellectuals and politicans; its historical aspects are reflected in the discussion of the development of contact with English in Ch. 3. The post-war quest for cultural identity, on the other hand, is much more complex, since defeat in the Second World War shattered the traditional value-system. Please note that the question of identity that is referred to here is essentially one of cultural orientation and *not* a problem of ethnic or group identity. It does not worry most Japanese, because, as Wagatsuma (1975: 313), in his perceptive essay entitled 'Cultural Identity in Modern Japan', points out, the 'Japanese know very well, perhaps too well, who they are and especially who they are not. For the Japanese, group identity is an assured given. They tend to believe that there is a greater degree of physical homogeneity among themselves than actually exists. They tend to believe that they look uniquely alike, and always look different from other Asians.' The function of *co-identification*, of course, in no way implies the negation of this core Japaneseness but means that, on a physical level, the following of a Western life-style is often considered desirable and appealing, especially among those under 40; the accusation of disloyalty to Japaneseness is no longer applied to the pursuit of such a life-style as it was before the war.

direct borrowing. This strategy provides an easy and convenient means of securing referential sufficiency for the community, resulting in the welter of English-based jargon and the abundance of foreignisms denoting material items of Western origin. This point has been illustrated in Chapter 4, where a full discussion of the socio-linguistic functions of this strategy—specialization, modernization, and acculturation—can also be found.

Although acculturation and co-identification may appear somewhat similar at first sight, their distinction is formally reflected in the different contact-patterns they are associated with. Acculturation is clearly denotational in character and is the function behind the high number of loans for Western phenomena that have become part of everyday Japanese life and are now established, codified borrowings. Such loans include words derived from *fork, spoon, bed, blanket, curtain, carpet, sofa, toast, jam, hamburger, boots, overcoat, suit, shirt,* and *jeans.* Co-identification, on the other hand, has more to do with the westernizing, upgrading connotational values of the donor language and the societies from which they derive, which are the motivation behind monolingualism and code-mixed styles. For example, consider the following two cases of such fusing co-identification:

Tarzan, 223, 28 December 1994 (Chapter 4, Fig. 4.6)

Note this text heading is not represented in syllabic script and no native terms are used, although equivalents for all the English words are available.

Misty love *itsumo no yō ni*
Midnight call *yoru ni hibiku*
Ring my bell *denwa no mukō ni* (Chapter 5, Fig. 5.2b)

The third strategy, *obscuring,* selects foreign resources in order to decelerate or even hinder decoding. A number of social functions can be satisfied through its implementation:

- *Politeness:* The avoidance of the harsh or undesirable impact of instant decodability by means of English-based euphemisms. An example is *etchi suru* (< pronunciation of English letter H, which stands for the Japanese word *hentai* 'perversion' + Japanese: 'do').
- *Rebellion:* The restriction of decoding access to insiders by using anti-language constructed by groups, such as criminals or adolescent (would-be) rebels, either firmly outside or trying to put themselves outside the

mainstream. Clipping or oblique referencing often serves to render such vocabulary opaque to outsiders: *torabu suru* (> *troub[le]* + Japanese: 'make'). Such patterning clearly belongs to the realm of word games (see below). The same opacity is a feature of the English graffiti in romanized script found in various Japanese public contexts. Rebellion against the mainstream is here achieved basically through two linguistic processes. First, resources from a foreign language are selected for the negative, instead of the usually posit-ive, evaluation of a significatum. Secondly, deviant lexical innovation is constructed which challenges and breaks away from standard usage. Such linguistic nonconformity is also deeply connected with the related function of derision, which is a widespread characteristic means of demonstrating opposition through the linguistic medium.

- *Elusion and derision*: The obscurity of words composed of English ele-ments protects the producer and user from feeling too guilty about their derision of the referent: *DC Burando* (< DC < discount on famous brand goods = students whose school records consist primarily of low C and D marks); *sebun-irebun teishu* (< English: *seven-eleven* (name of a grocery chain) + Japanese: 'husband' = a husband who leaves home early in the morning and returns home late at night long after the children have gone to bed). This is similar to the way euphemisms operate to obscure the un-pleasantness of the referent. A prominent feature of these examples is their punning on consumer-related items. This kind of derisory slang works through indirectness and substitution. It does not refer to something by means of its usual name but spotlights certain semantic aspects of a com-mon foreignism in order to achieve the negative impact. Another pattern of English-based derision involves metaphorization, which is a salient method of achieving linguistic mockery in communities throughout the world. Here the decoder of the metaphor is obliged to take the responsibility for perceiving the derisive implication of the sign through its symbolic comparability. Examples of this have been given earlier in this chapter. The fact that this negative downgrading is in direct conflict with the first strategy of upgrading accounts for its shock-appeal; its ploy is to violate mainstream strategies that aim to enhance referents through Anglicization.
- *Group solidarity* is a function that is closely related to elusive, deviant Angli-cization and can be seen at work in the slang of youth and the underworld, where it serves as a marker (or badge), identifying, demarcating, and uniting those who share its employment in a rebel view of referential reality.[13]

---

[13] Cf. Halliday (1978: 172): 'An antilanguage is the means of realization of a subjective reality; not merely expressing it, but actively creating and maintaining it. . . . The reality is a counter-reality . . . it implies a preoccupation with the definition and defence of identity through the ritual functioning of the social hierarchy. It implies a special conception of information and of knowledge . . . the language is secret because the reality is secret.'

Furthermore, the transgression of standard linguistic behaviour, through either deviant foreign lexical innovation or adoption, can provide covert prestige for members of a subculture, in the same way that dress and other social symbols can. Those who dare to join in the obscurant's game of anti-language based on external lexical resources are simultaneously signalling their group membership, usually to their own kind. The closed nature of access to the decoding acts as a bond between those who share the secret understanding, and bolsters their sense of solidarity.

The term 'language game'[14] is intended to emphasize the entertainment value of the obscuring strategy, even while it may be simultaneously functioning to express rebellion and derision. The most courageous risk-takers[15] in the game are able to enjoy the power of neologizing, while the majority of the players content themselves with the pleasure of only 'cracking' and sharing the subcode. Why then are foreign lexical resources conceived of as 'toys' in this strategy? Simply put, they appear to lack the 'real' significatory force of the Japanese language. It must be remembered that those involved in such deviant innovation generally lack a working knowledge of the contact language; its forms tend to lack psycho-semantic reality—being studied only through translations and dictionaries in school—and thus some teenagers do not hesitate to 'play around with' it. Such an approach ensures the supply of fresh slang expressions when older terms have lost their impact. Of course, deviant foreign-based innovations will eventually also lose their appeal through conventionalization, either within the subcode or by adoption into general usage, but new ones will continue to be coined.

The fourth strategy, *intentionally miscoding* for humorous purposes, may

[14] As Sornig (1981: 76) explains: 'Apart from rule-governedness there are other aspects to justify the Wittgensteinian comparison of language use with playing a game: you normally need a partner to play games, games are played because not only can one win or lose, but above all because games are fun or meant to be fun i.e. for at least one of the partners. Playing the game as an exponent par excellence of creativeness contains a fair amount of individualistic sophistication and waywardness'. Cf. Halliday (1978: 180): 'Antilanguages are typically used for contest and display' where 'a speaker is using language just in order to secure for himself the rewards that accrue to prowess in the use of language'.

[15] Cf. Sornig (1981: 75): 'Linguistic innovation is always a communicative *risk*. Slangisms—as parts of a lexicon in the making—have to take the risk of sounding misplaced and unsuitable, which must have been the case with those innumerable tentative lexical innovations, singular acts of performance that have never been taken up by a second speaker. As a rule in cultural history, failures are not recorded. To overcome a risk of this kind is what may set free a peculiar sense of humour as a symptom of a mental attitude that would not take everything seriously, because it refuses to take anything for granted, for inevitable or unalterable.'

include the parodistic deformation of familiar English-derived resources into hybridized macaronisms[16]—cf. English *twiggez-vous* for the French *parlez-vous*. This is particularly common among young students: *konjō-resu* (< Japanese: 'guts' + English: *less*); *pā-peki* (< English: *per[fect]* + Japanese: *[kan]peki* 'flawless'); *bai-nara* (< English: *bye* + Japanese: *sayonara*), *kaer-ingu* (< Japanese: *kaeru* 'go home' + English: *-ing*). Also in this category are those cases of stylistically inappropriate or intolerably lengthy foreign transfers already discussed above. The humour in all these instances ultimately derives from the recognition of their transgression of community norms by both sender and receiver.

I hope that the model of contact strategies is now sufficiently clear, and makes sense. Of course, the model is concise and does not cover every individual context, each of which contains its own internal set of functions. The model does not, for example, treat the obvious functions of advertising-language which external resources are often selected to fulfil (the need to attract attention, create conviction, and prompt desire to be translated into action). The satisfaction of those needs are best handled under the rubric of 'advertising strategies', which include audience targeting for sex and class. Such varying context-dependent strategies should not be confused with the community-wide contact-strategies of this general model.

Finally, it is essential to realize that the model represents only one dimension within the total set of stylistic options available to the community. Sino-Japanese (*kango*) and pure Japanese (*wago*) resources constitute the other necessary lexical elements in the production of Japanese texts, with their functional range covering all the needs of Japanese society. Nevertheless, it is worth reflecting on the question of how external resources are weighted in relation to native ones. The following stylistic criteria have been found to operate, for instance, in the selection of shop names from either external linguistic or (Sino-)Japanese resources:[17]

- Degree of community familiarity with the form.
- Degree of difficulty in pronouncing the form.
- Degree of difficulty in remembering the form.

---

[16] *Macaronisms* 'result from the general delight in mixing divergent language elements. The deliberate, illegal mixing of vernacular and (familiar) foreign language elements has a humorous effect; it is the parodistic delight in the mischievous deformation of things familiar' (Sornig, 1981: 77–8).

[17] These criteria come from Satake (1981). For his findings, see App. 4.

- Associative qualities of the form.
- Aesthetic quality of the form.

The investigation into the stylistic decision-making procedure of foreign lexification in relation to other vocabulary options in the Japanese language is a topic that cannot be directly discussed here, but typical patterns for (intuitively) judging the stylistic appropriateness of foreignisms may be inferred from their categorization in the model in the column headed Textual Realization, which reveals that foreign resources are often considered suitable for headlines, names, labels, cant, slang, euphemisms, and pejoratives, among others. Texts particularly compatible with foreign lexis, as we have seen, include those of a technical and academic nature, pop songs, and mass-media and advertising formats. From this it is evident that intensive lexification with foreignisms often serves as a register feature[18] and constitutes one of the principal methods whereby the community can expand its stylistic repertoire in response to contemporary social changes and needs.

This chapter has presented an original interpretation of the socio-functional strategies involved in contact with external languages such as English in Japan today. Obviously, it is the lexicon and not structure or function words which can be most easily manipulated and shaped by producers of text; it is on the lexical level that a refashioning of reality can be most readily pursued. This model reveals that a purely structural account of language contact is inadequate, because structural gaps provide the motivation for only one strategy, that of *compensation*. However, the other three strategies are equally important in an explanation of contact behaviour in Japan and they arise from non-structural, communicative needs and goals.

Finally, it must be admitted that socio-linguistic work suffers from a serious problem concerning the clear relation between abstract notions of social structure and behaviour and the actual details of communication. As yet there is no accepted theoretical framework which 'specifies what processes of, for instance, intentionality, symbolization, interpretation,

---

[18] '*Register features* may take the form of choices of lexis (the open-ended sets of choices in language) or of grammar (where the sets of alternatives are closed). In the following English examples, a contrast in formality is shown by a contrast of lexis alone: 1. He donated some volumes to the institution/2. He gave some books to the school' (Ure and Ellis, 1977: 203). As for the term *register* itself, it is confusingly and closely related to style. 'A register in a given language and given speech community is defined by the uses for which it is appropriate and by a set of structural features which differentiate it from the other registers in the total repertory of the community' (Ferguson, 1977: 212).

and negotiation are involved in making the social structure's distribution of relationships visible and observable in the actual behaviour patterns ... of people in interaction' (Gal, 1983: 65). In spite of these problems, it is hoped that my interpretation makes some kind of contribution towards attaining a model of social causation which is based on rationality and intentionality rather than on static sociological categories and relationships.

Conclusions

Because of the lack of a comprehensive and readily available theoretical and methodological paradigm for analysing language contact as a social process, a unifying framework for identifying contact phenomena in relation to specific settings was expounded in Chapter 1.

Chapters 2 and 3 then applied this typology to a macro-sociolinguistic account of the two-thousand-year evolution of language contact inside Japan by scrutinizing and classifying its channels, agents, domains, phases, motivations, attitudes, and linguistic consequences. From this chronology, language contact emerged as an almost permanent process in Japanese linguistic history, in spite of anti-contact intervals. Above all, the crucial role of political circumstances in the initiation and maintenance of linguistic associations is discernible. The distant, non-bilingual setting clearly stands out as the most characteristic type of Japanese contact-setting over the millennia. In fact, there were only two phases of diglossic bilingualism, in both cases among a small élite—in the eighth century and again in the mid-nineteenth century. The significance of contact experience with Chinese was emphasized for its effect on orthographic practices and its culmination in a system for integrating foreign items that was later extended to European donors. On another level, the analysis in Chapter 2 indirectly proves the case for a socio-linguistic approach to diachronic data.

The second half of the book, from Chapter 4, presents original research-findings, exploring and systematizing the synchronic, societal forces promoting large-scale contact with English by focusing on its formal and contextual variation. In order to capture the socio-linguistic dynamics of this contact-in-the-making, various fieldwork methods were employed, including the observation and investigation of mass-media data and the statistical analysis of community attitudes.

Chapter 4 explained the five stages of lexical innovation and integration involved in Japanese language-contact and demonstrated that the contemporary institutional setting for the acquisition of English was incapable of securing a foundation for community bilingualism. Interestingly enough, contemporary contact-phenomena, which include hybridization, monolingual Anglicization, acronaming, local English-based coining, and code-switching and -mixing, do not neatly correspond to the 'distant, non-bilingual setting' typology set up in Chapter 1. Instead they are much more associated with a diglossic situation of a High language leaking through into a Lower one, or with a dominant bilingual society. The major reason for the prolific character of present-day Japanese contact with external lexical resources is the existence of an economically and technologically based global communications network employing English as its principal medium and intensifying the flow of language contact. This makes Anglicization a late twentieth-century procedure *par excellence*, for only in this age can linguistic contact be carried out over such a distance at such a speed within a predominantly monolingual society. Internally significant factors for the massive linguistic importation are the 130 years of orientation to American and European models of modernization, and the strong appeal of external lexical resources as a means of satsifying certain social needs principally connected to the power and prestige of a Western-based image. With regard to the latter, however, it was observed that the semantic reference of foreignisms appears to be related more to the material than to the abstract aspects of acculturation.

The preference of 'modernizing' agents in the fields of technology, commerce, and mass media for external lexical resources makes the Anglicization of headlines, names, labels, slogans, and decorative signs in public communication predictable.

The systematization, given in Chapter 5, of orthographic variation in representing English highlighted the complexity and diversity of code-alternating patterns. The underlying importance of the Chinese contact-model was brought out in the analysis of locally created morphological processes which modify English elements though compounding and clipping. The ensuing divergence from donor norms seems to be legitimized by the fact that the remodelling operates for the benefit of the Japanese community and is not sanctionable by any norm-enforcing authority.

According to the results of the socio-linguistic survey conducted into community attitudes and described in Chapter 6, the degree of community resistance to language contact appears relatively low, in spite of a high degree of unitelligibility of its forms among older and less educated sections of the community. This tolerance of contact provides the basis for its persistence and further advance from now on, provided ecological conditions remain constant. The potentially most active disseminators and supporters of external lexical contact in the community turn out to be those with one or more of the following characteristics: a university education, a professional or white-collar occupation, and membership of the age band between 18 and 29. Sex does not appear a significant variable in the spread of foreignisms.

The wide-ranging applications of external linguistic resources, including the initially unexpected negative encoding for anti-language, euphemisms, graffiti, and pejoratives, were ultimately synthesized, in Chapter 7, into a socio-functional model consisting of four primary strategies. The motivation for contact was interpreted as a set of four planning choices: upgrading/westernizing, compensating, obscuring, or intentionally miscoding. Each of these strategies is connected to definite textual forms and to the satisfaction of specific social needs. Prominent among the latter are image-building, in-group boosting, entertainment, terminological specialization, modernization/westernization, politeness, elusion, rebellion, derision, and humour.

The ideas and data in this book should be of value to various researchers in the field of linguistics, as well as to other social scientists interested both in the general problem of human adaptation and, more specifically, the maintenance and transformation of social and symbolic order through the assimilation and manipulation of language. Many important insights have been offered here concerning the causes and patterns of linguistic change through external contact. Moreover, this research offers a significant explication of contact processes taking place in the rarely researched monolingual setting. It also applies a socio-anthropological perspective to phenomena usually handled purely structurally, and it does so using a novel theoretical and methodological approach.

Finally, the information describing the modifications undergone by the English language in a non-native context will certainly be useful for those seeking cross-cultural comparisons and universals, and for those desirous to fathom the relentless internal bonding of English with alien systems that is destined to expand and intensify into the next century.

APPENDIX 1

Negative Community Attitudes towards Foreignisms in Print

The following extracts represent a range of regularly publicized hostile reactions to different forms of language contact, deriving principally from newspaper-readers' letters; it should be noted that young as well as older persons express concern, and that a number of different groups in society are attacked for unnecessary or excessive borrowing.

1. '[Borrowing] can be viewed . . . as the result of having no pride in the [Japanese] language . . . I feel it urgent to set some guide-lines and limits on bewildering usages of foreign terms. Otherwise we only add to the reputation of Japan being an "impersonator" or "forget"'. (Teacher, 47)[1]

2. 'I think the mass media, the *shinjinrui* [new breed of Japanese] and frivolous entertainers are doing a lot of harm to the Japanese language. Erosion of the Japanese language is erosion of Japanese culture . . . The press, which is responsible for transmitting and preserving correct Japanese, should stop trying to copy Western culture and should stop mindlessly promoting Western fashion and trends.' (Company employee, 29)[2]

3. 'It's quite natural that Japanese people cannot speak English very well. There aren't many signs in English in the country because Japan isn't a colony of an English-speaking country. I wonder why so many Japanese are shamed into trying to improve their English and into putting up signs in English.' (Student, 26)[2]

4. '. . . the Japanese language is being badly corrupted at present. Male vocabularies are being used by young schoolgirls, and various foreign expressions are being coined by the mass-communications industry. I understand that foreign expressions can sound good to the ears. However, the adoption of such expressions in everyday language is being taken too easily. It is sad that beautiful Japanese words are gradually becoming "dead" language because of the abuse of foreign words. We should reconsider the use of our beautiful language, which provides many shades of meaning to express our feelings.' (Housewife, 26)[3]

[1] Letter from Toshihiko Kobayashi, in *Daily Yomiuri*, 12. 9. 87.
[2] From readers' letters column, *Yomiuri Shimbun*, 4. 11. 87. Extract (2) was sent in by Hiroyoshi Wada and extract (3) by Shiro Inoue.
[3] From readers' letters column, *Yomiuri Shimbun*, 4. 6. 86.

5. 'Recently, many film-titles are in *katakana* of original English titles—for example, *Footloose*, *Splash*, and so on. This may be designed to appeal to young people's feeling, but can many people understand these titles? Before this tendency became popular, many of the film titles were named for the contents of the films, not the original titles . . . as a film fan, I hope that film companies do not use long English titles or titles incomprehensible even with the aid of an English–Japanese dictionary.' (Teacher, 22)[4]

6. 'While dining at a restaurant, I happened to notice a cardboard box with the words "Chiba Nashi" [pears of Chiba] printed on it . . . I wonder why the trade name was printed in English.[5] Are the producers worried that their pears would appear inferior without slogans written in English? If they insist on using a foreign language, they should at least get it right and use the words "Chiba Pear". The message will then be clear and they can expect to get it across.' (Pensioner, 73)[6]

7. 'It's a wonderful job.'
   '*Kōtingu staffu* [> *coating staff*]? Well the *katakana* is all very nice, but do you know what kind of a job it is?
   'No, I don't really.'
   'You'll be amazed, I'll tell you. It's just an ordinary *penki-ya* [wall painter]'[7]

8. 'I was very surprised when I found that a list of ingredients and opening-instructions on a packet of sliced bacon I bought recently were written in English. The bacon was produced by a popular Japanese manufacturer . . . The bacon was produced for domestic sale, not export. There are many similar examples of such unnecessary English. A countless number of signs are written in poor English, and T-shirts are printed with English phrases that are so ridiculous they are embarrassing. As an English teacher I am angered by this phenomenon. Japanese people boast that Japan is the economic giant of the world, but they use foreign languages sloppily in places where is it unnecessary because, deep inside, they have an inferiority complex towards Caucasians. If Japan is to become a giant, in the real sense of the word, we should place more value on our native language—Japanese.' (Teacher, 59)[8]

9. 'Politicians and government officials should speak in plain language, but instead they often use jargon. Fox example, they describe events as being "drastic" or speak of a "global partnership", which is not very intelligible to most of us. I was disgusted to hear a Foreign Ministry official refer to "logistic support"

---

[4] From readers' letters column, *Yomiuri Shimbun*, 15. 10. 84.
[5] In fact the language criticized here is the representation of Japanese in roman script, which may be interpreted as a compromise between Anglicization and Japanese.
[6] From readers' letters column, *Yomiuri Shimbun*, 11. 10. 82.
[7] 'Katakana' in *Guidepost* (4. 4. 88, no. 180, p. 1), Tokyo: ICS Kokusai Bunka Senta.
[8] From readers' letters column, *Yomiuri Shimbun*, 8. 10. 89.

during a Diet session on Japanese assistance to the multinational forces in the Gulf War ... It is important for us as members of the international community to be able to speak other languages, and I hope more of us will learn to speak foreign languages better. At the same time, however, we should respect our own culture as well as others. Excessive use of foreign words will no doubt serve to detract from our culture and undermine our efforts to internationalize mentally.' (Translator, 52)[9]

[9] From readers' letters column, *Yomiuri Shimbun*, 1. 5. 81.

APPENDIX 2

The Questionnaire
(English translation)*

Questionnaire on Loan-Words

THIS IS NOT A TEST
Circle the item that applies to you.

1   Male   2   Female   3   Year of birth:

4   Place of longest residence:
    Hokkaido Tōhoku Kantō Tōkai Hokuriku Kinki Chūgoku Shikoku
    Kyushu Other

5   Location of current residence:
    Urban   Rural

6   Occupation:
    Retired
    If not retired, state occupation:
    .... Housewife   Student   Part-time

7   Last stage of education:
    Primary Middle High University graduate

8   Study of foreign language during schooling:
    Name of language and length of study
    ....

9   Self-rating of English ability:
    Non-existent A little ability Reasonable ability

10 If you have studied a foreign language at a private school, name
    language and length of study: ....

* All romanized Japanese items underlined here were, of course, presented in Japanese
script to the informants. The English translation in brackets had been added for the benefit of
readers unfamiliar with the original Japanese.

11 Have you lived abroad? If so, where, why, and for how long (not including holidays)? ....
....

12 Do you use a foreign language at work? If so, which language and how?
Speaking/Reading/Writing/Listening.
If it is not English, circle your assessed level of proficiency:
Non-existent/A little ability/Reasonable ability

13 Do you use another language apart from at work?
At home With friends Other situations (explain):
....

---

1   **Circle one item you usually use and like from the choices below**

rēnkōto / reinkōto (< raincoat)
bitamin/ vitamin
ripōto/ repōto (< report)
tsūrisuto/ tyūrisuto (< tourist)
terefon/ terehon (< telephone)
uirusu/ bīrusu/ bairasu (< virus)
handobaggu/ handobakku (< handbag)
zenerēshon/ jenerēshon (< generation)

---

2   **Express in Japanese**

SUMMER GIFT ....
DRINK MENU ....
fresh meat ....
vegetables ....
COFFEE JELLY ....
FAMILY ORANGE PACK ....
Please enjoy your taste ....
Hello! This is bike paradise ....
For peace and better life ....
In Kobe the history of Japanese coffee drinking hangs in the air ....

3　Circle the number of the following words which you often use:

1 *chansu* (chance)
2 *baibai* (byebye)
3 *sankyū* (thankyou)
4 *kontorōru* (control)
5 *nanbā* (number)
6 *OL* (office lady)
7 *kyaria* (career)
8 *Q & A*
9 *purēgaido*
　 (play guide)

10 *ekizochikku* (exotic)
11 *amenitī* (amenity)
12 *gōruin* (goal-in)
13 *pudingu* (pudding)
14 *imēji-chenji*
　　(image change)
15 *puraibashī* (privacy)
16 *shinpuru* (simple)
17 *herushī* (healthy)
18 *unīku* (unique)

19 *dorasutiku* (drastic)
20 *ekisaito* (excite)
21 *yangu* (young)
22 *ririfu* (relief)
23 *komyunitī*
　　(community)
24 *furīwākā*
　　(freeworker)
25 *shinseritī*
　　(sincerity)

4　Circle the item which you think fits best

1 *Restoran de '................. kudasai'.*
　At a restaurant: '.............please'.
　gohan/raisu
　rice

2 *Terebi-bangumi de 'Konya wa subarashī .... o goshōkai shimasu'.*
　On a television programme: 'Tonight I'd like to introduce some fantastic ......'
　okyakusan/gesto
　guest

3 *'Sumimasen .... wa doko desu ka'.*
　'Excuse me, where's the ....?'
　o-tearai/toire
　toilet

4 *Chīsai ko ga okāsan ni kikimashita: '........ wa doko ni iru no'.*
　A small child asked his mother: 'Where's ....?'
　otōsan/papa
　daddy

5 *'Okina .... ga ī ne'.*
　'A big .... is best, isn't it?'
　gamen/sukurīn
　screen

---

5 **What do you feel about this advertising language? Select your response from** (a)–(o)*

(a) very attractive
(i) quite appealing
(u) evokes nothing
(e) strange
(o) ridiculous

1–	4–	7–	10–
2–	5–	8–	
3–	6–	9–	

1 *za gaman*
** < the endurance
2 *hōmingu nyūsu*
  < homing < news
3 *uerukamu dorinku ken o purezento*
  < welcome < drink ticket < present
4 *study zemi-ryokō*
  < study (German:) < seminar journey
5 *sukī no tame no kanten na sutorecchi & torēningu o shōkai*
  for the purpose of < skiing, an introduction to simple < stretching and < training
6 *futari no pāsonariti to wakamonotachi ga isshō ni mai-terebi o tsukuri-ageru yūniku na bangumi*
  two (TV) < personalities and youngsters together create < my (= individual), < unique < TV programme
7 *yonme ijō no gurūpu wa daikin sono mama de wan-rūmu OK*
  (for a) < group of over four the cost is < OK as for < one < room
8 *tennenboku no pākketo-furoā o nanimebari ni shita ni-kai no rofuto-sutajio o, gyararī fū ni kōdineito shita shiō-rei*
  (an) example of natural wood for < parquet < floor that has been < coordinated in the style of a < gallery with the panelling of the second floor < loft < studio
9 *bīchi hoteru wa sūpā-derakkusu, derakkusu-rizōto, eguzekutibu, kurippa no kakukurasu kara erabemasu*
  as for the < beach hotel you can choose from each < class (of either) < super-deluxe, < de luxe resort, < executive or < clipper
10 *komynikēshon bōdo by supōtsu pīpuru & supōtsu shoppu*
  < communication < board < by < sports < people < & < sports < shop

* The ordering is a basic Japanese series based on the sequence of the syllabic symbols.
** In this Appendix the symbol < indicates a loan item, including nativized forms and monolingual transfers.

6 How do you react to the following opinions? Mark the reaction from 1–5 which corresponds closest to yours.

	1 STRONGLY DISAGREE	2 SOMEWHAT DISAGREE	3 NEITHER AGREE NOR DISAGREE	4 SOMEWHAT AGREE	5 STRONGLY AGREE	
1 The Japanese have progressed and become international, so it is natural they borrow many words.	....	....	....	....	....	1
2 Now that Japan is a world leader, learning foreign languages is unnecessary.	....	....	....	....	....	2
3 Western culture is more advanced than that of the Japanese.	....	....	....	....	....	3
4 Japanese succumb too easily to Western things, and over-borrow.	....	....	....	....	....	4
5 Too much adoption of foreign things is not good.	....	....	....	....	....	5
6 Borrowing is not an important issue, just a matter of fashion.	....	....	....	....	....	6
7 Contact with foreign things can enrich Japanese culture.	....	....	....	....	....	7
8 Borrowed words bring a fresh feeling.	....	....	....	....	....	8
9 Japanese ought to try harder to know foreign culture.	....	....	....	....	....	9

10 Foreign ways of thinking have a bad effect on the Japanese.	....	....	10
11 The more borrowing increases, the lower the value of Japanese becomes.	....	....	11
12 Since too many loan words are being used, control is necessary.	....	....	12
13 Japanese can profit considerably from contact with foreigners.	....	....	13
14 It's not wrong to borrow words from the West.	....	....	14
15 Japanese words are more beautiful and deeper than borrowings.	....	....	15
16 The flood of borrowing is a sign that pure Japanese is not respected enough.	....	....	16
17 Foreign life-style does not suit the Japanese.	....	....	17
18 Knowing about foreign culture can broaden the Japanese.	....	....	18
19 Loan words are important and useful for Japanese.	....	....	19
20 The Japanese way is better than imitating the foreign way.	....	....	20

APPENDIX 3

The Historical Division between Japanese and Chinese-based Literary Genres

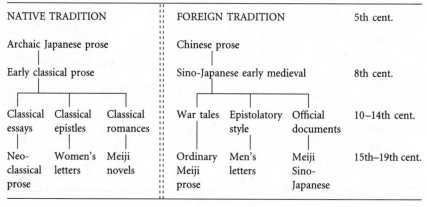

NATIVE TRADITION			FOREIGN TRADITION			5th cent.
Archaic Japanese prose			Chinese prose			
Early classical prose			Sino-Japanese early medieval			8th cent.
Classical essays	Classical epistles	Classical romances	War tales	Epistolatory style	Official documents	10–14th cent.
Neo-classical prose	Women's letters	Meiji novels	Ordinary Meiji prose	Men's letters	Meiji Sino-Japanese	15th–19th cent.

Source: Sansom (1928: 61).

APPENDIX 4

Lexical Resources in Contemporary Japanese Restaurant-Names (%)[1]

	Japanese-style food	Western-style food	Chinese-style food	Coffee-shops	Pubs
Pure Japanese (*wago*)	24	9	10	16	20
Foreign lexis (*gairaigo*)	1	39	3	39	30
Chinese-derived (*kango*)	9	8	33	8	8

[1] Missing percentages for each category relate to unclassifiable words such as names and nonsense creations.

Source: Satake (1981).

References

AIKIBA-REYNOLDS, K. (1983), 'Reconstruction of *nu: A Hypothesis for the Origin of Japanese', *Papers in Japanese Linguistics, 8*, Tokyo: Kaitakusha.

ALATIS, JAMES E. (1970) (ed.), *Bilingualism and Language Contact* (Washington, DC: Georgetown University Press).

—— (1978) (ed.), *International Dimensions of Bilingual Education* (Washington, DC: Georgetown University Press).

AMUDA, A. (1986), 'Language Mixing by Yoruba Speakers of English', Unpub. Ph.D. thesis, Univ. Reading.

ANDERSON, R. W. (1982) (ed.), *Language Form and Linguistic Variation* (Amsterdam Studies in the Theory and History of Linguistic Science, 4: Current Issues in Linguistic Theory, xv; Amsterdam: John Benjamins).

APPEL, RENÉ, and MUYSKEN, PIETER (1987), *Language Contact and Bilingualism* (London: Edward Arnold).

ARAKAWA, SOBEI (1931), *Nihongo to natta Eigo* (Japanized English) (Tokyo: Kenkyūsha).

—— (1977), *Kadokawa gairaigo jiten, dai-ni-han* (Kadokawa Loanword Dictionary) 2nd edn. (Tokyo: Kadokawa).

BAILEY, RICHARD W., and GÖRLACH, MANFRED (1982), *English as a World Language* (Cambridge: Cambridge University Press).

BARNLUND, DEAN C. (1975), *Public and Private Self in Japan and the United States* (Tokyo: Simul Press).

BARTSCH, RENATE (1987), *Norms of Language* (London: Longman).

BREITBORDE, L. B. (1983), 'Levels of Analysis in Sociolinguistic Explanation', *International Journal of the Sociology of Language*, 39: 5–43.

BROWN, PENELOPE, and LEVINSON, STEPHEN (1978), 'Universals in Language Usage: Politeness Phenomena', in Esther N. Goody (1978) (ed.), *Questions and Politeness* (Cambridge: Cambridge University Press), 56–289.

—— (1979), 'Social Structure, Groups and Interaction', in Scherer and Giles (1979) (eds.), 291–341.

CARTER, WILLIAM R. (1983), 'Kikaijin', in *Kodansha Encyclopedia of Japan*, iv. 205 (Tokyo: Kodansha).

CLYNE, MICHAEL G. (1967), *Transference and Triggering* (The Hague: Mouton).

—— (1978), 'Some (German-English) Language Contact Phenomena at the Discourse Level', in J. Fishman (1978) (ed.), 113–28.

CLYNE, MICHAEL G. (1988), 'The German Australian Speech Community', *International Journal of the Sociology of Language*, 72: 67–83.

COBARRUBIAS, JUAN, and FISHMAN, JOSHUA A. (1983) (eds.), *Progress in Language Planning* (Berlin: Mouton).

CONRAD, ANDREW W., and FISHMAN, J. A. (1977), 'English as a World Language: The Evidence', in Fishman *et al.* (1977) (eds.), 3–76.

COOPER, ROBERT L. (1982) (ed.), *Language Spread: Studies in Diffusion and Social Change* (Bloomington, Ind.: Indiana University Press).

—— and FISHMAN, JOSHUA (1974), 'The Study of Language Attitudes', *International Journal of the Sociology of Language*, 3: 5–19.

CORDER, S. P. (1983), 'Strategies in Communication', in Faerch and Kasper (1983a) (eds.), 15–19.

CRAIG, DENNIS R. (1978), 'Creole and Standard', in Alatis (1978) (ed.), 602–20.

CRUSE, D. A. (1986), Lexical Semantics (Cambridge: Cambridge University Press).

DANIELS, F. J. (1948), 'The Vocabulary of the Japanese Ports Lingo', *Bulletin of the Society for Oriental Studies*, 12: 805–23.

DOI, TOSHIO (1983), The Study of Language in Japan: A Historical Survey (Tokyo: Shinozaki Shorin).

—— (1984), 'On the Hypothesis of the Pidgin-Creole Origin of the Japanese Language', MA thesis, Southern Illinois Univ.

DRESSLER, WOLFGANG E. (1982), 'Acceleration, Retardation and Reversal in Language Decay', in Cooper (1982) (ed.), 321–35.

ELLIS, JEFFREY, and URE, JEAN (1982) (eds.), *Register Range and Change* (*International Journal of the Sociology of Language*, 35; The Hague: Mouton).

ELLIS, ROD (1985), *Understanding Second Language Acquisition* (Oxford: Oxford University Press).

FAERCH, CLAUS, and KASPER, GABRIELE (1983a) (eds.), *Strategies in Interlanguage Communication* (London: Longman).

—— (1983b), 'Plans and strategies in Foreign Language Communication', in id. (1983a) (eds.), 20–60.

FASOLD, R. (1984), *The Sociolinguistics of Society* (Oxford: Basil Blackwell).

FERGUSON, CHARLES A. (1959), 'Diglossia', *Word*, 15: 325–40.

—— (1977), 'Baby Talk as a Simplified Register'. In Catherine E. Snow and Charles, A. Ferguson (1977) (eds.), *Talking to Children* (London: Cambridge University Press), 219–36.

FISHMAN, J. A. (1971), Sociolinguistics: A Brief Introduction (Rowley, Mass.: Newbury House).

—— (1978) (ed.), *Advances in the Study of Societal Multilingualism* (The Hague: Mouton).

—— (1983) (ed.), *Levels of Analysis in Sociolinguistic Explanation* (*International Journal of the Sociology of Language*, 39; The Hague: Mouton).

—— *et al.* (1977) (eds.), *The Spread of English* (Rowley, Mass.: Newbury House).

GAL, SUSAN (1979), *Language Shift* (New York: Academic Press).

—— (1983), 'Comment', in Fishman (1983) (ed.), 63–72.

Gendaiyōgo no kisochishiki (Basic Knowledge of Contemporary Technical Terms): see under KAMEI, HAJIME (1985) (ed.).

GIBBONS, JOHN P. (1983), 'Attitudes towards Languages and Code-Mixing in Hong Kong', *Journal of Multilingual and Multicultural Development*, 4/2 and 3: 129–47.

—— (1987), *Code Mixing and Code Choice: A Hong Kong Case Study* (Cleveland, UK: Multilingual Matters).

GILES, HOWARD (1977) (ed.), *Language, Ethnicity and Intergroup Relations* (London: Academic Press).

—— and POWESLAND, P. F. (1975), *Speech Style and Social Evaluation* (London: Academic Press).

GONZALEZ, ANDREW (1982), 'English in the Philippines', in Pride (1982) (ed.), 211–26.

GOODMAN, JOHN STUART (1967), 'The Development of a Dialect of English-Japanese Pidgin', *Anthropological Linguistics*, 9/6: 43–55.

GUMPERZ, JOHN J. (1964), 'Hindi-Punjabi Code-Switching in Delhi', in H. Lunt (ed.), *Proceedings of the Ninth International Congress of Linguists* (The Hague: Mouton), 1,115–24.

—— (1982), *Discourse Strategies* (London: Cambridge University Press).

HAARMANN, HARALD (1989), *Symbolic Values of Foreign Language Use* (Berlin: Mouton de Gruyter).

HABEIN, YAEKO SATO (1984), *The History of the Japanese Written Language* (Tokyo: Univ. Tokyo Press).

HALLIDAY, M. A. K. (1978), *Language as a Social Semiotic* (London: Edward Arnold).

HAMADA, ATSUSHI (1955), 'Kanji' (Chinese Characters), in *Kokugogakujiten* (1955), 206–9.

HAMMITZSCH, HORST (1981) (ed.), *Japan-Handbuch* (Wiesbaden: Franz Steiner).

HANNAH, JOHN ADRIAN (1986), *Die Annäherung von Lehnelementen aus dem Englischen an das Deutsche als analogiebedingtes Interferenzphänomen*, Ph.D. diss. Ruprecht-Karls Univ. Heidelberg.

HATCH, E. (1976), 'Studies in Language Switching and Mixing', in W. C. McCormack and S. A. Wurm (1976) (eds.), *Language and Man: Anthropological Issues* (The Hague: Mouton), 201–13.

HATTORI, SHIRO (1967), 'Descriptive Linguistics in Japan', in Sebeok (1967) (ed.), 530–84.

—— (1974), 'The Japanese Language', in *Encyclopedia Britannica* (1974), x (Chicago: Encyclopedia Britannica), 93–7.

HAUGEN, EINAR (1953), *The Norwegian Language in America* (Bloomington, Ind.: Indiana University Press).

HAYASHI, DOI, and YAMADA, TOSHIO (1955), 'Nippon ni okeru kanji' (Chinese Characters in Japan), in *Kokugogakujiten* (1955), 204–6.

HERMANN, P. (1866, repr. 1970), *Prinzipien der Sprachgeschichte* (Tübingen: Niemeyer).

HINDS, JOHN (1986), *Japanese* (London: Croom Helm).

HIROSUE, HAJIME (1984), 'Kodomo to gairaigo' (Children and Loanwords), *Gengo Seikatsu*, 391: 63–6.

HOLMQUIST, JONATHAN (1987), 'Style Choice in a Bidialectal Spanish Village', in Cooper (1987) (ed.), *Language in Home, Community, Region and Nation* (*International Journal of the Sociology of Language*, 63; Berlin: Mouton de Gruyter), 21–30.

ISHINO, HIROSHI (1983), *Gendai gairaigo-kō* (Thoughts on Contemporary Loanwords) (Tokyo: Taishūkan).

—— and TSUTSUMI, TETSURO (1979), *Wakamono no gengo ishiki* (Young People's Linguistic Consciousness) (Tokyo: Chikuma Shobo).

JAHR, ERNST HAKEN (1992) (ed.), *Language Contact* (Berlin: Mouton de Gruyter).

JAKOBOVITS, L. A. (1971), 'The Psychological Bases of Second-Language Learning', *Language Sciences*, 14: 22–8.

JAPANESE NATIONAL LANGUAGE RESEARCH INSTITUTE (1964), *Bunrui-goi-hyō* (Lexical Classification) (Tokyo: Shueisha).

JIBRIL, MUNZALI (1982), 'Nigerian English: An Introduction', in Pride (1982) (ed.), 73–84.

JORDENS, PETER (1977), 'Rules, Grammatical Intuitions and Strategies in Foreign Language Learning', *Interlanguage Studies Bulletin Utrecht*, 2/2: 5–76.

KACHRU, BRAJ B. (1981), 'The Pragmatics of Non-native Varieties of English', in Smith (1981) (ed.), 15–39.

—— (1982) (ed.), *The Other Tongue: English Across Cultures* (Urbana, Ill.: University of Illinois Press).

—— (1983*a*), *The Indianization of English* (New Delhi: Oxford University Press).

—— (1983*b*), 'Models of New Englishes', in Cobarrubias and Fishman (1983) (eds.), 143–70.

—— (1986), *The Alchemy of English* (Oxford: Pergamon Press).

KAMEI, HAJIME (1985) (ed.), *Gendai-yōgo no kiso-chishiki* (Basic Knowledge of Contemporary Technical Terms) (Tokyo: Jiyū-kokuminsha).

KAMEI, TAKASHI (1954), 'Chinese Borrowings in Prehistoric Japanese' (Tokyo: Yoshikawa Kōbunkan).

KARLGREN, BERNHARD (1926, repr. 1957), *Grammatia serica recensa*, 29 (Stockholm: Museum of Far Eastern Antiquities).

KASAGI, MASĀKI (1983), *Mass Media in Japan* (The Japan Foundation Orientation in Seminars on Japan, 14; Tokyo: The Japan Foundation).

Kokugogakujiten (National Language Dictionary) (1955, repr. 1963), compiled by the Kokugo-gakkai (Tokyo: Tōkyōdō).

Kokuritsu Kokugo Kenkyūjo, see under National (Japanese) Language Research Institute, below.

Lambert, W. E. (1967), 'A Social Psychology of Bilingualism', *Journal of Social Issues*, 23: 91–109.

—— et al. (1960), 'Evaluative Reactions to Spoken Languages', *Journal of Abnormal and Social Psychology*, 60: 44–51.

Lebra, Takie Sugiyama (1976), *Japanese Patterns of Behaviour* (Honolulu: East-West Center Press).

Lehiste, Ilse (1988), *Lectures on Language Contact* (Cambridge, Mass.: MIT Press).

Lewin, Bruno (1981), 'Sprache', in Hammitzsch (1981) (ed.), 1717–802.

Lewis, Glyn E. (1978a), 'Migration and the Decline of the Welsh Language', in Fishman (1978) (ed.), 263–351.

—— (1978b), 'Types of Bilingual Communities', in Alatis. (1978) (ed.), 19–34.

Lieberson, S., and McCabe, E. (1982), 'Domains of Language Usage and Mother Tongue Shift in Nairobi', *International Journal of the Sociology of Language*, 34: 83–94.

Loveday, Leo John (1986), *Explorations in Japanese Sociolinguistics* (Amsterdam: John Benjamins).

Lyons, John (1977), *Semantics*, i and ii (London: Cambridge University Press).

Macaulay, Donald (1982), 'Borrow, Calque and Switch: The Law of the English Frontier', in Anderson (1982) (ed.), 203–37.

Mackey, William F. (1983), 'Models for Comparing Cases of Language Contact', in Nelde (1983) (ed.), 71–94.

—— and Ornstein, Jacob (1979) (eds.), *Sociolinguistic Studies in Language Contact* (The Hague: Mouton).

Martin, Samuel E. (1975), *A Reference Grammar of Japanese* (New Haven: Yale University Press).

May, Tim (1986), 'Finding a Way to Figure out Japan', *Daily Yomiuri*, 16 Nov., 7.

McMahon, April M. S. (1994), *Understanding Language Change* (Cambridge: Cambridge University Press).

Mehrotra, Raja Ram (1982), 'Indian English: A Sociolinguistic Profile', in Pride (1982) (ed.), 150–73.

Miller, Roy Andrew (1967), *The Japanese Language* (Chicago: University of Chicago Press).

—— (1977), *The Japanese Language in Contemporary Japan* (AEI-Hoover Policy Studies, 22; Washington DC: American Enterprise Institute for Public Policy Research).

—— (1980), *Origins of the Japanese Language* (Seattle: University of Washington Press).

—— (1982), *Japan's Modern Myth* (New York: Weatherhill).

232   *References*

Mosha, M. (1971), 'Loan-Words in Luganda', in W. H. Whiteley (1971) (ed.), *Language Use and Social Change* (Oxford: Oxford University Press), 288–308.

Motomichi, Kōno, and Bowles, Gordon T. (1983), 'Ainu', in *Kodansha Encyclopedia of Japan*, i. 34–6.

National Japanese Language Research Institute (Kokuritsu Kokugo Kenkyūjo) (1962), *Hōkoku*, 21: *Gendai zasshi kyūjusshu no yōgo yōji, i: Sōki oyobi goi-hyō* (Vocabulary and Chinese Characters Used in Ninety Contemporary Magazines, i: General Introduction and Word-Frequency Tables) (Tokyo: Shūei Shuppan).

—— (1963), *Hōkoku*, 22: *Gendai zasshi kyūjusshu no yōgo yōji, ii: Kanjihyō* (Vocabulary and Chinese Characters used in Ninety Contemporary Magazines, ii: Chinese Frequency-Tables) (Tokyo: Shūei Shuppan).

—— (1970), *Denshi keisanki ni yoru shimbun no gōi chōsa* (A Computer-Based Survey into Newspaper Vocabulary) (Tokyo: Shūei Shuppan).

Nelde, Peter Hans (1983) (ed.), *Theorie, Methoden und Modelle der Kontaktlinguistik* (Bonn: Dümmler).

Neustupny, Jiri V. (1978), *Post-structural Approaches to Language* (Tokyo: University of Tokyo Press).

Norman, Arthur M. Z. (1954), 'Linguistic Aspects of the Moves of U.S. Occupation and Security Forces in Japan', *American Speech*, 29: 301–2.

—— (1955), 'Bamboo English: The Japanese Influence upon American Speech in Japan', *American Speech*, 30: 44–8.

Norman, Jerry (1988), *Chinese* (Cambridge: Cambridge University Press).

Ozawa, Katsuyoshi (1976), 'An Investigation of the Influence of the English Language on the Japanese Language through Lexical Adaption from 1955–1972, Ph.D. diss., Ohio Univ.).

Parasher, S. N. (1980), 'Mother-Tongue-English Diglossia', *Anthropological Linguistics*, 22/4: 151–68.

Peng, Fred C. C. (1975a) (ed.), *Language in Japanese Society* (Tokyo: University of Tokyo Press).

—— (1975b), 'Sociolinguistic Patterns of Japanese Kinship Behaviour', In id. (1975a) (ed.), 91–128.

Pfitzner, Jürgen (1978), *Der Anglizismus im Deutschen* (Stuttgart: Metzlersche).

Pietersen, Lieuwe (1978), 'Issues and Trends in Frisian Bilingualism', in Fishman (1978) (ed.), 353–99.

Platt, J. W., Weber, Heidi, and Ho, Mian Lian (1984), *The New Englishes* (London: Routledge & Kegan Paul).

Pride, J. B. (1982) (ed.), *New Englishes* (Rowley, Mass.: Newbury House).

—— and Holmes, J. (1972) (eds.), *Sociolinguistics* (Harmondsworth: Penguin).

Richards, Jack C. (1985), *The Context of Language Teaching* (Cambridge: Cambridge University Press).

Rubin, Joan (1968), 'Bilingual Usage in Paraguay', in Fishman (1968) (ed.), 512–30.

SAITO, EIZABURO (1985) (ed.), *Gaikoku kara kita shingo jiten* (Dictionary of New Words from Abroad) (Tokyo: Shueisha).

SAITO, SHIZUKA (1968), *Nihongo ni oyoboshita orandago no eikyō* (Dutch Influences on Japanese) (Tokyo: Shinozaki Shorin).

SANDEFUR, JOHN R. (1982), 'Kriol and the Question of Decreolization', in Graham R. McKay (1982) (ed.), *Australian Aborigines: Sociolinguistic Studies* (International Journal of the Sociology of Language, 36; Berlin: Mouton de Gruyter), 5–13.

SANKOFF, G. (1971), 'Language Use in Multilingual Societies: Some Alternative Approaches', in Pride and Holmes (1972) (eds.), 33–51.

SANSEIDO-HENSHŪSHO (1979), *Konsaisu gairaigo jiten* (Concise Loanword Dictionary) (Tokyo: Sanseido).

SANSOM, GEORGE (1928), *An Historical Grammar of Japanese* (Oxford: Clarendon Press).

SATAKE, HIDEO (1981), 'Wago-nazuke-ryūkōka' (Hit Songs with Pure Japanese Words in the Title), *Gengo Seikatsu*, 359: 46–52.

SAVILLE-TROIKE, MURIEL (1982), *The Ethnography of Communication* (Oxford: Basil Blackwell).

SCHERER, K. R., and GILES, H. (1979) (eds.), *Social Markers in Speech* (Cambridge: Cambridge University Press).

SCHUMANN, JOHN H. (1978), *The Pidginization Process: A Model for Second Language Acquisition* (Rowley, Mass.: Newbury House).

SCOLLON, RONALD, and SCOLLON, SUZANNE (1979), *Linguistic Convergence: An Ethnography of Speaking at Fort Chipewyan Alberta* (New York: Academic Press).

SCOTT, CHARLES T. (1966), *Preliminaries to English Teaching* (Tokyo: The English Language Education Council).

SCOTTON, CAROL MEYERS (1983), 'The Negotiation of Identities in Conversation', *International Journal of the Sociology of Language*, 44: 115–36.

—— and URY, W. (1977), 'Bilingual Strategies: The Social Functions of Code-Switching', *International Journal of the Sociology of Language*, 13: 5–20.

SEBEOK, THOMAS A. (1967) (ed.), *Current Trends in Linguistics*, ii: *Linguistics in East Asia and South East Asia* (The Hague: Mouton).

SEELY, CHRISTOPHER (1991), *A History of Writing in Japan* (Leiden: E. J. Brill).

SHIBATANI, MASAYOSHI (1990), *The Languages of Japan* (Cambridge: Cambridge University Press).

SMITH, LARRY E. (1981) (ed.), *English for Cross-cultural Communication* (London: MacMillan Press).

SONODA, KOJI (1975), 'A Descriptive Study of English Influence on Modern Japanese', Ph.D. diss., New York University.

SORNIG, KARL (1981), *Lexical Innovation* (Amsterdam: John Benjamins).

SRIDHAR, KAMAL K. (1988), 'Language Maintenance and Language Shift among Asian-Indians', *International Journal of the Sociology of Language*, 69: 73–87.

STANLAW, JAMES (1982), 'English in Japanese Communicative Strategies', in Kachru (1982) (ed.), 168–97.

STEVEN, ROB (1983), *Classes in Contemporary Japan* (Cambridge: Cambridge University Press).

SUGIMOTO, MASAYOSHI, and SWAIN, DAVID L. (1978), *Science and Culture in Traditional Japan* (Cambridge, Mass.: MIT Press).

TAKAHASHI, KENKICHI (1965), *Eigaku kotohajime* (The Beginning of English Studies) (Tokyo: Kadokawa Shoten).

—— (1967), *Kaikoku-ki no Eigo* (English at the Time of the Country's Opening) (Tokyo: Sanichi Shobo).

TAMAMURA, FUMIO (1981), 'Wago no hataraki' (The Functions of Pure Japanese Lexis), *Gengo Seikatsu*, 359: 36–45.

TANABASHI, ISHINO, and SUZUKI, SEIICHI (1912), *Nichiyō-hakuraigo-binran* (Everyday Dictionary of Imported Language) (Tokyo: Kōgyokukan).

TATSUKI, MASĀKI (1979), 'The Effects of Loanwords on the Phonology of Contemporary Japanese', unpub. MA thesis, Univ. Victoria, BC, Canada.

TAY, M. (1982), 'The Uses, Users and Features of English in Singapore', in Pride (1982) (ed.), 51–70.

THOMAS, CEINWEN H. (1982), 'Registers in Welsh', *International Journal of the Sociology of Language*, 35: 87–115.

THOMASON, SARAH G., and KAUFMAN, TERENCE (1988), *Language Contact, Creolization and Genetic Linguistics* (Berkeley: University of California Press).

TRUDGILL, PETER, and TZAVARAS, GEORGE (1977), 'Why Albanian-Greeks are not Albanians: Language Shift in Attica and Biotia', in Giles (1977) (ed.), 171–84.

TSUKISHIMA, HIROSHI (1967), 'Historical Linguistics, Including Affiliations with other Languages', in Sebeok (1967) (ed.), 503–29.

UMEGAKI, MINORU (1963, repr. 1978), *Nippon Gairaigo no kenkyū* (The Study of Japanese Foreignisms) (Tokyo: Kenkyūsha).

UMETOMO, SAEKI *et al.* (1961) (eds.), *Kokugogaku* (Studies in the National Language), in *Kokugokokubungaku kenkyūshi-taisei*, xv (A Complete History of Studies into National Language and Literature, xv) (Tokyo: Sanseido).

URE, J., and ELLIS, JEFFREY (1977), 'Register in Descriptive Linguistics and Linguistic Sociology', in Uribe-Villegas (1977) (ed.), 197–243.

URIBE-VILLEGAS, OSCAR (1977) (ed.), *Issues in Sociolinguistics* (The Hague: Mouton).

VELTMAN, C. (1983), 'Anglicization in the United States', International Journal of the Sociology of Language, 44: 99–114.

VIERECK, WOLFGANG (1980) (ed.), *Studien zum Einfluß der englischen Sprache auf das Deutsche* (Tübingen: Gunter Narr).

VOS, F. (1963), 'Dutch Influences on the Japanese Language', *Lingua*, 12: 341–88.

WAGATSUMA, HIROSHI (1975), 'Cultural Identity in Modern Japan', in G. De

Vos and L. Rom Anucci-Ross (1975) (eds.), *Ethnic Identity* (Palo Alto, Calif.: Mayfield. 307–34).

WEINREICH, URIEL (1953), *Languages in Contact* (The Hague: Mouton).

WHITNEY, CLARA (1981), *Clara's Diary* (Tokyo: Kodansha).

WHITNEY, W. D. (1881), 'On Mixture in Language', *Transactions of the American Philological Association*, 12: 1–26.

YAMADA, TOSHIO (1967), 'The Writing System: Historical Research and Modern Development', in Sebeok (1967) (ed.), 693–731.

YAMADA, YOSHIO (1940), *Kokugo no naka ni okeru kango no kenkyū* (A Study of the Chinese Words Borrowed into the Japanese Language) (Tokyo: Hōbunkan).

YANO TSUNETA KINENKAI (1986), *Nippon: A Chartered Survey of Japan. 1986/7* (Tokyo: Kokuseisha).

YOSHIKAWA, KŌJIRŌ (1975), *Jinsai, Sorai, Norinaga* (Leaders of the National Studies Movement) (Tokyo: Iwanami).

ZUGHOUL, MUHAMMAD R., and TAMINIAN, LUCINE (1984), 'The Linguistic Attitudes of Arab Minority Students', *International Journal of the Sociology of Language*, 50: 155–79.

ZWENGLER, JANE (1982), 'Kenyan English', in Kachru (1982) (ed.), 112–24.

Index

238

Index